CW00881434

WORDS FROM

# Awaki

The Third and Final Covenant Vol. III

BERNETHA GEORGE, MD

authorHOUSE®

*AuthorHouse™*
*1663 Liberty Drive*
*Bloomington, IN 47403*
*www.authorhouse.com*
*Phone: 833-262-8899*

*Published by AuthorHouse 08/16/2021*

*ISBN: 978-1-6655-3487-1 (sc)*
*ISBN: 978-1-6655-3488-8 (hc)*
*ISBN: 978-1-6655-3486-4 (e)*

*Library of Congress Control Number: 2021916339*

*Print information available on the last page.*

*All Scriptures were taken from King James Version of the Bible.*

*This book is printed on acid-free paper.*

This book, the end of a trilogy, is dedicated to Future Generations with apologies. For, had we touched your Ancestors with this knowledge your lives would be different.

# Contents

# Acknowledgements

God gave me Benjamin Lester to help make the journey of this Trilogy of His information available to the masses. Thank you God and thank you Ben.

Thank you Calvin Styles for telling me I would do it when my faith was absent.

# Preface

*REV 22:10 SEAL NOT THE SAYINGS OF THE PROPHECY OF THIS BOOK FOR THE TIME IS AT HAND.*

*LUKE 10:9 ...AND SAY UNTO THEM, THE KINGDOM OF GOD IS COME NIGH UNTO YOU*

*LOUANN CHAN, PROPHETESS: "THE HOLY AWAKI DID NOT VISIT AND BESTOW KNOWLEDGE AND WISDOM SO THAT IT COULD BE JEALOUSLY HOARDED AMONG A SELECT FEW. THIS IS INFINITE MIND'S GIFT TO ALL."*

These words are being written for those yet to come. They are written less for those (faithless) who are already here.

You may be questioning why the Creator did not warn you of the changes you see? Why didn't He alert you earlier to the chaos and turmoil? He did. Just as He empowered the Prophet John, The Revelator, in Revelation to warn us all, He empowered Prophets and others to warn you.

He awakened, prepared and charged Prophets, told people with Divine Gifts of Healing, Oneness of Mind, Multitudes, Presence of The Angels, Self - Taught Spiritual Gifts and others to tell you this was coming. This happened, in this universe, from November 3, 1995 through May 15, 1996 in Baltimore, Maryland mostly at the Home of Omni located on 3617 Howard Park Avenue which became "The Temple of Angels."

During those visitations, a 28 year old male's body (Nathaniel Keys) was invaded (they just took it) by 7 Angels: Awaki, Shakardak, Laiki, Melchizedek, Myackaoka, Marchardack, Azreal variably, and he was rendered unconscious. Each angel, using his unconscious body, spoke to those present, via The Prophet (Thomas Gains), and dialogue began.

Thomas sat directly in front of Nathaniel, the "Host," so called because he "hosted" the angel in his body, touching knees to knees, holding his hands and resting them on both their knees.

That took place 40-50 times throughout the 6 months. Each occurrence lasted 45 minutes to 1 hour, variably. It happened, multiple times during one day, once a day and other days no visitations at all, changeably.

Many people, at least 100 at the Home of Omni that I am personally aware of, were told the entire 6 months, not to hold back the information that was being given to them. "Go out and tell others" is what they were told.

This book, the end of a trilogy, all with the same name, is a culmination of 25 years of intense study of those visitations. It gives 10 real accounts of people whose lives personified the "madrids" (thousands upon thousands) spoken to worldwide then. It is written to pass on the information exactly as it was given to the people herein. Their sessions represent all of the concepts that were taught.

Omissions, distortions, erroneously reported revelations all are sought to be rectified through these publications. To that end, many different holy writings were consulted in preparation of this book. Much of what we have been fed for generations, over centuries, has landed us here; replicating that had to be avoided. Minimally, the attempt had to be made, therefore every quote herein is verbatim, thanks to technology. No liberties were taken with the words of the Angels. The Characters' names are ficticious but no liberties were taken with their words either.

As time passes the authenticity of what you read here will be borne out. It already has been for me in just the past quarter-century. Being a part of a world that's changing, continually in one steady direction, while the masses of its Beings move steadily and unceasingly, in the opposite direction, is my greatest paradox. How do you get them synchronized?

Perhaps the generations here at the coming of the Angels were unable to believe in the possibilities of their being possible, but you, for whom this is written, will have lived through enough that your faith will have been fully born and well - honed in you, to believe and benefit from it, prayerfully.

# Prologue

*REV 17:14 THESE SHALL MAKE WAR WITH THE LAMB AND THE LAMB SHALL OVERCOME THEM: FOR HE IS LORD OF LORD AND KING OF KINGS AND THEY THAT ARE WITH HIM ARE CALLED, AND CHOSEN AND FAITHFUL.*

*LUKE 10:1 …THE LORD APPOINTED OTHER SEVENTY ALSO, AND SENT THEM TWO AND TWO BEFORE HIS FACE INTO EVERY CITY AND PLACE WHITHER HE HIMSELF WOULD COME.*

*LUKE 10:3 GO YOUR WAYS, BEHOLD I SEND YOU FORTH AS LAMBS AMONG WOLVES.*

*LUKE 10:9 AND HEAL THE SICK THAT ARE THEREIN*

God sent us 7 Angels directed by Awaki, The Spirit of Angels, also known as Archangel Michael, to this universe. Their purpose was to awaken, enlighten and charge or instruct madrids of people throughout all nations, simultaneously. They began making contact with people in this universe November 3, 1995 and stopped coming May 15, 1996. They pulled people to hear them explain why they were here by their sheer power, many, not all (you weren't allowed to choose not to go to them, if you did they overrode that choice in the end). They bestowed upon those people the Divine Gifts of Prophecy, Healing, Multitudes, Oneness of Mind, their presence, affirmation of Self-Taught Spiritual Gifts and to others the charge to just live their lives in faith and obedience before the masses using their inherent spiritual gifts, all from God.

Those chosen to go, hear and see, from all over the world, what went on then, have kept it very quiet ever since. That is understandable because they knew, if they spoke up, no one would believe them in the first place, and worse, they would be called crazy. That being the undisputable case, did not prevent their being called and sent to you, nevertheless. So as you read what's written here, believers, try not to judge too harshly those who failed to enlighten you. Non- believers, (if any of you dared crack the covers and continued to read) you are the epitome of why all that is currently being experienced had to come to be; up to and including the muted paralysis of those who were unable to share this with the world (faithless).

To one of the many, whom you will read about here (provided you dare read on), one Angel said, "this is a display unto the hosts of this universe that we may teach and bring unto those who seek truth, before the Third Covenant, the 11 and 40, that they may come into obedience of your God in faith and all understanding, as in your history in this universe. We have been sent unto those who have displayed an openness to receive and to help prepare the hosts of this universe in wisdom. For unless you are in faith and wisdom and can choose of us or not of us, then you cannot be expected to do what is your destiny for lack of understanding, for you are imperfect. That is why you have been chosen. You have been summoned unto us that you may achieve the knowledge that you need, that you may not mislead the multitude."

Even with this well delivered explanation from an Angel of God Himself it was not enough to overcome that inertia, felt by those spoken to, to go out and tell those who were not spoken to, anything. They simply kept it all to themselves, for the most part, and let the chips fall where they may.

Let me make this clear from the outset so that, as you read on, you may not feel that expectations have been placed upon you that you are unprepared to meet. Spiritual battles were and are reserved for those chosen and prepared to fight them. Other publications available may have misconstrued them to be the responsibility of all mankind but assuredly they were and are not. When questioned by one, chosen for preparation to assist in the sharing of this new knowledge with the masses, if they (the masses) should be told that they were going to be fighting Spiritual Battles, Awaki was explicitly clear. *"They will not be in battle; ONLY those who have been chosen by your God will fight the battles in this time and space as we direct them and we will fight the spiritual battles in the air for you."* Additionally, it was assured by him that, *"Victory has already been claimed for you. In the far reaches of heaven, these battles have already been fought and won millions of times. How you interpret your faith will determine the outcome in this universe."*

All of this notwithstanding the information is here for you now, my apologies for all things bygone, and I invite you to read on to understand where things are in this day and time, please.

# Chapter One

## The Gratest Spiritual Leaders

The Prophet learned from the first visits the purpose of the appearance of those, "Emanations of the first thoughts of God" as they described themselves, whom we called Angels. He questioned the Angel Shakardak, the Warrior Angel, the Angel of War, when he prompted him to do so.

"There are many questions that you wish to ask" he told Thomas. "Those that I can, within your understanding, I am charged to do so. You must ask the question, for unlike the Holy Awaki, I cannot probe your thoughts."

"The first question I have is, how should Nathaniel and I prepare for the holy battles, for the holy spiritual battles, that are to come? We were told by the Holy Awaki to read the scriptures, to read the Bible, which we've been doing. Some of the questions that we have are: if our preparation is also to involve other people, and if we're to take the role of trying to convince others?" the prophet asked.

"This Host is preparing to our delight. And in the case of involving others, can there only be a battle of one?" Shakardak responded.

"No," the prophet said.

"Then, it is within your understanding. This Host will begin with a circle within his creative forces. He will deal with those and those will deal with others," the angel explained.

"I see. So then the preparation of others will come through conversation, through discussion?" Thomas asked.

"Just like we are different in our gifts with the Infinite Mind, so shall

1

the approach be different with each. Some will have to see and they will believe and some will not see and they will believe. Others will hear and they will believe, others will not hear and they will believe. And there will be those that will see and they will not believe, and there will be those that will hear and they will not believe," Shakardak explained. "But I told you before, that as we continue to re-engineer the physical body of this host, he will start to change physically. His speaking will start to change. His persuasion and control over others will be magnified to serve the purpose and our purpose only."

"Is there anything he should do to assist in this preparation, to assist in the re-engineering of his body?" Thomas asked.

Shakardak answered, "He has already done that which was required of him. This process will be complete with the first of 12 (January: the 1st of 12 months)."

"Is that on his birthday or his next birthday?" the Prophet asked.

"What you will label 'birthday' in this universe, at this time, we have no resistance of such for this host and this spirit was born many times before, and we know them all. But, in this universe, the significance of this date coincides with the year that this host came into existence in this universe. It coincides with the year all your greatest spiritual leaders was teaching all teachings to humanity."

Thomas was just told of past births and past lives of his cousin Nathaniel, whom he knew well. Yet he let it go right over his head. This gives you some insight into the mind set of people herein, when they sat in the presence of the Angels.

Instead of delving into that with pertinent questions he asked, "Who was the teacher to whom you were referring?"

Shakardak let it drop, too, and just answered the question he was asked.

"In your universe and time he was known as Martin, but to us he was known as Mahaladek, 'The Bringer of The Message.' In this, I made one mistake," he said. "In his generation I brought forth two of your greatest spiritual leaders for the spiritual battle and I could not guide their destiny until it was too late."

"Who was the second?" the Prophet inquired.

2

"There is no 'second' for they were equal in our eyes," Shakardak corrected him.

"Who was the other?" he asked.

"The other spiritual leader in this universe was known as Malcolm, known to us as Simeon, 'The Fighter'. It was not our intentions for the two to be at great distances from the one. So, in order that we may begin again in the next generation, it is necessary that he who has seen the face of God and heard the voices of the Angels, that the Testators must leave this universe. But, in your mind you may believe this to be harsh. But, it was not out of cruelty of us, but of man's humanity in this universe that will kill their greatest spiritual leaders. But, they were sent unto us because I did not complete my mission.

"When I first came unto you I told you that I was Shakardak, The Warrior Spirit. I have fought many battles in many universes. I have been in charge of directing yours in your universe. I bring forth now another generation of Great Spiritual Leaders, all with a different mechanism. But, this time the same message to bring forth the preparation for the coming of the truth, the light and the life. I am still here, speak unto me," he directed the Prophet.

"I am listening, Shakardak," he said. "So, you're saying that the work of Martin and Malcom is still being done, it's not yet completed?"

"That is within your understanding," Shakardak answered yes.

The Prophet hesitated and then let out a barrage of questions, "How? Will he be a part of that work? Will Nathaniel and I be a part of the completion of that work?"

"You are already a part," Shakardak said. "The Host (Nathaniel) before you is chosen of that generation and the message in 12 and 40, when he reaches the point of power will be the message, and there will be others. The mistake that we made is also that we put our faith too much in humanity and the chosen people of the Infinite Mind. And, we brought forth one with peace and love and the other with truth and understanding, that at the elimination of those two there were not others. This time we bring forth many of all nations and nationalities, that the message will be one: truth, light and life."

"What is the message, Shakardak?"

"The message will be, 'repent for the kingdom of the Most High God

3

is at hand.' In order for humanity to exist into the third and final covenant, the Infinite Mind, where He will take His place with His people and live in harmony and love; there must be a universal reverence and repentance before judgment."

"Is that how we are to save ourselves: through 'universal reverence and repentance'?" asked the Prophet.

"Only until the masses turn away their faces from idolatry and sinful behavior, will He that gave all the heaven and earth unto them, will return and remove from this place, the existence of which you call hell. Life here on earth, in this universe, hell and heaven are conditions of your life." Shakardak answered.

The Angel of War, dropped what sounded like "info bombs" all at one time. Those, needed more in depth exploration so we could reconcile what we were told: Angels made a "mistake"? We needed to understand how this information lined up with what we knew. Also, and most profound, we had to reconcile our long time understanding of the concepts of Heaven and Hell: "conditions of life" not "places"?

# Chapter Two

## First Born Spiritual Leader

<u>Malcolm X</u>

Those revelations by Shakardak were among some of the most shocking of all. He was actually telling us that two of the greatest known civil rights activists in history were also two of our greatest spiritual leaders in history. They were sent to us by God Himself to fight Spiritual Battles! Civil Rights Battles equated Spiritual Battles? Civil Rights activities are a harbinger of that chaos prophesied in Revelation; that to which they had come to awaken us? That for which we were being prepared to help prepare others; Spiritual Battles? All of this was one and the same? Spiritual Battles were Battles for Civil Rights of Human Beings?

Additionally, his admission that they made a "mistake" in guiding their destiny strongly challenged our perception of Angels being perfect in all of their doings. "They are emissaries of God, for God's Sake, are they not perfect in all of their doings," our prior thinking. No longer, he made that clear.

At the writing of this, the 20th, year of Armageddon, the entire world is engulfed in worldwide turmoil stemming from the most heinous violation of a human being's physical and spiritual rights May 25, 2020. An horrific murder, by pressing a knee into a person's neck for almost 9 uninterrupted minutes, by a policeman on duty, was viewed via video by billions around the globe. As a result, what erupted from billions around the globe, from all nations and all nationalities, was civil unrest and the cry, "Black Lives

Matter." Without any doubt, if Malcolm and Martin were here they would have lead that hue and cry.

The first to have been born was Simeon, "The Fighter." He was born in this universe May 19, 1925 and given the name Malcom Little in Omaha, Nebraska. He was born to activist parents, Earl Little from Georgia, of the United States, and Louise Helen Norton-Little from the country of Grenada. Both parents were removed, early, from Malcolm's life leaving him to be reared in the Foster Home System. His daddy died when a street car struck and killed him under dubious circumstances. His controversial death was ruled an accident. His mother suffered a nervous breakdown some years later and was institutionalized for almost a quarter century before being released.

Malcolm's life took him on a journey that involved a stent in the United States' prison system. While there he found guidance through religion. He aligned himself with the Nation of Islam, which was under the leadership of Elijah Muhammad another native of Georgia, USA. There Malcolm became a Minister and rapidly excelled. The Angels explained he was given the Divine Gift of Multitudes. This explained his meteoric rise, world-wide, in the organization.

His elevation, in the arena of civil rights activism, catapulted him to the highest levels of scrutiny by his own religious organization, national government organizations, international government organizations and their respective agencies. He espoused the philosophy of self-determination for his people "by any means necessary." He was unwavering in his tenacity for truth and justice and vocalized that stance constantly and consistently. This unyielding position conjured up fear and opposition among many powerful forces and arguably propelled them into offensive modes.

There existed a chasm between Malcolm and the other spiritual leader, centered for one on their differing philosophies, which the Angels admitted they were unable to bridge until it was too late. Malcolm was murdered February 21, 1965 (age 39) by agents of those opposing forces. At his death he had pilgrimaged on a metamorphosis of names, outwardly, from Malcolm Little, to Malcolm X to finally el-Hajj Malik el – Shabazz. Inwardly, there was a metamorphosis in his philosophy regarding the coexistence and cooperation on all levels of human beings, to the end that his fight expanded from civil rights to that of human rights for his people.

Shakardak's acknowledgement of their misplaced faith in man's humanity, which allowed them to murder their spiritual leaders, and in God's chosen people, as being responsible for Malcolm's death, gave great credibility to Malcolm's lifelong fight and his philosophies.

# Chapter Three

## Second Born Spiritual Leader

<u>Martin Luther King, Jr.</u>

The other spiritual leader of that time was Martin Luther King, Jr. ((MLK) born Michael King, Jr. (after his father) January 15, 1929. He was born 4 years after Malcolm. He is "Mahaladek, the bringer of the message" before the Throne and the Angels of God. He later changed his name, as did his father, who was also Michael King initially. His father, an activist Baptist Minister, who fought for the civil rights of his people was born 1899 in Stockbridge, Georgia. After visiting Germany and becoming familiar with the German religious activist, Martin Luther, he named himself after him, Martin Luther King, Sr. His son Michael King, Jr. renamed himself, likewise, and became Martin Luther King, Jr. (An interesting caveat here: Malcolm X's father was born in the state of Georgia as was Elijah Muhammad as well.)

Like Malcolm X, MLK was given the Divine Gift of Multitudes also. He gained notoriety which propelled him to fame nationally and internationally when he assumed leadership of a historically famous bus boycott in Montgomery, Alabama. A major civil rights battle which ended with the Supreme Court outlawing segregation on buses within the United States. This success lead to nationwide efforts, among King's people, to earn freedom in varied aspects of their lives.

Their religious leaders established an organization through which to accomplish this and elected this Spiritual Leader, Mahaladek, as its

President: the Southern Christian Leadership Conference (SCLC). His participation in the organizing and speaking at a March on Washington, DC by hundreds of thousands of people, marching for Civil Rights on August 28, 1963, earned him his constant surveillance by the Federal Bureau of Investigation (FBI), a national law enforcement agency, until his death. It is felt by many that that agency was complicit in his assassination on April 4, 1968.

He advocated for acquiring civil rights for his people peacefully with nonviolent means of protest. This garnered great support, worldwide, for him and his followers who numbered in the millions. It also brought great angst, distrust, resentment and eventually his death from those who opposed his efforts. After his death, his followers were successful in having numerous streets, bridges, schools buildings and various other highly visible public mementos named for him.

He and Malcolm X differed decidedly in their methodologies for attaining the civil rights their people were due. Malcolm advocated doing so "By any means necessary" and MLK restricted any gains that were made be made by "peaceful passive non-violent" means, strictly. Malcolm X advocated for equality being attained "separately," MLK sought "integration" as a means of attaining equality.

They operated from completely different ends of the spectrum in their efforts to attain equality of civil rights for their people: a shared, common people. A people believed by many to be God's chosen people. Both were assassinated for their efforts: Malcolm X February 21, 1965, age 39; MLK April 4, 1968 (some 3 years latter) age 39.

# Chapter Four

## The Home Of Omni

<u>Louvinia Mariner</u>

A place known to me since 1984 as a place to learn meditation and grow spiritually, became a place more reverenced than any other place known on earth, in 1996. It became the Temple of Angels (The Home of Angels) instead of the "Home of Omni." It was located in Baltimore, Maryland on Howard Park Avenue. On numerous occasions the angels engaged the "called" and the "chosen" day and evening at that Temple to bestow knowledge on them for themselves and for the masses.

A husband and wife lived there together for decades, prior to the arrival of God's Angels. They taught classes and various and sundry means of spiritual development in which countless people participated and developed, for years.

On 3/16/1996 the angel Awaki remarked, "The Spirit of this Temple, speak unto me. I hear the voice, the question of the gift. What is your confusion?"

He spoke to the wife, the owner of the Home of Omni during one of their many visits to the Home.

"Of whose gift? My gift?" Louvinia, the wife, responded to him.

"It is within your understanding," he answered her.

"My gift, it is within my understanding," she said.

"It has been difficult for you," he said.

Her response was immediate, "No."

"Then you are obedient unto your God," he lauded her, praising her for her strong discipline.

Her response was immediate again, "Trying to every day, every minute, every second!"

"Then, I say unto you, that within the next 40 of your days there will be change in this place. Be not alarmed for you are already accepting our presence with cheer in your spirit. But, in the shadows of the Temple there will be Angels descending. Is this within your understanding?" he asked.

"Yes, it is," she said.

"Awaki is this the Temple for the Angels of God to descend upon in this universe?" Thomas, queried Awaki.

"That is within your understanding. For, I have spoken unto you these words: we have sealed this place unto us," Awaki agreed.

He confirmed that God's home for His Angels, in this universe, was now Louvinia's home that she had lived in for many decades with her husband.

The Prophet continued, "It is a holy place where no evil can come, where the elium lords cannot dwell. Is that correct?"

"They cannot, but they will try," Awaki agreed and continued his conversation about the owner of the Temple over the next 40 days. "And, in this she will see, in the shadows, the battles of the spirits."

"Is there anything for her to do other than her obedience to her God in terms of just carrying out her gift?" Thomas asked for her benefit.

"She has been instructed and when she sees the changes, and when she feels the breeze, and when she hears the stillness of the Temple of her God, then pray," Awaki spoke to her directly.

"And do what, pray?" she asked.

"It is within your understanding?" he answered her.

"Yes," she said.

The Home of Omni, was the "Home for all seekers of spirituality and God" for decades, prior to this. Many souls, seeking, had found themselves there under Louvinia's tutelage, myself included. It was no wonder that God chose her home as one for His Angels to do His work here in this universe: awaken and prepare those of us whom He had chosen to assist Him in the last days.

Those people were spoken of in the Bible but no one knew who they were; not even they themselves. So when the enlightenment started person after person was awakened to who they were, what their purpose was, and what the callings were that God had on their lives. They also became acutely aware of the freedom they had to do their own will in that regard. Louvinia was light in the lives of countless people and often led them to the path of light in their own lives. So what occurred there was in perfect order and of God.

"It is I," the Angel spoke on 2/21/1996.

"Is this the Holy Awaki?" the Prophet asked, as usual, when he engaged the angels at the beginning of a session.

"It is within your understanding," Awaki answered.

"Hello Awaki. We're here this afternoon with Louvinia. There are questions that she has, information that she seeks."

Present in the sitting room were the prophet, the Host, and Louvinia whose bodies could be seen. Awaki had invaded Nathaniel's body and was unseen but heard. He had dispatched Nathaniel to another realm. As always in the sessions, his body appeared limp, lifeless and comatose except for the movement of his lips.

From his lips the surly voice of Awaki was heard.

"The second entity. A special one. Have her come unto me," he instructed the Prophet Thomas.

"Very well," he said and had Louvinia sit in his seat in Awaki's presence.

She sat knees to knees directly facing Awaki. This was the standard posture taken by all who went before the Angels direct presence. All others took a seat within the room.

Awaki proceeded, "Take the hands of this Host into your hands."
She did.

He then continued, "Jah, when He walked in this time and space, was special not because He was sent to you by the Infinite Mind. He was special because He was the first and last to take on your form, your feelings, your experiences, in purity of spirit with a incorruptible soul. His wisdom was that of obedience and deliverance unto He who sent Him.

"When He chose His followers He spoke only unto them, 'if you believe, follow me.' And they did so. They did not question His existence. They were imperfect in the midst of perfection and could not understand His manner of wisdom and from what source did it come. But, still, they followed Him and left all that existed in their creative force behind. When Jah was questioned by one who had followed Him, to leave His presence to go back among those of his inheritance for a ceremony of resurrection, Jah said unto him, 'let the dead bury their dead.'

"And, when they moved on there were those who thought that His wisdom was at their discretion and for their superficial uses for insignificant and nonexistent problems in their creative force. But Jah said unto them, 'I am about my Father's business in obedience and deliverance. Through my display is my gift to you. Foolish and unlearned questions we will not deal with for I am flesh as you are but I am spirit unto my Father and I am here only to redeem unto Him that which He has created.' And then He fulfilled that which He came to fulfill. Ask the question."

"Are you speaking of the Christ?" she asked.

He answered, "Jah the Son Universe, Jesus, Yahweh, all are one. I am here to speak all manner of wisdom unto you that you may understand who Jah was and His mission, and Infinite Mind and His creation, and what is to come. That which is in your creative force is not my concern. When you draw your sword and choose of us then we guide you. When you choose not of us you have chosen your own destiny. Ask your question. I am within your soul. I can feel what you feel. I can see what you hide. Speak unto me."

"My soul seeks, I seek an understanding of this path that will lead us back, all new, to the source from whence we came," she explained.

That was an expected response from Louvinia, as that was the life she lived, that we knew. That's why we all visited her home, seeking, for years.

"You are speaking of your direction in this space and time. But that is not what you seek, for you can only seek those ends unto yourself and not unto others. Through your faith you can direct others but when they draw their swords they must choose. You seek the answer to your own salvation. Is that within your understanding?" He enlightened and asked her.

"Yes," she replied.

"You have been chosen. This host and our Prophet were sent unto you that the superficial display of our Father's may benefit those who seek the truth through purity of heart. This is only a beginning of the end and the end of the beginning. You are the mechanism through which the Infinite Mind will work His ends and His ends only. Other than His glorification and His preparation for the 11 and 40 unto us is foolish and unlearned, and in the 11 and 40, it will not exist. Be not concerned with it in this time and space.

"Our lessons unto our prophet have been that of obedience and he has learned to let go of the foolishness of men and in doing so he has experienced a divine guidance unlike any in your time and space. As I sit before you I sit before many in this universe. As I speak unto you in your tongues, I speak unto many, in their tongues, in this universe. This is occurring now, here and there and there and here. You have been given the opportunity to be a vessel for the ends of the Infinite Mind through your desire to know the truth; and the truth is this: obedience unto He who has created you will bring unto your creative force love and happiness. Ascension and resurrection are those things that have been distorted by the hosts of this universe. Ascension is possible for all who reach that level, but in order to reach that level you must be given a spiritual gift and you must use it to glorify the ends of the Infinite Mind. Should you corrupt His Divine Gift then ascension is not within your means. Is that within your understanding?"

"Yes," Louvinia said.

Awaki continued to enlighten her, as the task she had before her was colossal and specific to her only.

"You have learned the foolishness of men. The training and the knowledge that was not inspired, in all cases, by us. There can be no spiritual gift unless it is given unto you by He who has created you and is not given without your knowledge. Is that within your understanding?"

"Yes," she answered.

"For, He cannot hold you and charge you with that which you cannot understand. And you have the teaching of men and the spirit of He who has sent you. I have been charged in the 11 and 40 to prepare all who seek the truth, of the truth.

"This is your day to draw your sword and be resurrected in the truth and the light of the Infinite Mind. That which you have known and learned is the foolishness of men. Put all in the past from you and begin to understand that the Infinite Mind wants you to know the truth.

"You ask a simple question and listen for a complicated answer- for that is not of us, for we are simplistic that you may understand the truth. That is His will and that is our command. Is that within your understanding?"

She said, "Yes."

"Ask the question," he instructed her.

"Am I moving or in my teaching, those that come to me, am I using the wisdom of God in helping them?" she asked.

"That which you speak unto them is confused," he said. "Your heart cries unto us for that wisdom but your mind that is in the universe embraces the teachings of men. Is that within your understanding?" He didn't give her time to answer, he just kept talking. "It is not your charge, to speak unto others wisdom, unless you have been charged by Infinite Mind.

"The Infinite Mind charges those and He gives them all manner of wisdom and these He calls His Prophets. They have been sent unto this universe, since it has been created. All others who attempt to understand the wisdom of the Infinite Mind fall short because they have not been given the true wisdom.

"You are in the wisdom and the power of He who has created you because you seek that true wisdom. That is why you are a vessel to the ends of the Infinite Mind. Your gift from Him is not that of prophecy or all manner of wisdom. Your gift from Him is not to heal those stricken with inadequacies. Your gift from Him is us that we are in this place to protect you, and bring unto you that which you seek.

"You have access to those who we have given the gift of healing unto. You have access to our prophet. You have access to us and as I have already spoken unto you, the keeper of the gates, Melchizedek, resides in this place, to keep it holy, that when we come unto this place that we are entering into the gates of holiness. That is why he was sent unto you for he is the keeper of the gates of the universe. That is your gift from us. Is that within your understanding?"

"Partially," Louvinia said.

This was a big surprise because it was rare that Louvinia did not understand what was spoken.

He told her, "Ask the question."

"How do I know? Is it a feeling or hearing, that---"

He stopped her immediately. "You hide your unreadiness in your place and time. There are times throughout your existence when you are nervous, when you have feelings that come upon you. That is because we move in this place and allow you to feel our vibrations when we touch you. You see things in this place. That is because we have sought out you to see them. There have been things unexplained that have occurred in this place. That is because we have so did them. You only need hear the bells and we are present.

"Yes, you are charged. I heard your voice. You are charged," he spoke to his Prophet.

Awaki did that often when he found the person to whom he spoke was unable to fully understand what he was saying to them. He would "charge" his prophet to make it clear to them.

Thomas spoke. "Remember when you were a child in school, when the bell would ring? All would stop and stand still and would not move again until the bell rang. When you get that feeling, be still. Not a literal bell."

"I understand. I understand," she said to Thomas.

"Ask the question," Awaki instructed her again.

"When I had the feeling of that which came to me to start a meditation class and I asked the question what do I do when confronted by those souls that have studied the Bible, I've never been a Bible student, and I was told to open my mouth and the words would be given unto me and that which I would speak of would be for the day. The Bible was written for yesterday. Yet there were times when I was sent to the Bible to get certain things to talk about. I was also told that that which I delivered would be understood by a 10 - year – old child. That's how simple it would be. I am wondering---"

Awaki stopped her again. "This is your response from this day forward when you're from the truth. The truth is this: obedience unto your God is your salvation. You prepare yourself. The end is the beginning and the beginning is the end. Once you have prepared yourself with that knowledge, then all else will be simplistic.

"You did not understand but our prophet is charged. When I have left this house our prophet will speak all manner of wisdom unto you. The end is the beginning and the beginning is the end. Be only concerned with that message.

"Pass that knowledge on to those who place themselves in your creative force and leave all other knowledge unto us for we will be in this place at your command. This host and this prophet will always make themselves available for the ends of the Infinite Mind for this is His will. Speak unto me."

This was brand new for Louvinia. She had been teaching all things of spirituality for years and years to all who entered the Home of Omni and beyond. She traveled far and wide (worldwide) to teach and be taught. She connected with her daughter, now transitioned as she, Corinnia Newcomb, a renowned spiritualist and lecturer, and they both taught, worldwide. So this change was shocking for her: these limitations and restrictions on her teaching, from an Angel of God, speaking for God Himself.

She asked him, "Am I to understand that out of all the readings and all the lectures that I have attended, I can put aside?"

"In your reading and in your lectures were we there?" he asked. "Speak unto me?"

"It was my feeling that you were there," she told him.

"Did I, or any of the Angels of God, speak unto you as I speak unto you now?" he asked.

She hesitated before she answered and then stammered when she did. "Some, not all, ...I did not,... deep within myself---"

He stopped her the same as before with an abruptness some may have thought rude.

"Do you understand who sits before you? I am Awaki, the Angel of Spirits. There is no spirit of the Infinite Mind that can move without me. For, the Infinite Mind has charged me and I am obedient unto His will and they are obedient unto mine and we are commanded by He who has created all. Do you understand?"

She answered, "Yes."

He continued.

"Then if we were not present and spoke all manner of wisdom unto you, then you have done what the hosts of this universe have done since it has been created and that is misconstrued and deceived and created your own wisdom.

"Throughout the creation of this universe, the Infinite Mind has sent His wisdom and His Angels unto those He chose. Those are prophets and those blessed with divine gifts unto his hosts. Man in his vainness has attempted to speak unto his God in disobedience.

17

"If it was possible for so many to have the wisdom of the Infinite Mind, what would be His need for Prophets in your time and space, since your creation, to deliver unto you His wisdom? Speak not to me of man's foolishness for there is only one God and one truth and one wisdom and it is delivered unto you by us to His Prophets, and only His Prophets. Is that within your understanding?"

"Yes," she said.

He did not let up. "For man has created a philosophy and a theory but he cannot know the truth unless it is spoken unto him. For, his philosophies and theories can be destroyed with a thought from He who has created all. For a philosophy is merely his opinion and a thought is merely His creation. And, any destiny, any direction can be changed by a thought from the Infinite Mind or a touch from His Angels. As we have touched your lives, we are changing that which you knew, that which you know, and that which you will know. Is that not within your understanding?"

She said again, "Yes."

"Ask the question," he said, "And, you, in your wisdom, must grow outside of your physical existence to receive pure truth and understanding. You have to allow to pass from you those emotions and fears. You have to embrace obedience and with obedience you will love all in your spirit. Allow no one to consume you with vainness, jealousy, dishonesty and deceit, and in turn, you live your life in that manner. Heal those misunderstandings one to another. These things that I speak of, you know of. Speak unto me."

"I have surrendered unto the Infinite. Every breath that I take is of the Infinite," she told him.

"Then you have understood the beginning of wisdom and knowledge," he began again, "which is obedience unto your God. Also you seek answers to problems of those who exist in your creative force and those who are of you. It is done.

"Be not concerned with their direction for your existence, they are blessed. As we have spoke unto you before, meditate unto your God only and He will answer for He has promised you and cannot break His promise unto you,"

Louvinia asked Awaki about another matter.

"Tell me, what is a salamander? What does that mean?" she asked.

"Unto us it has no meaning. Unto you, it is your creation. There is only one meaning unto us and that is obedience unto the Infinite Mind. What is the Parousia? Have you not heard us speak of it?" he asked her.

"Parousia? No," she said.

"Then, that is not within your understanding. When we last came upon this place we spoke unto the Parousia, but entities that were in my presence had no knowledge of it, but we said it and we can explain it, because we are it, so therefore it is.

"What you asked unto me, you cannot explain it, you did not create it, and you are not it, so therefore it has no meaning. Everything that we depart upon the hosts on this universe is of the Infinite Mind. It is carried out by us so we are it and we can explain it that you can understand it in its detail.

"But you speak unto me things that man has created and you do not understand it because it does not exist and you are not it and it cannot be explained for it is a creation of philosophies and theories and mind and man's foolishness," he said.

She persisted. "Is it possible that this is something that comes from eons of time before now?"

"In your present universe in time, you are able by means in the number of years you exist. Is that within your understanding?" he asked.

"Yes," she said.

"So in this present space and time your name in number. Speak unto me. Are you not 84? Is that within your understanding?"

"Eighty four?" she asked.

"Is that within my understanding?" he asked.

"You've written in years I didn't know about. Eighty two. I'll be 83," she corrected him.

"You are in this time and space 200 of your years unto us. Numbers are deceptive. You say 82 in your years. I spoke unto you eight and four in my understanding. And, in Infinite Mind's creation you are 200 of your years, existed in our presence. Now do you understand why the things of this universe concern not He who has created all?" he asked her.

"Yes," she said.

"You have been created in this time and space for this period in your re-engineering of this universe, to serve as a vessel. You have been allowed to continue your life for you have earned it and you are blessed to see and speak unto the Angels of your God. In your time and space. I would not have a number name for I have no number, for I have existed before this creation and I will exist unto all creation. Speak unto me. Do you understand why we transcend time and space?"

"Yes," she answered.

"And where did you get your understanding?" he asked her.

"I had an experience in which, at the time, I experienced my whole body on fire," she began. "And there was a feeling that something was being drawn through the top of my head. As I looked up there was a white cloud going out."

"That does not apply to us" he said and repeated, "Do you understand why we transcend time and space? You cannot transcend time and space because you exist within this time and space and this universe."

She just continued, "I felt that I was dying, that I was leaving this physical body," as though he had not spoken.

"That is within your understanding for your spirit can move on to other universes, to other experiences," he admitted. "But even in that, if you are not a prophet unto Infinite Mind to speak all manner of wisdom, to ascend, then your spirit moves on to another consciousness, another time and space. As I speak unto you in this time and space, I am also unto another universe, speaking in their time and space. Is that within your understanding?"

"That's within my understanding, yes," she said.

"Our Prophet, at Infinite Mind's command," he continued, "will ascend from this time and space unto others, to speak all manner of wisdom, and he will transcend time and space and move here and there and there and here, but you will only be able to leave here and go there. Is that within your understanding?"

"Are you speaking in terms of astral projection?" she asked him.

"You are speaking in terms of man's scholars," he told her. "We are speaking in terms of Infinite creation which your scholars cannot understand. Astral is a word your scholars created to explain travel through a universe, but yet they cannot travel to other universes. Why is that? It is because they do not understand and they do not know the truth. Their obedience to their God is the key to their technology and to salvation of this universe.

"It is time, but you must understand this: Angels of the Infinite Mind exist within this place to keep it pure that those may depart unto His prophet and His prophet unto the entities of this universe, the coming of the Third Covenant and the Parousia and the truth of all things. That is your blessing."

"May I …" she started to speak and stopped.

"Speak unto me," he encouraged her.

"Why do this body that you speak through, the face disappears? I am not using the third eye, I am looking through two physical eyes and it disappears," she asked him.

"It is a power of your faith and your reverence unto your God," he told her. "And, I have sealed this place unto us."

With that proclamation from Awaki the "Home of Omni" became "The Temple of Angels" their "Home" in this universe for the remainder of their time with us.

There were visits to the Temple, before this, when Louvinia encountered Awaki, 1/20/1996 was one such visit.

"I hear voices," Awaki declared. "There are entities with many voices. Ask the question," he instructed them.

"Will you address the voices that you hear and the entities that you hear them from?" the Prophet asked.

"The voices that I hear come from her who has asked the question. She is amazed by the display before her. She has many concerns. Many concerns about family members, but first we must deal with that which she really wants to know: the existence of spirituality and the direction of humanity. Ask the question," he invited them again.

"Can you give her information that she desires in that respect?" The Prophet asked him again.

"Her questions and her concerns are many. One that is of her (Corinnia Newcomb) and one that is not and their direction. The one that is of her is of us and has been given many spiritual gifts. And, as we speak, unto her direction is being changed. She is being re-engineered to move on to other spiritual gifts.

"Her other that is not of her, she is desirous of his direction. His direction is one of the sword. He is now placed in the valley in which he must draw his sword, and he has not chosen. Her questions and concerns

21

about humanity and that that deals with spirituality have to do with her role in the lives of others as she wants to teach and make them understand that it's within their power to control their lives and existence, that it's within their creative beings to bring unto themselves that which you refer to as a 'heaven,' peace of mind, and well-being.

"Be not dismayed for what you see is of the Infinite Mind. Ask the question," he encouraged her.

"About the child, the baby, that was born October 28, 1995," Louvinia spoke up, "what are his purposes for incarnating at this time?"

"The question that you asked is simplistic," Awaki answered her. "You talk in contents of time and space. You talk in contents of reincarnation. First, you must assume that there is death in your universe.

"To you, moving on to another consciousness and other experiences in the Infinite Mind, is your death. Death does not exist. There is no death. This child that you speak of who is not of you, that I spoke of, has not been placed in a position. He is in the valley in which to draw his sword. His destiny has not yet been chosen. Ask the question. You are confused."

"This present time, I desire to know if I'm moving in the right direction spiritually, to achieve, or to be of service, to mankind?" she asked him.

Louvinia passed right over, without giving any attention to the profound revelations that" there is no death," and no "reincarnation," concepts engraved in her. Concepts passed on to others by her too many times to count, during her lifetime.

Also, the issue of "destiny being predetermined before birth" was addressed and shattered by the truth of "his destiny has not yet been chosen." They all went totally without response from her.

"You, again, talk in time and space," he answered her. "You have already drawn your sword and chose. You are of one of us and we have been with you and will be with you, until you receive your gift from the Infinite Mind and move on to another consciousness and time and space. You are as you are. Is there truly perfection in the belief of the Infinite Mind, or is there improvements and choices for which you have drawn your sword to lead you in the direction of that which you seek, eternal and forever. Ask the question."

She remained silent.

"You are still concerned about the child," he said. "I say unto you today, for his Angel sits before the Throne of the Infinite Mind and will guide his path as he draws his sword through this time and space on your universe.

"Confusion is not something that is within our understanding, for we hear all your thoughts. Understand that you are, for if you were not, I would not have been sent by the Infinite Mind. Were you not, you would not be witnessing what you see before you today. You are humanity's choice, you are for service. Ask the question."

"Should I assist his mother in the certain materials that will help her---"

"You have already chosen," he interrupted her. "You have drawn your sword. This is your choice and we will look over you, guide you."

The Prophet intervened, "Awaki, perhaps the question is how could she better assist this mother in the development of this child, in order to lay the groundwork for him to make a choice that is in concert with the desires of the Infinite Mind?"

"Is she of us?" he asked him.

"She is," he answered.

"Have you not faith in He who created all?" Awaki asked her.

"Yes," she said.

"Then, you have already laid the groundwork. Your presence in anyone's creative force, in itself, is guidance," he told them.

Now, the Prophet persisted. "Awaki, I still think that she's asking on a practical level, if there's anything that needs to be done in our universe, in our space and time."

Awaki responded, "Then she must remember this lesson that was taught by the Son Universe: your purpose is to be of service to those who are poor of spirit and lack faith, within your creative force. Is that within your understanding?"

"Can you explain please?" the Prophet asked.

"She has powers given unto her by us. She has need but to use them in all that she desires to do. Then, she will direct anyone who is within her authority. Is that not within your understanding?" he said.

The Prophet responded, "It is within mine. Do you understand Louvinia?"

"Yes, yes," she answered.

23

"For we draw not the sword, for it is yours to control. Ask the question," he said again.

"My daughter," (Corinnia Newcomb) Louvinia said.

"That which is of you?" Awaki asked.

"Of me," she replied.

"She is our gift to you," he informed her. "And all that she has done, and all that she is about to do; there will be uncertain changes in her direction. There will be physical discomfort as she is being re-engineered to take on her new and Divine task.

"That which she has done is over. It is time now that she moves into a Divine spirit. Then she will be exposed to different people and cultures so that she may influence our will on their swords. You have earned that honor. That is why we have been with you throughout your time in this universe. Ask the question."

"My grandson, my daughter's son, his purpose?" she asked.

"He is in the valley of decision," he told her. "He has not yet chosen. He will soon draw his sword and he will choose that of which you have shown him, that of which has been shown unto him, but he will need help and understanding, for his deliverance comes by his own hands. Ask the question."

"Should I remain in this house, this city, and this state for the duration of my time?"

"Your question is not that which you ask. Your question is should you move on to other places to influence the minds of others, to lead them to that which you know exists, and to teach and to love? This deals with the essence of humanity in your creative force. It is within your choice, for where you go, the Infinite Mind shall be with you, and what you do, the Infinite Mind shall manifest, for you are kept and blessed for your faith. Your direction, your influence on humanity, is already done. You think in time and contents, we know all there is to know. It has been delivered unto you. Where you are, it is. Is that within your understanding?"

"Yes, yes," she answered.

"Ask the question," he invited her again.

"I am aware... I recently became aware of the energies that... I know the energies are the same but there are differences in the vibrations of energies," she explained to him.

"You speak of energies of this universe, in this time concerns. The energies are creations and emanations of your creative forces. We have sent unto this Host (the Spiritual Leader whose body he was in), a warrior of spiritual battles, which is pure energy.

"You seek that understanding but you can't understand that which is not of this universe. But, there is a spirit of the Yad Ying in this house. There is a spirit of Melchizedek, in this house. These have been sent unto you to guide you and to keep you in this time for which you have to draw your sword and choose.

"And, these were sent to protect and to uphold your faith in all that you have done and all that you have seen. In your prayers, when you pray, and your meditations, we hear the voices as you call upon, the spirits and the angels of the Most High, to give you strength for that task which you are about to undertake, and for those decisions that you were about to deliver. He is the keeper of the gates, He opens and closes the doors of many universes."

The Prophet intervened again, "Do you speak of Melchizedek?" he asked.

"This is within your understanding." Awaki answered, yes. "He controls, for the Infinite Mind, the doors for the universe. That is your power. Is this within your understanding?" he asked Louvinia.

"Yes," she said.

"Ask the question that is within your mind," he asked her and went on to explain without waiting for her to ask it. "You, again, need for me to clarify who he is in your universe and time. Melchizedek has many names in many universes. In your universe, he is known to you as the Archangel, the Holy Gabriel, that which controls the doors of the universes for the Infinite Mind. Ask the question."

"How does the Ascended Master, St Germane---" she started.

"St Germane is in your universe, a theory, a philosophy, a possible existence, a creator of other men's talents and desires," Awaki answered before she finished. "He is just what you have created him to be, a philosophy and a theory. That which existed to create for others, is a spirit, sent by the Infinite Mind for a purpose, to create a mechanism for the hosts that dwell in this universe. For, greatness is chosen and there must be a Divine Mechanism to achieve our ultimate end. Is this within your understanding?"

"Can you explain more?" the Prophet asked.

"Not quite," Louvinia said.

"You talk of a man, a theory, a philosophy, that we know as a Divine Spirit, sent to guide the hosts of this world in this time that the Divine Mechanism, which Infinite Mind has bestowed upon many men, could be developed and created. Is that within your understanding?" Awaki told them.

"I think…" she began and paused.

"Ask the question. For it is time," Awaki told her.

"Are there any questions?" the Prophet asked.

"No," she said.

"Understand this," Awaki continued. "Those in your universe that have reached a level of greatness spiritually, sustenance-ly, mythology, in all those areas, were given a Divine Mechanism to serve a purpose for the Infinite Mind. It can come in many forms, but only your faith can believe in the possibilities, and the possibilities in all things, is your faith."

She asked Awaki, "Are you saying to me that this entity, St. Germane, has been presented in my mind through books and other things, and feelings I have… it has come to be?"

"This is within your understanding," he reassured her. "There are many things in your universe that have been created by the possibilities, and the possibilities of faith in all things. There have been men who have taught about gods with heads of animals. There have been men who have taught about goddesses who create beauty and fashion, but you know us through the greatness of those we choose, and those we choose only. It is time," he said and exited the Host.

They both thanked him as he left.

Weeks after Louvinia had been given the parameters limiting and restricting her teaching of spirituality, the subject of it surfaced again. Awaki visited the Temple to bestow Divine Gifts on those who were chosen to receive them on 3/7/1996.

The Prophet engaged him in the usual manner, after which Awaki told him, "There are questions that you have."

"The only question I have pertains to Louvinia," he said, "and her role, because you know she has the Friday groups. She and I had talked briefly, and I have spoken to her as instructed. And, of course, as you know, I will be coming on Friday evenings. The question is her role and her role as counselor versus her role as speaking prophecy- she's clear on that point."

"Do you remember, as I spoke unto you, when this host asked for the 'wisdom' of Solomon?" Awaki asked him.

"Yes, I remember your answer," the Prophet answered.

"And, I said unto you, it was not wisdom but what you would call 'common thinking?'"

"Yes," the Prophet said.

"Then her role as an advisor pertaining to the things of this universe is within her ability. Pertaining to the things that are not of this universe and time and space, only the prophets chosen by Infinite Mind can be charged. Is this within your understanding?" Awaki asked him.

"It is. It is clearly within my understanding," he answered.

"Is that within your understanding?" Awaki asked Louvinia.

"Are you speaking to me?" she asked.

"I speak unto you," he answered.

"Yes. I am not to speak of things of wisdom that is not of this space and time," she told him.

"Then, it is within your understanding," he acknowledged.

"Yes," she said to him.

He continued and told her, "For, we give all manner of wisdom of Divine truth unto the prophets chosen by He who has created all, and He was sent unto you, that these things will work to the ends of your God. Is that within your understanding?"

"Not quite," she said.

"Your confusion is separation between the ends of the Infinite Mind and that which you can speak of," he told her and gave her some specifics. "Remember this: those things that man has created over your time and space through theory and philosophy are yours to ponder. Those things spoken unto our prophet, all manner of wisdom sent by He who has created all, is the only truth and not of this universe. For you cannot understand the truth of He who has created you, and His purpose and His ends unless we are sent unto you. And, that we give all manner of wisdom unto you as we have been commanded to give unto our prophet. Zimblach."

27

That expression "Zimblach" signaled the end of a session of instructions, to which everyone had become accustomed. That ended the session.

Jasper Mariner

On 1/20/1996, Awaki spoke in the Temple, "I hear many voices, that of a second entity. He has no thoughts about what he sees. Believe in the possibilities of true faith, comes from the experiences that you, in this universe, have. He is well of heart, strong of spirit, but has many experiences. His faith is in that who has created all, the Infinite Mind. But, he deals with thoughts of spiritual hosts. Ask the question."

The Prophet responded, "You say he has thoughts of the spiritual hosts. Can you explain what you mean by that?"

"He is a host for his spiritual soul, which is strong, and will be with him for many of your years. But, he has questions regarding faith, the possibilities of all things, is the true definition of faith, as we have discussed."

He was addressing, the husband of Louvinia, Jasper Mariner, The owners of the Home of Omni, now the Temple of Angels. One of the experiences that Jasper shared with me and others that helped him to develop his faith, occurred many, many years prior to this encounter with Awaki.

As a much younger man, (he was approaching 90 at the time of Awaki's visits) he sought to become a member of a secret spiritual society. One task required of him for membership was that he speak Japanese during the intake ceremony. He spoke only one language, English.

"When his turn came to speak Japanese during the ceremony, he spoke it fluently. He told the story with much laughter, each time, because it gave satisfying, convincing and living proof of the amazing power of God in our lives; if we only chose to believe. The laughter was total acceptance of the possibility of all things being possible, including his speaking Japanese with zero knowledge of the language.

Awaki continued to speak of him, "The second entity who is among us, he has a question, he does not want to ask."

"Jasper, is there a question that you have?" the Prophet asked him directly.

"Yes," he said, "I would like to know if my positive agreement, to speak to young people at schools, will be beneficial to them."

Awaki spoke directly to him. "Again, as the other entity (Louvinnia), you have been chosen. Your union was not by coincidence. You were chosen for each other. Your spirit is strong. Your faith must be strengthened. Your desire to be an influence is beyond that which you ask.

"You have only to draw your sword and choose but you feel that you are not capable, but you possess a strong desire. You are, and will be, a strong and creative force in the lives of those whom you speak. Your time in this universe is growing short. Do as He in the Son Universe, and be of guidance to those who cannot guide themselves. Is this within your understanding?"

"Uh Huh," Jasper said.

The Prophet overheard the exchange and knew Jasper was confused over what Awaki had explained to him. They, along with the wife, Louvinia, had a long time relationship for years studying spirituality. So he knew him really well.

He spoke up, "I think, also Awaki, he wants specific information. He understands what you're saying, that it would be for a good purpose. But he wants specific information about any pitfalls in terms of carrying out this activity."

Awaki addressed Jasper, directly. "Throughout your existence in this universe, have you experienced disappointments? Is this within your understanding?"

Jasper hesitated and did not respond.

The Prophet intervened, "It's within mine. Do you understand Jasper? He's asking you, throughout your life have you ever experienced disappointments?"

"Oh, Yes," Jasper then replied.

"Are not you still in existence? Have not you conquered that which has attempted to destroy your sustenance?" Awaki asked him.

"I can't understand," Jasper said.

"He's not understanding you, Awaki; not understanding specifically what you're getting at," the Prophet stepped in again.

Awaki explained more to Jasper. "You have been given the ability to choose, and you chose that of the Infinite Mind. Throughout your existence in this universe, you have experienced downfalls and catastrophes but you have, through your faith, overcome all that has been laid before you.

"Then, doubt not now your ability to overcome and conquer that which cannot stand before you. Strengthen your faith and thine can create all things. The possibilities are faith, and anything, in faith, is possible. Is that within your understanding?" he asked him.

"Uh, huh," he answered, the same as before.

The Prophet asked Awaki specifically, "Is there anything he should do to protect himself from any persons who will be involved in his speaking to the students at the school, for the purposes they may have that are not in concert with the Universal Mind?"

"He needs not to protect himself for we are with him and have been," Awaki reassured them both.

"Is there anything that he should know in that regard?" the Prophet persisted.

"Remember the love that was shown you as a boy in your time of need, and manifest that love through your faith to help those who need of you," Awaki told Jasper.

"Any other questions that you have?" the Prophet asked.

"No that's it," Jasper said.

Some were blessed to have multiple encounters with the Angels; Jasper was one of those. On the afternoon of 3/27/1996 he sat in the presence of Awaki again.

"Hello, Awaki. This afternoon, as you know, we're at the Home of Omni again and we have Jasper with us," the Prophet told Awaki.

"There are voices in his mind. Come unto me," Awaki called Jasper.

He left his seat and exchanged places with the Prophet. He sat directly in front of Awaki; knees to knees almost touching but not quite.

"What is that you ask of me? I hear voices of your mind but there are those who cannot be where I am. Speak unto me. What is it that you ask of us? You are concerned about this time and space and your existence here and there. Is that not within your understanding?"

Immediately the Prophet helped Jasper with the question, "Is that correct or do you want him to be more specific?"

Jasper answered them, "Yes, I'd like to know about my spirituality.

Why I'm….. How I can be more in possession of spirituality. What is the holdup? Why I've not been enlightened like most people?"

"Why are you concerned with, in this time and space, is it not your physical existence? Do you not think often on this place and that place that you will pass upon? Is that within your understanding?" Awaki questioned him.

"Yes," he admitted.

"He's asking you if you often think about your transition," the Prophet said to him.

"Yes, yes I do." Jasper admitted again.

"Then, that is the essence of your spirituality; that which you feel has not been given unto you," Awaki told him.

"Can you explain that in more detail, please?" the Prophet asked.

"It is he, whose thoughts are on this time and place, and not on what has been done. Let go of that which you think of for even I know not your God's time. For, He stands outside, and when your transition is inevitable, thus will He send us. Is that within your understanding?" Awaki told them.

The Prophet, explained it to Jasper. "He said you should stop focusing and concentrating on when your transition will take place because even he, as one of the Archangels, does not know the time of your transition. And, that your God stands outside of time and space and when He commands your transition to occur then that's when the angels will come. But before that time they don't know."

"Is that within your understanding?" Awaki asked Jasper again.

"Yes," he said.

Awaki continued, "And when you let go of that, of this time and space, then shall you experience that which you ask in faith. We have spoke unto you and have said that in this place thee are blessed. For we have sealed this Temple unto ourselves. Worry not for where you go in the time that your God sends us so shall you live and be as us. Is that within your understanding?"

"I'm afraid not," Jasper said.

"For your choices, when you drawed your sword has continually been of us. As you continually ask yourself 'am I doing the will of my God? Am I submitting unto His ends?' That say ye unto your God and He has thus rewarded you. Be not concerned with the time of your transition and your spirituality will become a living spirit unto your faith in your obedience. Is that within your understanding?" Awaki clarified further for him.

"Yes," he answered.

Even though Jasper admitted understanding what had been said to him, Awaki still told him, "Ask the question," and he did.

"My question is my association with a group of fellows who have a very negative attitude. Do I continue that with them, discussing pros and cons of what's happening on this earth, or should I let go of them?" he asked.

"Do as you will; for we are with thee," Awaki began, "But, know this, that those who wrestle with truth cannot find the path unto their God. And when it becomes foolish and unlearned then they have chosen and it was not of us. For those who are of us open their minds that they may seek true knowledge and wisdom and choose of us and we guide their paths. Those who close their minds to our knowledge of their existence and unto their God, have chosen their own path. Is that within your understanding?"

"Yes," he said.

Awaki told him, "Their foolishness has no determination upon your truth."

He kept Jasper in his presence and continued to probe him.

"There is another question. It is concerning she who has been chosen for you. Ask the question,"

Jasper started, "I'm quite concerned about healing abilities. Do I possess the healing abilities---"

Awaki stopped him. "That is not the question. Your question is about she who has been chosen for you. For you are concerned about her and her abilities and her physical existence. You have often thought, and have been concerned, and we have heard you. For, this is now the time to ask unto us."

"I don't understand," Jasper told him.

The Prophet spoke up again, to help him out. "What he's saying is that you have questions about she who has been 'chosen for you,' or Louvinia. They're saying that you should discuss and ask about those things now, because this is the time for it."

"My concerns about Louvinia?" he asked.

32

"Yes," the Prophet answered.

"Oh my goodness, real concerns about her!" Jasper said and turned his concerns to Awaki.

"You've explained about my transition and I'm often concerned about how she will live," he stated.

"This is not what we have just spoken unto you," Awaki told him. "Are you not concerned about her time and space, in this plane, in this universe? These are the things that you must not be concerned for you to become truth in spirituality and understanding. For, we have taken unto ourselves her soul. As we have spoken unto you, this place is a Temple, sealed unto your God. Be not concerned about that, nor concerned about her abilities and what she has to do to be obedient unto her God for she is walking in obedience. It is difficult what is being done and her God is pleased. Now, ask the question."

"Do I have a guardian angel that protects me as I go through life?" Jasper asked.

"As you call 'angels,' there are many that are charged to take care of those who have been chosen and given spiritual gifts. You do not have what you call an 'angel.' Is that within your understanding?" Awaki answered.

"Explain, please," the Prophet asked.

"Is this within your understanding?" Awaki questioned Jasper.

"No, I don't understand," he told him.

"You speak as if we are assigned unto you, one unto a host, one unto a host. This is not. We are many. We are here unto all, unto your wave of your hand and a nod of your head. Then, they shall be upon you. Not one, not two, but madrids upon madrids upon madrids, if your God so commands. Is that within your understanding?" Awaki explained.

"No, it's not. Could you explain that please?" Jasper asked.

"You are charged," Awaki instructed the Prophet to tell Jasper what he just told him.

"What he's saying that is that you're speaking in the context of just having one guardian angel. What you refer to as 'Angels,' they refer to as Spirits of God. You have many more than one, and they're assigned not only to take care of you, but all those who walk on the path of righteousness. They are available to you with a wave of your hand and with a nod of your head, as God commands them to be available to you. And it's madrids. It's thousands upon thousands of them to assist you and to help you and to take care of you. You have many more---,"

Awaki stopped him and asked Jasper, "Is this within your understanding?"

"Yes, I understand it now," he said.

"Speak unto me," Awaki told him again.

"What are your other questions or concerns?" the Prophet explained.

"I have one more question," Jasper added. "The question is, did I hear voices that call my name, and sometimes I think my wife called me. When I answer her she says she hasn't called me."

Awaki told him, "I spoke unto her, the Spirit of this Temple, and we had told her that there will be changes unto this place, that there will be many spiritual battles, in the shadows. Did not we speak unto you? That which you hear are many voices. As they move here and there you will hear beautiful psalms of rejoicing. Be not dismayed for it is your angels' psalms of victory in this place."

Jasper moved back to his original seat after he received the answers to his questions.

"There is another," Awaki said.

"I have a question." Louvinia, Jasper's wife, also present, spoke up. "The question I have is concerning Jasper's daughter. I think he spoke in terms of her having some concerns about her spirituality. She is teetering, you know, straddling the fence."

"Come unto me," Awaki said. "He who she speaks of."

Jasper returned to the presence of Awaki and again sat in front of him.

"Do you understand why I spend this time on you, dealing with things that do not concern this? Is this within your understanding?" Awaki asked him.

He did not respond but just sat silently.

The Prophet intervened. "He's asking if you know why he's spending the time talking with you now."

"Yes, I understand why he's spending time talking to me," Jasper said.

"Then, why is that?" Awaki asked him.

"To answer the questions I have in my mind for a long time," he answered.

"This is not within your understanding," Awaki said, no it isn't and continued. "For, I have only been charged to prepare this universe for the Parousia and it does not need for me to fulfill the understanding of the hosts of this universe. I spend time unto you because she who has asked is concerned about you. And, we have given unto her a gift and that gift is our presence. And, so shall she ask the question, am I commanded to answer. And I will answer unto you.

"Be not concerned for those who are of you that are in the valley of decision, for they have to choose. You can only do as your God did for He (Jesus) who He sent, and that is, give unto them knowledge and understanding of what is to come, then they must choose. When they draw their swords, it must be in obedience to their God, or disobedience to their God. Each will be rewarded equally.

"In obedience, we shall guide and protect as we did with He who was sent unto you. And in disobedience, you choose your own path and that which you create, suffer unto yourself. Then, they must understand that. Speak that unto them and then you must let go, as your God has done. For, they have been given the gift of choice. Is there a question?" He asked Jasper.

"Yes," Jasper answered, "I am quite concerned about, there seems to be a little dissension within this family, and I am a man who loves family unity. Am I---"

"You are." Awaki answered Jasper's unasked question. "Are not you given unto them? Are not they given unto you? It is within your ability to speak unto them that which we have spoken unto you, and then once you have done all that you can do, then call upon your God and ask, and it shall be given unto you. Is that within your understanding?"

"Yes," he answered.

"Zimblach." Awaki said, and ended the conversation.

On yet another occasion, 3/30/1996, he was blessed again to be in Awaki's presence,

"To those, there is a voice, come unto me." Awaki spoke. "It is he who is of the spirit of this home. Speak unto me." He invited Jasper to come sit in his presence as on occasions before.

Jasper obeyed and placed himself in front of Awaki. "What do you want to know?" he asked him.

"Why do you wrestle with us so?" Awaki asked him.

35

"I try to be very spiritual," Jasper said, "I didn't know I wrestled with myself. Can you explain what you mean when you say I wrestle with myself?"

"You are not satisfied when we speak unto you," Awaki explained. "For, you see the countenance of others and wish unto yourself these things. And, you question why, and you, even after we have spoken unto you, are still preoccupied with your transition. Do you know what your gift is?"

"No I don't," Jasper answered.

"Were you aware of a gift?" he asked him.

"No," Jasper said.

"Do you desire from your God this gift?" Awaki asked.

"Yes, I do, very much," he answered.

"Then this is your gift. You, throughout your life and existence on this earth, have chosen of your God when you were in the valley of decision and had to draw your sword. And, we have guided you here and there, there and here and you have experienced many things, and you are set among men in your generation for who you are.

"You depart wisdom upon those generations below you and you are on the Council of Elders before your God. So why do you wrestle so with all that you have been given with this space and time? You were not given a gift like those who have been charged because you have been before your God all of that time and blessed and held, and you sit before your God on the Council of Elders.

"Do you desire your transition or do you seek to enjoy the presence of the Angels of this Temple? It is your choice," he told Jasper.

Jasper laughing, spoke immediately. "I desire the Temple of Angels, not my transition."

"Then wrestle not with us again with these things. Zimblach." Awaki ended his conversation.

The Prophet asked Jasper, "Do you have any other question?"

"I don't know exactly what my gift is," Jasper lamented.

"You sit with the Council of Elders before God---" the Prophet started to explain.

"You are charged, not at this time, there are others. Zimblach." Awaki stopped the conversation a second time.

"And remember this, that we monitor your thoughts and are forever in this place so think not you hide these things from us. Do you know why I called you before me?" he admonished Jasper.

"I think it was to tell me my gift," he answered.

"I was answering the prayers and the anguish of the Spirit of this home for we are to do as commanded and she asked and so we have given you understanding of who you are. Go thee therefore," and with that he dismissed Jasper again.

"Thank you, Awaki." Jasper accepted and ended the conversation too.

# Chapter Five

## Spiritual Leader Nouveau

### Nathaniel Keys

<u>Spiritual Battles</u>

When you hear the term "Spiritual Leader" you immediately envision a church associated person: a Pastor, a Deacon, a Sunday school Teacher, or some such person, most likely. You would least likely think of a 28 year old, medically disabled, retired policeman, as such. Also, you would not likely associate such a person with Angels.

That was the case here. Nathaniel Keys, at his designation as such, was 28 years old, married father of three children; living the life of father, husband, and steady working state employee. A steady, stable, normal young man, doing what young people did at that age. Prior to retiring he admitted being a regular, typical cop, doing what cops do inside and sometimes outside, (or not strictly "by the book,") the law.

He came to my life via his cousin who was my attorney and a formally trained priest. He and I went to dinner one December evening in 1995. He wanted to discuss with me and invite me to some gatherings he and his cousin, the attorney, were hosting. He told me a most bizarre tale. He related, Angels were using his body, through which, to talk to people. He was rational, calm and sincere in his invitation and tale.

I committed, verbally only, to attending-- unknown to him. He took me seriously as he respected me as a physician, a member of the organization he had just joined with me and generally as a human being.

He had no reason to doubt me when I said I would attend. I just did not--- contrary to my promise to him.

Fast forward to 2 ½ years later, when I received proof of all that he told me that evening. I was granted access, June 1998, to all recorded notes and tapes (video and audio), of every documented gathering they hosted. Those gatherings happened for a six month period, from 11/ 3/ 1995 to May 15, 1996. In those records were accounts that proved his body was used by at least 7 different angels (Awaki [Micheal], Shakardak, Laiki, Melchizedek [Gabriel], Azreal, Myackaoka, & Marchardak) who spoke to 75-100 people (myself included), during that 6 month period.

To add intrigue to intrigue, it was proven, via the records and my own evaluation of him, as a physician, that he was unconscious, oblivious to each occurrence, out of his body (NO palpable or observed body life functions), and replaced by an angel in his body during each occurrence, save one.

The very first recorded session said it all, though no one knew what it meant at the time.

The first audio recorded session by his cousin Thomas, 11/3/1995, was heard from his body, while he appeared sleep and lifeless, except for what was heard coming out of his mouth.

He recorded a voice which was raspy and softly spoken, like a whisper. "I am Shakardak, Shakardak, Shakardak."

Thomas engaged the voice, which clearly was not Nathaniel's. "Shakardak, we know you are of the light. Tell us about your assignment. Tell us about your dominion. Tell us how we can assist you."

The voice responded, "I am one of thee, I am one of you. I belong to Awaki, the Angel of Spirits."

Thomas continued, "Can you tell us exactly what 'Shakardak,' what the translation for it is in English; to get a greater understanding of your energy and your role and where you stand in front of the Throne?"

"I am 'The Deliverer' and a 'Warrior.' I have fought many battles. I am Shakardak. I belong to Awaki."

"What kind of battles have you fought? And, what were the purposes?" Thomas asked.

"I have fought many battles for those who are not for the Great Transition. My spirit is strong, but it has been at rest."

"Why was your spirit at rest?" Thomas questioned him.

"The battles over a period of time continues in the Universe. I have now been awakened to again fight the battles for Awaki." Shakardak told him.

"What can we do to assist?" Thomas inquired.

"Do what you must," he told him.

"We desire to know specifically, how can we do to stand strong in the light for the Great Transition of which you speak?" he asked Shakardak.

"You cannot stand strong in the light," Shakardak told him.

"Is it because we are incapable or that that's not our position or our role?"

"Your role is to do what you will." Shakardak responded. "Your spirit have not passed on, for He who have given it, the Infinite Mind. You have not the energy to fight."

Thomas continued to probe, "And what are we supposed to do, here on this side or at this time, in this body, in this matter, in this world?"

"Prepare. Prepare for battle." Shakardak told him.

"How do we prepare?"

"Do what you will. Do what you will." Shakardak repeated himself.

However, he did explain a bit more. "You will be given guidance and direction. And I, Shakardak, will give you spiritual guidance on how to win the battle."

"When will you give us that guidance?" Thomas asked.

"At your will," he said.

"We desire it now."

He responded to Thomas, "First you must understand the spiritual battles, transform war. In your present host is spirit occupied. You must seek, and I'm to transform and strengthen his spirit. For there will come a time the Infinite Mind will transform you into warriors. Help in the battle against darkness, evil. The Elium Conqueror, at that point in time, will defeat the elium.

"The lord of death will seek to destroy all those in your universe that have become a Spiritual Leader for the battle of 12 and 40. He will come for you. He will come when the signs are given to devour the host Spiritual Leaders. Those have already been chosen for the battle of the 12 and 40," he explained to Thomas.

"Will he (the elium) destroy all?" Thomas asked.

"No," Shakardak answered him.

"Who will he devour?" Thomas questioned him.

"Those that do not prepare themselves. Preparation. How do you prepare? That is your question," Shakardak said.

"Yes," Thomas answered.

"Each of those who has been chosen at the same point in time in this universe are experiencing what you may call 'phenomena'. All different. None have the same spiritual gift. But each, at the appointed time will guide to those that can teach them, prepare them, on how to use their gifts. And if they do not prepare, they really won't know it will devour them." Shakardak gave him more details.

"Will they rise again even though they are devoured?"

"No," he told Thomas.

"What will happen to their spirits and to their souls?" Thomas asked.

"Their spirits will be held in transition. Their souls will remain here until the completion of the Great Transition." Shakardak explained.

"And what of us who prepare? What will happen to our souls?" Thomas continued.

"Those who prepare will have to fight the physical battle of the elium lords who look like them. They come out in Transition. They walk among them. As the Infinite Mind prepare those who have been chosen, by awakening, so does the elium lord prepare those who have been chosen for the battle. They walk among us.

"You will not know them at the time, but they will know you. If properly prepared, those who have been chosen, will be protected by our light that will glow." Shakardak, answered him.

"You keep saying 'prepared.' Can you explain in more detail what's necessary for preparation?" Thomas asked.

"True light. Spiritual growth. Remove from the host spirit, at our direction, that that has confined his spiritual evolution," he answered.

"There is not a blockage inside to his spiritual evolution that should be removed. What are the confinements?" Thomas asked on Nathaniel's behalf.

"Confusion. Confusion of who he is," Shakardak explained. "He has been chosen. Chosen because he is so active in displaying the openness of his mind."

"Can you answer the questions that he has so that he can hear them after you leave him as a host? He's very much concerned about the purpose of all of this. Not just the purpose of why he was chosen, but what he is supposed to do with the information."

Shakardak responded, "I will answer the questions that he has. The purpose of this is the purpose of the Infinite Mind. He has been chosen because you gave him a gift and he looked with his heart and mind."

Nathaniel told me, Thomas gifted him a crystal ring before the angels began to use his body. The day he received and arrived home with it, the "ring began to chant." He immediately called and told Thomas, who went to him. Upon hearing and questioning the sounds Thomas realized, from his Priesthood background, that Nathaniel was being used to allow angels to speak to us through his body.

"How can he learn the purpose of the Infinite Mind?" Thomas asked

"He cannot learn that which he is incapable of understanding," Shakardak informed him.

"How can he know? He desires to know," Thomas pleaded.

"He has become your charge to help him to understand," Shakardak assigned Thomas.

"Very well. The charge is accepted. He also wants to know how we, he and I, are supposed to distribute information or disseminate information to other like souls. Is this our duty, is this our role at this time?"

"Prepare. As you properly prepare him, this host, what your kind may do, to his spirit, take on the task to create." Shakardak answered.

"He is not prepared at this time," Thomas acknowledged and said, "Sometimes the bird only flies when it's pushed off the ledge."

No one we knew, was prepared for any of this. Angels taking over someone's body, literally, and then talking to others through it. No, he definitely was not prepared for that and neither were we. Not any of us.

Shakardak then said, "This host is omnipresent in many universes."

He let Thomas know just how prepared Nathaniel was: he existed in all of God's countless universes. He just wasn't "prepared" here in this universe.

"Understandably," Frank responded. "Is now the time to eliminate those confinements?" he asked.

"That is your charge," Shakardak reminded him of his assignment again.

Thomas said, "Hmmm."

Shakardak continued, "As I go to other energy impulses of this host, I feel his feelings, I hear his thoughts, I know his actions."

"Speak to him," Thomas told Shakardak.

"Yes, I have, and I will," he assured him.

"Very well," Thomas said.

What else could he say? He was facing a daunting task which he committed to God to do. He had to convince a 28 year old novice, of things of the spiritual world, to willingly let a foreign subject take over his body, 100 percent, send him out of it as though he were in a coma and be "ok" with that. And, this was to take place at the sole discretion of the foreign subject.

"I have traveled a long distance. I have crossed many deserts and many skies," Shakardak intimated.

That announcement made it all seem more real and plausible. We all knew what "skies" and "deserts" were. Imagining the long travel was easily possible, even. We think of the habitat of Angels as being quite some distance away from us, normally and in general. So his report of his journey to reach us kept it in the realm of possibilities and easier to accept as being real for us all.

"Can you describe them?" Thomas asked.

"Deserts are made of white sand. The skies are black dark. Travel, darkness, brilliant light, the stars, the tunnel," he said.

"Will the Spirits of Light be successful in the battle of which you speak? In the battle that is to come," Thomas questioned him.

"The Spirit of Lights have already won," he answered.

"Will Infinite Mind be glorified?" Thomas continued to probe.

"He is already," he said.

"Will this be the way for more people and more spirits---"

Sharkardak stopped Thomas.

"Universe wars adjust the will of the light with Infinite Mind. Your Universe wars against the Sun Universe to cause the spiritual Armageddon;

must take in your Universe and then will Infinite Mind be glorified. Your Universe is one of the last universe that has not met the elium lord defeat. Your Universe is about to come alive 12 and 40 with the other Universes of the World Savior. Evolution, spiritual evolution, 12 and 40 will take place in this universe. Angels will then become your friends. They will speak to you. They will walk among you. They will teach you 12 and 40. But first the battle, if you properly prepare. Prepare with what you have been given, the battle is already won," he told Thomas.

"Thank you," Thomas said. "We want to, desire to train the energy, to train the light. We are very, very thankful for all things that you have told us. And we thank from the bottom of our heart of hearts. Please be gentle in leaving this host. Is there anything else you want to say at this time?"

Shakardak said, "You really want to concentrate on past spiritual battles so you can understand why they took place. The past spiritual battle of this universe was for---"

Thomas interrupted, "What type battles are you referring to? What we call wars?"

"---battles of the spirit." Shakardak finished his statement.

"Again for clarification and my understanding?" Thomas asked.

"The last days. Last days." Shakardak said.

"I understand. The last days in the sense… the last days of an age, or a particular time?" Thomas questioned.

"The Universe," Shakardak said.

"I understand," Thomas acknowledged.

Shakardak exited Nathaniel's body.

Nathaniel was out--- unconscious, and out of his body--- throughout that entire 45 minute ordeal. He was allowed to hear what transpired from the tape when he awoke, after Shakardak had commandeered and invaded it.

Upon awakening and listening to that tape he learned that Thomas was spoken to by an Angel named Shakardak. He learned that this angel had come to gather and prepare warriors (an army of sort). These warriors had to do what they "must" to help fight up – coming spiritual battles (a war) and he and Thomas were two of those warriors. He did not believe ANY OF IT.

Also those warriors had to be prepared for those battles against the

"Lord of Death" (Satan) who would be coming to destroy them. The war that was coming was a war against evil and was to take place to defeat evil.

He heard it all and was still unable to accept it, believe it or deal with any of it. Thomas had his job cut out for him: make Nathaniel allow it against this strong doubt, disbelief and unconsciousness? Colossal charge.

Within 7 days 11/10/1996, there was another encounter where Nathaniel had to submit his body to be used, sans his consciousness. The usual prologue or greeting occurred.

"In English please," Thomas said. "Whenever you're ready to speak we're ready and willing to listen," he told the incoherent visitor who had taken over Nathaniel's body.

"Myackaoka, Myackaoka, Myackaoka," was what Thomas heard.

"Whenever you're ready to speak in English, we're ready to listen," he repeated.

"Myackaoka, Mayackaoka, I am here. Where are you?" The voice continued.

"Who do you seek?" Thomas asked.

"Thee I seek, I have found. Myackaoka, I am here, where are you?"

"I am---" Thomas started and was interrupted.

"I am Myackaoka, speak."

"Can you tell me what Myackaoka means?" Thomas asked.

"Myackaoka," the Angel repeated.

"Myackaoka, what does it stand for?" Thomas asked again.

"Divine Evolution, in the Creator Spirit," the voice said.

"Myackaoka, what is your relationship to Nathaniel?" Thomas inquired.

"Divine guidance. The Great Transformation," Myackaoka responded.

"When do you guide him?" Thomas asked.

"At his will," he answered

"Do you guide him in his dreams?" Thomas continued to query him.

"No," the Angel replied.

"Why does he dream so much about outer space?" Thomas asked.

"I guide him in all his existences, in every universe," Myackaoka informed Thomas.

He confirmed what Shakardak had told Thomas earlier, that Nathaniel was present, simultaneously, in all of God's other universes just as he existed in this one. Thomas let that "go over his head" just as he did the first time it was revealed.

He ignored that revelation but probed other areas, "What about the different visions he has of the earth, which you know about?"

"All of it he understands, that as he exists here, so does he exist in all the universes," Myackaoka told him.

"Can you explain to him the significance of the numbers 1, 2, 2, 7 or 1, 2, 7, 2 and why those numbers are so important to him."

Getting that answer was of crucial importance for them to understand because the angels gave numbers from the beginning of their coming but no explanation as to what any of them meant.

"That is the time of the coming of the rebirth of the spiritual evolution. That at the time that all of those born in what you call 'the year of your Lord' were born in all the universes." Myackaoka told Thomas.

"Shall we take those years in their literal sense or in their numerological sense?" He asked.

Myackaoka explained, "To take, to understand that the Divine Creator, Infinite Mind, that inhabits all things, control all time, space, evolution, does so in accordance to the times of the various universes.

"12 in your universe, depicts the coming of the Disciples. 12 years from now, he will come all spiritually powerful (12 years from 1995 meant 2007). 12 is the time of the spiritual arrival.

"27 denote the time that the Infinite Mind has awakened throughout all universes those who will be part of the spiritual battle in the last days of the last generation."

"And 72?" Thomas asked.

"Denotes Royalty of the Most High," Myackaoka replied.

"What is Nathaniel's role in his life, in this universe at this time?" Thomas asked.

"He has none," he said.

"What is his purpose?"

"To be guided by the Divine Spirit as an earthly host for the spiritual battles," He answered Thomas.

"Can you tell us more about the spiritual battle? You've mentioned it before," Thomas asked.

"They have descended," Myackaoka said. "The spirits of all who will be chosen to fight the universal spiritual battle."

He explained further, "There will come a time in 12 and 40, when the battle must be physically fought in the flesh, here in your universe. 1967 was a year the generations were born of those who will be prepared to fight the spiritual battle in 12 and the number of your Lord the Divine Creator, 7, 40. 40 years of earth time; (they will be 40 years old). 12 years of now and then (1995 to 2007 equal 12 years). The spiritual battle will be complete. In 12 there will be a physical spiritual battle, in which he will have to endure, 12, 27, 7, 40."

Thomas asked, "What is the best way to endure?"

"I must leave you now," he said abruptly. "I must leave you now and yes."

He left uttering unknown words in that "chanting" like manner, as they all did when they came and went. Before he left though, he had cleared up the meaning of those numbers. The 12 was twelve years from that time, 1995 to 2007. The 40 was Nathaniel's age at that time (in 2007) as he was born in 1967. The 72 was an indication of Royalty.

"Thomas, Thomas."

Yet another foreign voice was heard coming from Nathaniel's body, immediately, with no physical change; just the voice emanating from it had changed.

"Yes," Thomas responded.

"The questions and the answers are for me to answer. Laiki, the Spirit unto you, this host to divinely guide. Thomas. Thomas."

"Yes," Thomas responded again.

"Ask what you will, because this will be the last time you speak with me."

"Shall I ask for Nathaniel or shall I ask for myself?" Thomas questioned.

"Ask what you will, for this will be the last time you speak to me." Laiki repeated.

"Nathaniel wants to know, if there is a Jesus?"

Thomas posed an age old question, which embodied great doubt.

"The Son of the Living God, the Son Universe, exist in all universes." Laiki told him.

"How do we best bring the existence of Jesus here and now in this

47

universe at this time? And, what is my role and what is Nathaniel's role in doing that?" Thomas asked.

"It is not His (Jesus') time. He comes at the appointed time. You must understand. You have to prepare the 12. In 12 years of your time will be 2000 and 7. The 7 depicts Christ, 27 for 2 is infinite. 27 denotes the time in which the relationship with you was guided and reinforced. (Nathaniel was 27 when he and Thomas were brought closer together). In 12, which depicts the Disciples and the Masters of the Universe, in 12 we will have 40 generations of the Divine Spirit. At his age 40, will he become spiritually aware and strong enough to fight the battle on your planet, in your universe, in your known existence," Laiki explained.

"How do we prepare for the spiritual battle, of which you speak?" Thomas asked.

Awaki who had, unobtrusively, entered, responded. "That's not the question you wish to ask. Ask the question," he told Thomas.

"Then if you know the question that I should ask, why do you ask me to ask it?" Thomas said.

"Because you also must understand, it's not by accident that this young man was sent to you. Your purpose is to guide; your purpose is to lead; your purpose is to keep him open; your purpose is to protect," he told Thomas.

"Is that the question that I should ask, what my purpose is in relationship to Nathaniel?" Thomas asked him.

"That was your question," Awaki told him.

"You are correct, of course," Thomas admitted. "What is my relationship to others?"

"Your purpose in relationship to any others that walk this universe is determined by you. Your Divine responsibility now, is to guide," Awaki informed him.

Just as suddenly as it was heard, Awaki's voice was gone and replaced by the prior voice, which had returned.

"Listen and understand," Laiki said. "For, this will be the last time you speak with me," he told Thomas again.

"These are the things that you must watch for: this host has no knowledge of what will occur, but you will, so that you can guide. There will come a time as we begin to rearrange his spirit, things will become difficult to understand, for him. You need only to ask and an answer will be given unto you. There will come a time when the four (4) thoughts of his mind: intellectual, spiritual, artistic, and creative will unite. You will see these things occurring physically as he becomes spiritually stronger. Ask the question."

You're answering the question in terms of my role," Thomas remarked.

"Why now?" Laiki said.

"Why now?" Thomas repeated.

"Now because in 12, the physical battle will take place and those must endure. He is not the only one. There are madrids and madrids across your universe who are being spiritually awakened simultaneously to prepare for the physical battle of spirits." Awaki came back as quickly and answered.

"Will they come together or will they know who they are?" Thomas asked.

"In 12 they will begin to up-rise all over the universe and the message will be the same. That's when you will know. Now you must understand. There will be some things that will….." Awaki trailed off as he paused.

"There must be some things that I must understand…" Thomas said, repeating him.

"I am in many places at once." Awaki explained. "I am in many tongues simultaneously," he said.

"We appreciate your being in our tongue and in our place at this time," Thomas told him.

Awaki continued with Thomas.

"Understand this so you know that all these things that you hear are of the Divine Light. There will come a time in this host's development spiritually, that his energy will increase. He will be able to do things that only you will understand. He was given a gift and the gift was given by you. You are now responsible. You are responsible and we will be with you.

"Listen now and follow my commands. Remove the crystal from the neck of the host. The reason so that you will know, as time goes on, he will become stronger and stronger spiritually. Crystal will be incapable of dealing with the energy that he will be generating. It will become an irritant to him. It will become a thorn to his flesh. From this point on, even without his knowledge, he will not be able to handle, touch, any crystal for it will cause him great physical pain. He must use the stones given unto him, for his life here and for our purpose."

"Will he know the stones that he should use?" Thomas asked.

"The spirit that has been sent unto him to guide him will do so with your assistance."

"Very well," Thomas accepted. "What will be the outcome of the Great Spiritual Battle?" he asked.

"Ahhh life. Life unlike you ever imagined. Love everywhere. Great, great peace and tranquility. Peace. Ask the question."

"What other instructions are there at this time?" Thomas wanted to know.

"For you to know this, that through you will we succeed. Through this host, will you be rewarded. You simply need to ask and it shall be given unto you. We hear your thoughts. We hear your prayers," Awaki explained.

"I thank you for the answers to my prayers that you have already given."

"But Thomas, as I move out of this host, remember 12 and 40 years. Prepare yourself," Awaki spoke as he exited Nathaniel's body for that session.

The "creating" of Nathaniel was an arduous task that involved many, many invasions of his body by many Angels. It required that he altered his mindset. His inability to "just roll with" what was happening to him made adopting this new mind and knowledge, that much more complicated.

On 11/20/95 major instructions on preparation for the up-coming universal changes were given by Awaki.

"There are several keys to disciplining and learning to endure for the Great Transition," he said. "Remember these," he told Thomas.

"You have to teach, to attain the desires of the physical mind that it becomes more governable to your will, the books that you read from the Infinite Mind that were left to you as a rule and guide for your practice throughout this universe. Begin at the end and end at the beginning then you will see the truth. Ask what you will."

"I was listening," Thomas said. "Are there... what are the other keys? You said that there were more than one key. And, I heard what you said in terms of the books."

"Master the mind," Awaki answered. "It is a tool, and tap the resources of the spiritual over-self. This host must, on a regular basis, commune with himself... peace be still... to begin to master and allow the genetic re-engineering of his mind. You must find to discipline - his body - nourish that which his spirit occupies – this temporal building must become in tune with the spiritual over-self.

"Try, as you have been charged, through our direct, as we will remove from this day forward, without his desires. We have been attempting to re-engineer his total makeup of his physical self. This accounts for his discomfort that this host experiences.

"He has to understand purity in body is purity in mind and strengthening of the spirit. Fasting begins that discipline. To deny one's physical self that which one needs begins the discipline, the purification.

"Also, that which has been left for your – universe - written, are the fingers of the men guided by the spirits which I command and provided for you – the word of the Infinite Mind – begin from the ending and end with the beginning and you will understand that your ending is the beginning and the beginning will be your ending. Do you understand?" He asked Thomas.

"I understand rationally and logically. I want my soul to understand – explain," Thomas said.

"Your soul – feel this," Awaki told him. "The ending of the various interpretations of Yahweh's writings have been re-engineered. The ending is the beginning of the second coming and the beginning is the ending of the new order of things."

Those keys for preparation, served the purpose for which they came: to gather, to awaken and to prepare the spiritual warriors. Thomas could now provide that information to Nathaniel who needed to be prepared for the spiritual battles. Key was reading the Holy books he listed, in proper order: from the ending, Revelation, to the beginning, Genesis. Also key was meditation: communing with one-self to tap into the spiritual over-self. Another was to develop discipline by fasting and denying the physical self, that that it needed.

It was Thomas' charge to bring this to Nathaniel such that he accepted it and remained open to it. It had to become a regular part of his personal life. Along with these, Nathaniel had to accept the discomforting physical changes the angels made to his body. They were physically rearranging or "re-engineering" the total physical make-up of his body and his spirit during that time. These changes actually changed his insides and his outside physically.

One week, 11/27/1995, later when his body was commandeered and invaded again. Thomas brought a concern to Shakardak, the angel who invaded him.

"We do not know who we will speak to this evening but we have questions," he told him. "Nathaniel was involved in a project that came to him in his trainings about books that he writes or desires to write. You see his heart, you know the purity of his intentions. I see it and it is for the greater glorification of the Living God. Our question is are we to proceed in that direction? How it's to be done? My inclination is that there is someone who can be sent in the same manner that you have come to give us this information and to write these books? Is that the way this is to be done and how is it to be accomplished?" Thomas asked.

"That which you speak of are not books," Shakardak told him. "That which you speak of is a 'Mechanism' that will thrust him into his spiritual battles as they come.

"In your time and universe, your leaders must be developed. We choose the mechanism that they will acquire their leadership. In order for this physical being to be prepared, 12 and 40, he must be respected in your time and universe as a great spiritual mind. To you, books, to us, our 'Mechanism'.

"As he continues to progress through the system that has been set up, he will find himself always beset in spiritual disagreements with those uninformed. And, the battles will begin as he and others in this universe begin to say the same message at the same time. It is the beginning of the Great Transition," he explained to Thomas.

"The other question we have is whether or not you will send someone to communicate the process of the mechanism that you speak of---the mechanism with the books?" Thomas asked again.

That is my charge," Shakardak told him.

"I understand," he said.

This was yet another requirement Nathaniel had to accomplish to become a "prepared" warrior. He had to become respected as a "great spiritual mind," from the writing and use of a book, his "Mechanism."

That was the first recorded mention of writing a book for Nathaniel's preparation, very early on. The third time Shakardak spoke to them.

He made it clear that all Spiritual Leaders, in this universe, had to be elevated to a statute of prominence. Nathaniel was to become a "great spiritual mind" to the public via the production of his "Mechanism" a book.

Weeks later, 12/19/1995, the Mechanism or Book was mentioned again.

Nathaniel was invaded by Shakardak who told Thomas, "This which we occupy is beginning to come to spiritual enlightenment. He is starting to understand how to move away from the physical and into the spiritual body-- the ideal of things he is learning to become of service to others through the knowledge that you are providing him. We will continue to guide you but you must continue to guide him. The Mechanism is part of his conscious travel. Ask what he sees"

There was nothing in the documents pertaining to Nathaniel's visions for the creation of the book. It was assumed, however, that they talked about them during their private times.

Nathaniel was chosen for this. That was reiterated throughout the entire period of visitations by angel after angel. He had no prior personal knowledge of such things: angels taking people's bodies and talking through them. He was religious, not spiritual. He was an avid "church" goer.

During the first session with an audience, other than the Prophet, 12/27/96, an interesting revelation was made about his being chosen.

"The first teaching of the Son Universe (Jesus) is sacrifice of yourself to save someone else. Is this within your understanding?" Awaki asked Thomas.

"It is, Awaki. The good shepherd," he replied.

Awaki said, "You are learning but this Host (Nathaniel) is still in doubt and you must keep him open. Guide him. Teach him. For, he does not understand, nor does he accept. But, we understand and we are with him. And, Shakardak, who I have sent, will never leave him."

That was a telling revelation because it was then 6 weeks or thereabouts since the first invasion of his body. Nathaniel was still unaccepting, doubtful, resistant and without understanding of his body being invaded and taken from him.

The Prophet said, "He wants to know what --- he doesn't understand why this gift has been given unto him?"

"Then you tell him this: that if you do not open the door, then how can you enter?" Awaki told him.

"Is the door closed, Awaki?" Thomas asked.

"Your understanding is correct," he answered. "There is a difference between doing what you believe and believe what you are doing. He is connected in all his doings to the righteousness of Infinite Mind. Even before he came out of his mother's womb and was given physical life, he was already given spiritual birth. These things that you witness are predestined in 12 and 40. It is time."

With that Awaki took leave of Nathaniel's body and that particular session ended. That was one of those sessions wherein Thomas was faced with the true facts from God of what was happening with Nathaniel. And, the truth was Nathaniel wanted no parts of that even though he kept doing it. He was spiritually committed to God for it, from birth, but physically, not at all.

The preparation of Nathaniel's physical body for that brought on many interesting, and never before, known experiences. One such occurrence was witnessed on 1/4/1996.

"Who are you please?" Thomas questioned the arrival of an angel into Nathaniel's body.

"Here am I," the Angel responded.

"Are you the Holy Awaki?" Thomas asked.

"You are in my presence, for this is holy ground. I am: the spirit of Melchizedek, sent to complete the teachings."

"We're here, Melchizedek, waiting for your completion," Thomas said.

Melchizedek continued hurriedly, "This host, as you know from the teachings of Awaki and Shakardak, has been prepared for the Holy battles. You have many questions. There is only a short time for the life force of this host cannot sustain the glory that I have deposited within him now.

"I come to you only this time in this place to tell you to heed, for the time is at hand. The questions that you will ask will not be answered by me, but I am here to tell you that we are with you. Your guidance and your teaching is from heaven."

Then Melchizedek left Nathaniel's body abruptly. It was writhing and stressed to the max. His entire body was physically stretched out all over and his eyes were bulging. His body was raining with sweat. The obvious physical discomfort was almost intolerable and lasted only 2-3 minutes. Unlike usual, what Nathaniel said right after coming back into his body was recorded.

*"What was that!!?" He said, as he literally cried tears streaming down his face.*

*Thomas attempted to console him. "You okay?" he asked him.*

*"Yeah. What was that? My heart is pumping. I feel like I can't breathe!" Nathaniel continued through his tears and visible anguish.*

*"You're okay," Thomas said as he continued to console him.*

*"Oh my head hurts. I'm hot, hot. Look, my hands are sweating." Nathaniel stretched out his trembling, wet, shaky hands for Thomas to see them. "My hands are tingling; my feet – tingling; my chest is tight – hurt," Nathaniel complained.*

*As Thomas healed him, in his usual manner, and made him more comfortable he stopped crying. He described his leaving out of and his return to his body. His breathing was much less labored, easy and calm as well.*

*"This time when I left I felt like I was tumbling, tumbling, tumbling," he spoke rapidly.*

*As he described the departure from his body he did so in an animated manner. He was rolling his hands, over and over one another rapidly, to show how he felt as he tumbled over himself leaving. None of this was witnessed. Physically, it appeared as though, he never left his seat.*

*Then he said, "My return was immediate; like swoosh and I was back."*

*Again he became animated, and made a swooshing movement with his hands, sliding one hand over the other with open palms so as to show how quickly he was thrust back into his body.*

After he was fully recovered, Nathaniel was invaded again within a short time after Melchizedek's departure from his body.

"I am here," Thomas heard.

"Who are you please?" he asked.

"Shakardak," the voice said.

"Hello Shakardak. It has been a while since you've been in this host. Is there any information that you wish to give this evening?"

"I am here to answer the questions that you have. For, my energy is the weakest, for this host cannot withstand the spirit of the Holy Awaki at this time. I shall be your mediator," he answered Thomas.

"Thank you Shakardak. Who was the spirit that appeared earlier this evening?"

"That was the Holy Melchizedek," he answered.

"Melchizedek?" Thomas repeated.

"Yes. The keeper of the gates." Shakardak explained.

"Can you tell us why he came?"

Shakardak answered, "So this host's physical re-engineering will be complete. There were questions. There were questions and he came to dispel any further doubts that you have left; any that this Host is chosen. He is the "Keeper of the Gates" with much power. For, he answers the direction of the Infinite One. He opens the doors of the universes so that we may enter and exit."

"Is he known by any other names?" Thomas asked.

"He is he who stands on Holy ground. He is the power of all the universes. He is known in your universe as Gabriel the Archangel," he answered.

"Was there information that he was going to give us this evening that we would find useful?" Thomas questioned.

"That information was given unto you," Shakardak said.

"That is correct," Thomas agreed. "He also indicated though, there would be no answers given to any questions."

"He does not answer questions because he IS the answer to all things," he told Thomas.

"I see," Thomas said.

Shakardak explained, "This host before you has certain abilities hiding within him. For, he is not yet perfect in his understanding. He has an ability to communicate to all plainly. His presence in all the things that he has done has been attributed to his thoughts but nothing must stand in his way. He has prayed. He has asked for the power to overcome all obstacles and in his crude fashion, he maneuvers around that which stands in his way.

"This process of re-engineering is preparing him in 12 and 40 for the ultimate battle and believe me my son, as I speak to you today, it has already begun. There are Madrids of Infinite Mind's Angels descending upon areas of this universe, preparing, disturbing things, as you know it. The Hand of Divine Wisdom is touching all things that are wicked and bringing them to an end. It is time now to move out of this host. I will be gentle for I see this little one has been stressed." And with that, Shakardak left Nathaniel's body.

Again, an Angel of God, Shakardak this time, confirmed the book of Revelation was being manifest as they spoke in 1996. Their presence was proof positive that the book was being manifest.

He spoke specifically of the wicked things being brought to an end in the areas upon where they had already descended. Another mind blowing revelation that challenged our faith (already meager) and heightened our doubt (already abundant). We were creatures of little faith and much doubt who were called to them to be awakened and prepared; our prior status of having been identified before birth by God, for this feat, notwithstanding.

Relationship

Within ten days 1/14/96, there was another invasion of Nathaniel's body that pertained to him directly. As usual he was totally absent from it and Thomas hosted the visitation. This session included Nathaniel's wife, Mrs. Rebecca Keys.

Rebecca, mother of Nathaniel's three children: two boys and a girl all under the age of ten, at the time, (the oldest and youngest were boys), attended alone. The session began as usual when Thomas greeted and welcomed the invading angel.

"It is I," the Angel's voice spoke.

"Is this the Holy Awaki?" Thomas asked.

"It is of that you ask," it said.

"Hello, Awaki. Is there information you have for us this evening? We're here with Nathaniel's wife, Rebecca. There are questions that they have about their relationship; about her role in Nathaniel being your Host and the Host of Spirits. Is there information that you have in that regards?"

"There is," Awaki replied. "This host's re-engineering will be complete.

The discomfort that he has been experiencing will cease. The thorn which was to his skin will have no effect upon him anymore," he explained.

"What do you mean the thorn to his skin?" Thomas asked.

"When we began the re-engineering of this host, the energy levels were so high that that which he wore around his neck was a conductor. It will no longer be a thorn to his flesh," Awaki explained.

He had told Thomas all of this at the earliest visits and had him take the crystal from around Nathaniel's neck.

"That means he can wear crystals again if he so chooses?" Thomas asked.

"That is within your understanding," Awaki said, yes.

"So his re-engineering is it concluded now because we somewhat suspected that it would be on Martin Luther King's birthday, which is tomorrow in our time. Is that correct also?" Thomas asked.

"That is not within your understanding," Awaki told him, no.

"Very well. When will the re-engineering be complete?" Thomas asked.

"It was told to you, in the first of the 12 in 9 (January 9th : 1st of 12 months in 9 days). His re-engineering was completed at that time. At that time we set in motion, life events to correct that which disturbs his mind; that distorts his thoughts."

"Was that his birthday? That was Nathaniel's birthday." Thomas noted.

"In your universe, that is correct," Awaki agreed.

"Thank you. We did seek clarification of that when we were speaking with Shakardak," Thomas told him.

"What else does he need to do in relation to the re-engineering at this time? I know he would want to know." Thomas asked him.

"There is nothing that he can do but to keep himself open. That is your charge."

Awaki took this opportunity to remind Thomas, again, that they had given him the job of keeping Nathaniel open to all of this, especially letting them use his body.

"I understand," Thomas said. "There are other concerns that he has, as you know."

Awaki responded. "Those concerns are voices of the other entity. Ask the question,"

"Which other entity do you refer to? Do you mean his wife?" Thomas asked.

"Is there another entity present beside yourself?" Awaki asked him.

He never referred to her as "wife."

"Of course, Awaki, and we know that you meant that that entity is here."

"Ask the question," he told Thomas.

"The questions, as I said initially, were the relationship between Nathaniel and his wife. And, of course she has questions now, as to what it was that she sees."

"First," Awaki said, "They must understand, and you must explain, that there is no relationship. Those are words. She has been assigned to help this host and this host has been chosen to love this entity before they even knew that they would be together. The problems are lack of understanding by this entity. She has no faith."

"How can she begin to build faith? What kind of experiences must she undergo to build faith, if she so chooses that route?" Thomas asked on her behalf.

"Hear me now, my son. The Infinite Mind, The Jah, as He walked the earth in the flesh, of the Son Universe, there was a man, a man stricken of palsy who had four friends. Those four friends knew that the Infinite Mind was speaking in the house. They attempted to take their friend stricken with palsy, to him, and were unable to get in. They did not let that obstacle stop their faith for they climbed the walls of the house and removed the roof and lowered their friend, in his bed, and all his possessions, down into the house in the presence of the Jah, who said unto him, 'your faith hath healed you, your sins are now forgiven.'

"The Scribes and the Pharisees and the Priests said unto Jah, 'what manner of man can forgive his sins?' And He looked and He said unto them, 'that my Father who sent me, the Infinite Mind, has given me the power and the authority to forgive sins, and the power and authority to heal the sick.'

"And, He looked to the man with the palsy and He said, 'you are healed. Pick up your bed and go.' And, he did so. This was not for the four friends who already had faith that this could be. This was not for the man stricken with palsy who knew that this could be. It was for the doubters, the ones with lack of faith, the scribes and the Pharisees to see that He was.

"This that she sees before her, if it is not enough for her to believe that the Infinite Mind abides in her house, and if she does not have enough faith to conform to this Host, which is before her, who will be a great spiritual leader in 12 and 40 then she has chosen her own fate and has drawn her sword."

"Is there other information that she should know in this time in this respect?" Thomas asked him.

"There shall also be her understanding. Is this within the entity's understanding?" he replied.

"Are there any questions that you have in terms of what he said?" Thomas asked Rebecca.

"No, I understood," she said.

Awaki continued.

"She believes what she sees before her but she questions her own ability to conform simply because she does not know how. It is the charge of this host to be gentle, to be kind, to be loving, and to show her how. The re-engineering of this host was not only with his physical body but with his spiritual and emotional body.

"There will be more events set into motion by us to calm the storms of disagreement between these two. For, he must be allowed without noises, to complete the task which we have discussed.

"We have given you the Mechanism (the Book). You Thomas, before you see the changes in his thought pattern. You see the wisdom of which he analyzes all things. This did not come of his birth. It came of his openness and it will increase, as your abilities will increase.

"Be not afraid for you are in the presence of the Angels of God. Yah He Yah Weh, Jehovah, the I Am surrounds you and will be with you until you decide to draw your sword and not be with Him." Awaki told them.

"So He is with us in all times and all places... even in our darkest moments, even when we have doubts, even when things appear that He is not there---"

Awaki stopped Thomas before he finished. "That is when He is the strongest. "For the I Am is with the weak, the poor of spirit, the low of heart."

"How would this entity know that the I Am is present in times that her spirit is poor?" Thomas asked on Rebecca's behalf.

"Even now with her lack of faith has she had to find bread in the street, to beg for a dollar?" Awaki asked.

"No," Thomas said.

"Then the I Am has been merciful upon her. Ask the question," he continued.

"Is there any information that she should know in relation to her commitment to Nathaniel in terms of the task that he must perform?"

"She should know this, that if she walks in the valley of decision, she must draw her sword. And, when she draws her sword, she must decide and if she decides not to have faith in what is displayed before her today, then she will surely guide her own destiny," Awaki said.

Thomas responded, "Can you explain to her what you mean by drawing her own sword?"

"The sword of decision. We decide, when you walk in the light of the Infinite Mind, your fate. But, when you walk not in the light of the Infinite Mind, then you choose your own destiny and you are at the ends of this universe in this world," Awaki explained.

"I see. What of their children?" Thomas questioned.

"Their children are of the light and protected. As we speak, their Angels sit before the Throne of God simply because this host has decided that he will be a warrior for the I Am," Awaki told their fate.

"So their children's needs will always be attended to, and their earthly needs, of education, of health, again so long as they are children. When they become of age to choose, will that be the case?" Thomas asked.

"You are talking in contents of time. It is already the case," Awaki assured him.

"Well, as I sit here, I sense the same thing from Rebecca that Mary must have had in her concerns for Jesus as He walked in the context of her own children," Thomas explained.

"She is concerned about death," Awaki responded. "Death of this host, in time of spiritual warfare, the death of this host shall be surely imminent at the time the Infinite Mind deems, but you will have a long and prosperous life with him," he told her. "But, you have to develop the ability to have faith in Him who sent him, and yourself. For, surely this host will leave this universe before you because he has earned the right to do so and leave behind the hell in which rules this world; until the day that the Son sets His foot back upon this place."

"So the Son will return, the Son of the Living God?" Thomas followed up.

"We all will," Awaki said.

"There are those who teach that He is beyond this place protecting it and He will not return in the same manner in which He walked here before," Thomas said.

"There are those who teach that men have heads of birds. Does that make it correct?" Awaki asked Thomas.

"No, Awaki, that does not make it correct and I was asking because that was a question that I had some time ago, if the Son of the Living God will return on this plane on this earth," Thomas explained.

"Does the Holy writings say that He will?"

"They do," he answered Awaki.

"Then doubt not for surely His return is in the Third Covenant and there must be a spiritual battle," Awaki reassured him.

About a month later 2/16/1996 there was more personal discussion about Nathaniel.

"This entity (Nathaniel) has come into contact with that concept (Jesus' return) and it has confused. But, he was not aware that it was this that we are doing now," Awaki said.

"The time before that (Jesus' return), in two to the infinite to the infinite to the infinite to the infinite is the millennium (2000) and the end of your preoccupation. Then seven years (2007) of spiritual battles, then the Son will return to the earth to reign for another millennium of your years. That is the Parousia. Explain this unto him for he has gotten the knowledge confused," Awaki told Thomas.

"I will do that." Thomas committed to tell Nathaniel that, once he was allowed back into his body.

"The knowledge came unto him by way of a holy one who is himself, having difficulty understanding the difference between his religion and true righteousness. He is beginning to cross the bridge, as we speak, to the understanding of true faith. These things are displayed within his love to those he has been given charge." Awaki explained.

"Will Nathaniel know who this person is?" Thomas asked.

"He already knows," Awaki said. "For we have placed him as near to him as possible. There will come a time in the 11 and 40 that he will take his place to assist him with the spiritual battles that this host will undertake. His ideology is now being transformed so that he will be prepared to assist this host."

"Is this Rev. Kingston by any chance?" Thomas asked.

"It is within your understanding," Awaki agreed.

"So you're saying Rev. Kingston understands the Parousia? Is that the term?" Thomas questioned him further.

"That is not within your understanding. The Parousia, he does not understand in the true context of its meaning, but he is coming into the knowledge of the oneness of the Infinite Mind. This is done to assist this host in the 11 and 40 for you have lost one." Awaki clarified and then noted, "There is voices, there are many voices. Speak unto me."

"Which voices are you hearing, Awaki?" Thomas asked.

"That of the second entity," he answered.

"The questions that she has, can you speak to her voices?" Thomas asked him.

"They are not questions. They are doubts," Awaki said. "Her doubts stem from her lack of understanding. She feels rejected by this host. She cannot move into his creative force to keep up with the changes. We have spoke unto her before and she was told to submit herself to bring him peace unto this host. She has not done so."

"How can she submit and maintain her own identity?" Thomas asked.

Awaki answered, "There is no identities in our consciousness. We serve at the will of the Infinite Mind, to fulfill His ends. There are no identity. For, not to fulfill His will is certain destruction."

"I understand," Thomas said.

"We have talked about that particular point. She must draw her sword and choose. We are descending upon this host's home because the elium lords are attempting to destroy that which he resides, in an attempt to destroy him. We will be ever present with him," He told Thomas.

"Is that what happened yesterday?" Thomas asked.

"It has been an ongoing process," he revealed. "There have been several battles and they were not aware. This has disturbed their emotions. Their children are pure at heart, can feel the vibrations of the battles. They are at peace now because we cannot fail. But they will not give up. Those that are pure of heart and are in the valley of decision, who cannot draw their swords are protected each by the Angels. But, she is in the valley and can draw her sword and it gives them the opportunity to destroy by fear and uncertainty."

"Is there anything that can assist her that she would need to know in drawing her sword?" Thomas asked on her behalf.

"You have the knowledge departed unto you and I charge you to speak unto her about the one true teaching of Jah, obedience," Awaki told him.

"May I ask the question that she had? She wants to know, why was she chosen for Nathaniel?"

"For just that purpose," Awaki answered. "If she had not been guided by us, she would not be before you today. For, that which created her, in her creative force know not of us and have chose not of us," he said of Rebecca's mother. "To leave her would have destroyed her own life because she knew not and they knew not of the fear and the wisdom of the Infinite Mind.

"Her children are brought forth: the youngest of her sons, has been given a spiritual gift to see beyond space and time. It was difficult during the battles to hide ourselves from him for he witnessed our movements. But, as much as we could, we hid in the shadows of darkness. Ask the question."

"What did Natahniel see? What did Rebecca and Nathaniel see in their room?" Thomas asked.

"That was a descension of protective Angels," Awaki told him.

"I see," Thomas said.

Awaki continued with more details as Angels just appearing in a bedroom was much to take, at face value, just as talking to an angel through a body was.

"The one that she saw sitting in the corner of her room was Shakardak watching over her son, for they (demons) know of him as well, and will try and destroy him also and guide his life into destruction. But, we will not let it happen. But, she is allowing things to go on in her mind and her spirit," he explained.

"Nathaniel asked me to ask that, in the event the marriage does not survive, what will become of their children?" Thomas asked on Nathaniel's behalf.

"The oldest will become a Physician, a healer, in your universe. The youngest son will complete what this host will begin. And the girl will fulfill her destiny unto her mother."

"What do you mean by that?" Thomas asked.

"She will be the one that will take care of her in her days of old," Awaki explained.

"And what if the marriage does survive?" he continued to question Awaki.

"All that I have spoken will still come to pass. It has been written and it will be done," Awaki told him.

"Nathaniel asked me to ask if he may have the power to overcome the resentment, anger, and if he could be more at peace, more tolerant of people, particularly of those he loves. I think he asks this in the context of bringing peace to his family and to his marriage."

"This is not his question," Awaki responded immediately. "That question is the result of his ridicule from she who has been given unto him. He has been told that he is all of those things and he wants much to be like his God in all ways. He's battling with this flesh and his emotions. He has mastered his mind. But, these things can be given unto him. But, ask of the second entity if we fulfill your question and give you that peace, will you fulfill your destiny?"

"Can you explain to her in more detail?" Thomas asked him first.

Awaki responded, "As we have spoken unto her before, she was chosen for this host to give him peace. Block not his desire to follow his God and do that which he has been chosen to do. Give him peace and the things that he asks and we will give unto you that which you desire."

"Yes," the wife replied.

"And, you must understand that when we give a gift unto the hosts of this universe, as we will put this host through more re-engineering, and if you cannot fulfill your destiny, then the Angels sent to protect this host and all that is within his creative force, will surely turn against you to remove you as you have chosen your own destiny. And, there will be no peace in your life. Is that within your understanding?" Awaki asked her.

"Yes, it is," she said.

"It is still your desire for us to change this host and give you that which you ask for?" he asked her.

She sat, and did not speak, as though dazed or confused.

"Speak to him," Thomas encouraged her.

"I don't understand what you're saying," she said to Awaki.

"You asked for that which this host has thought of," he explained to her. "You want to be respected, reverenced and loved unconditionally. We will, at your request, re-engineer this host to give you what you desire, but you must fulfill your destiny and give him peace and that which he asks of you, out of love, and block not what he has been chosen to fulfill in following his God. Is this within your understanding?"

She answered, "Yes, it is."

"Is it still your desire?" he asked her.

"Yes," Rebecca said.

"Then it is done," Awaki told her.

"Ask the question," he invited Thomas to continue with the session.

He spoke, "Nathaniel also asked about having, on a conscious level, the wisdom, of Solomon."

"Solomon had no wisdom. That is the writing of men. The wisdom that Solomon displayed was what you call, 'common sense'. We spoke unto the prophet, Nahum, and Nahum advised Solomon. As we speak unto you, then you must advise this host for he is your charge.

"His ability to do what is wise has been impeded by his emotions to please all those he loves. But, she has agreed to fulfill her destiny and he must do what he has been chosen to do. Tell him it is done," he told Thomas.

At the end of the session when he prepared to take leave of Nathaniel's body he informed Thomas, "The leg of the host has been damaged."

"Which one, left or right?" Thomas asked.

"It would be to your right. At the conclusion, repair it. I must go," he said to him.

"Thank you, Awaki, and peace to you," Thomas said.

"Thomas, the damage to this host is to both legs and his arm. This is due to the request made unto us by the second entity. It was done as we spoke and not over time. I wanted this to be within your understanding," Awaki said.

"Very well. In other words it is not because of your coming into his body," Thomas remarked.

"That is within your understanding," Awaki said.

"I understand. And I will explain it to him," Thomas committed.

That was the second time, within the first 3 months, that Nathaniel's wife, Rebecca, had come into Awaki's presence. It was regarding their struggle in their marriage with his charge. It was not the last. She requested another session with him 6 weeks later. She had learned of another upcoming requirement that Nathaniel was to face. The reason for the requirement was known from very early on.

Their second recorded visit on 11/10/95, Shakardak told Thomas of Nathaniel undergoing physical changes. On another occasion, 12/14/95, Awaki mentioned his being re-engineered physically. Then weeks later, 1/4/1996, they explained Gabriel's entry into his body as being necessary for Nathaniel's physical re-engineering to be completed. At some point, the Angels had made Thomas aware of a specific time when even more physical changes would be made to Nathaniel.

On 3/3/1996 it was discussed.

"This host is afraid," Awaki told Thomas. "We said unto you that in 5 of 12 (May), that he would be re-engineered again for the ends of the Infinite Mind, and would not be able to host our beauty and energy for that period in your space and time. This is the reason for that to occur. For he is still not confident enough to withstand the ridicule. Yes, it is still to take place."

It was this planned occurrence, in May, that caused Nathaniel's wife to seek another audience with the Angels for a third time.

It was on 3/31/1996.

"It is I." Awaki appeared and gave his usual greeting.

"Good evening, Awaki. There are questions Rebecca has that she wishes to ask," Thomas responded.

"Come unto me," Awaki called Rebecca.

She left her seat and sat directly in front of Awaki, who had inhabited her husband's body. She therefore sat directly in front of her husband, physically.

"Take the hands of this host into your hands," Awaki told her.

She complied and took the host's...the Spiritual Leader's... her husband's hands, into her hands.

"What do you see before you?" Awaki asked her.

"What do you mean, what do I see before me?" Rebecca asked.

"What do you see before you?" he repeated.

"I see my husband before me," she said.

"That is within your understanding," he agreed with her. "Look beyond the physical, and what do you see before you?" he asked her.

"I don't know," she answered.

"Then, why have you come before me?" he questioned her.

"Because I wanted to ask, why does he have to go away in May?" she answered.

"If you do not know what you sit before, then who do you seek these answers from?" Awaki asked her.

"Who do I seek these answers from?" she repeated.

"Yes," he said, "That is within your understanding."

"I seek these answers from God," she said.

"Then, beyond he who was sent unto you, what do you see?"

"I'm not sure of the question," confused, she answered.

"You are charged," Awaki told Thomas.

"He's asking you, 'who is….are you speaking to'?" Thomas rephrased the question for her to help her understand.

"To you," she said directly to Awaki, as she looked at her husband's body.

"Who is he? He's asking who he is." Thomas clarified more.

"An Angel of God," she said finally.

"That's what he's asking," Thomas told her.

"Oh, okay," she responded.

"Is that within your understanding?" Awaki questioned her.

"Yes, it is," she replied.

"Have not we spoke unto you before?" he asked her.

"Yes," she said.

"Ask your question," he told her.

"What is the purpose of the trip in May?" she asked.

"You are concerned about these seven days, but your concern should be the rest of his life," Awaki said.

"Why is that so, Awaki?" Thomas asked him.

"She who is in the presence of who has been given the gift of multitudes does not see what he is or who he is," he explained. "Is it our understanding, should we allow such a entity to destroy that which your God has sent unto the universe to bring forth His ends? Is that within your understanding?" he asked Rebecca.

"Yes," she answered.

"She does not understand. You are charged."

He instructed Thomas again to make clear to Rebecca what he told her.

"He's saying to you that Nathaniel, as a physical person is very, very special and what he does, he does at the direction of God, and that should you not develop the proper understanding, then you will be a block. You will be an impediment and you will therefore destroy his mission, or more so even to destroy his spirit," he explained to her.

Awaki then continued to speak to Rebecca.

"Should not his mission be more important unto you than that which you ask? For, it is the rest of his life. For, his life was given by his God and his God has now recalled his life unto Him to serve His ends. And, it is our command to protect him. Is that within your understanding?"

"Yes," she said, again.

Whether she understood or not was debatable. Nevertheless Awaki took her at her word and continued with her.

"Then, you come to us to inquire about his God's command unto us. For, the prophet has been charged and he has been instructed unto him that which he is about to do, and you are only concerned with seven of those days, and at the end of those seven, then are you concerned?"

"Yes," she said.

"Then your question should be not of that which is temporary, but that which is permanent in your life. For, if you do not, you will lose unto yourself he who sits before you," he told her.

Frank intervened, "Explain that please."

"She has a difficult time understanding, even as I speak unto her, the noises in her mind," Awaki replied.

"Can you address those noises? Does she wish to address them privately?" Thomas asked.

"Those noises are of confusion," Awaki explained. "Confusion in all that she does. She feels that she has no place or part in that which is occurring unto he that sits before her, so they use this fear to destroy her and to attempt to destroy he who his God has blessed. And, in that destruction, so shall she destroy herself."

Thomas continued to probe while Rebecca, in her confusion, remained silent.

"What is her role?" he asked.

"We spoke unto her before when she asked of us to alter he who sits before her, and even then she did not honor. Then, why is she concerned about that which she cannot, and will not, be obedient to in faith, not in he who sits before, but in He who has sent us unto him. In her obedience should she accept this gift and in her faith should she support, as we have spoken unto her before, and fulfill her destiny. Is that within your understanding?"

Again, Rebecca said, "Yes."

"You are charged," he told Thomas.

She did not understand and as usual when attendees were too confused Awaki had Thomas intervene.

"He's saying that they've already spoken to you about what your role is, and why are you still having the same questions when it's already been laid out for you?" Thomas explained to her.

Then Awaki continued.

"It is not that she has not seen the power of her God. It has been displayed unto you in that place that you dwell through those who are of you and through he that sits before you. But, still you live in darkness and ignorance. Then, you come before us and you ask about this host and why his God has sent him on such a quest.

"Even I do not question the command and the will of He who has created all. In all that you have seen and heard, you question that which you know God has done. And you come back not to seek guidance, and then you ask unto yourself, why is he so unpleased with that place that he is? It is the same as it was with the institution. Prophet, speak unto her and that of the institutions," he instructed Thomas.

"Would you please clarify?" he asked Awaki. "I'm not sure of the institutions. Are these the institutions of the church?"

"The reason he left the institution," Awaki said.

"Ahh, thank you," Thomas said. "It's the educational institution. What he's saying is that Nathaniel got very, very frustrated in Morton because of the unrighteousness that was there. Because, he absolutely demands that things be right and that people do the things that they are supposed to do.

"What he's saying is that you're creating the same kind of atmosphere in your home and the same kinds of discord that he felt there that he's beginning to feel in your home, and that that is like pushing him away because he's already left the educational institution for that particular reason."

Awaki continued from there.

"And, just have we have recognized this, we have spoke unto our prophet that there is a place that will be prepared for him as we speak, and if he cannot abide in your presence, so shall we prepare a place for him that he not be destroyed. Is that within your understanding?"

"Yes," she said.

"You must step outside of yourself," Awaki told her. "You are not lost. If you only knew, this host would live in the streets before he will allow any harm to come unto you. But, yet, in all that he does in his logic and understanding that he is capable of, you do not reverence what it is.

"We asked unto you once before, in your dishonesty, have you ever begged in the street. Have you ever gone without the necessities while you have been unto this host? And your answer was 'no'. But, yet, in all that you have seen, you continue to become a tool for the elium lords and you do not respect your own dwelling. And, you demand much of this host, and he gives much. And, then you ask, 'why does he not come unto this place for refuge?' would a cat go into a pack of hungry dogs to seek salvation? Speak unto me."

"No," the wife said.

"Then, why should he who you have seen, and have been exposed to his righteousness, be comfortable as he is growing in spirit and truth and righteousness, come unto unrighteousness, turmoil and destruction? Is that within your understanding?"

"Yes," she said.

The Angel continued.

"You have drawn your sword and your intentions were to do that which you were called to do, but even you fight with your own thoughts.

You know what you should do, but out of anger and resentment you do that which you know you should not do.

"This is not wise. It is not in your ability to be equal unto this host. He is growing more spiritual while you are choosing not of us. It is your own doing for he fights the battle in his mind to defend himself against all. Is that within your understanding?"

"Yes, it is," she answered.

"It is beyond our wisdom, as we have come unto your home and cleaned it and sealed it, all unto your sight. We have touched unto he who is of you who has been gifted with sight beyond this universe to speak unto you what he sees, and yet you do not humble yourself before your Lord. And, you come before us and question your God's commands unto this host. Ask the question... You have a question... What is it that you can do now? Is that not the question?" he asked her.

"That is the question," she said.

"It is in obedience and faith that you will bring unto you these things again. But, you constantly interfere with his spirit when it does not please you, and who should he be pleasing? Is it you or He who can take life from all? Speak unto me," he told her.

"He should be pleasing God," she said.

"Is it not your God's will that it be obedient to Him?" Awaki asked her.

"Yes, it is."

"You are quick to say what you do not have and what is not being done that you may live in this universe. This universe is not of your God and He is not concerned about your foolishness. And, it will be your destruction if you do not step outside of these things. Obedience and faith. Ask the question. Ask the question," Awaki repeated.

"How do I get..... let's see......" she stammered.

"I hear the thought, but you must ask. It is a testimony to your faith." Awaki encouraged her.

"Okay. How do you get faith? How are you supposed to have faith and obedience?"

"Do you know Jah?" he asked her.

"Yes," she said.

"And, who was Jah?" he asked.

"I'm not sure. Who did you say?" she asked.

"Jah," he repeated.

"Who was Jah?" she asked.

Thomas answered, "Jesus."

"Okay," she said.

Awaki continued.

"Jah came unto the hosts of this universe and He raised Lazarus from the dead, and He healed multitudes with a touch, and He calmed storms with the power of His words. And, still it was those that saw, that heard, and they said, 'He is a sorcerer'. He is not God, the Messiah, He who we wait upon. He is of trickery. And they turned from all that they saw with their own eyes in foolishness and vainness and suffered their own destruction.

"You have been blessed to see with your own eyes, to hear with your own ears, and to feel with the physical, and you ask of us what do you need to have faith? Should not you know, or should you be like those who saw Jesus and turned their backs upon Him?

"It is your choice, choose ye this day for we told unto you when we spoke upon you before, that when you ask of us we will give you to fulfill your destiny. And, if you did not do so, that you would be removed with a swiftness of certainty, and it was to be, and you knew so for you could see and feel the change in this host. Is that not within your understanding?"

"Yes, it is."

"Then do you still understand the necessity for your obedience and faith?" he asked her.

"Yes."

"Do you know who and how great men are deceived in your universe and destroyed?" Awaki asked.

"Do I know?" she repeated.

"That is within your understanding?"

"No, I don't," she answered.

"Throughout your time and space, it has been through their arrogance and the love of a woman, for they have no discipline," Awaki told her. "That was our mistake and it shall not happen in the Third Covenant, nor shall your governments destroy those who we send to fulfill the Parousia. This is the power of your God in this time for there will not be a fourth. So, it will be all set unto the Son Universe. Is that within your understanding?" he asked her.

"Yes, it is," she said.

"So, be not concerned about the commands given unto this host by your God for you cannot question His wisdom, and you cannot match His power. For, His power is mine and my power is obedience unto Him. Should I question in disobedience, should I be certainly destroyed.

"Then I have only the power that He gives. And you have none of His power. And you question. Do not. Live in faith and you have been given those tools of faith. Know ye this day that he who sits before you is greater than he who you love.

"Question him not again on these things of his God but he loves and he will teach you, as he will teach many others. For, he is gifted with multitudes. Do you not see this in all that he does?" he asked her.

"Yes, I see it," she admitted.

"Have you not seen us bring him from nothing to greatness in all that he accomplishes and does? Speak unto us," he told her.

"Yes."

"Then, obedience unto your God and faith unto he who has come unto this host in his burdens, and question not again," Awaki admonished her.

"Awaki, what is Rebecca to do when she feels that Nathaniel is responding to her out of his imperfections and out of his shortcomings as a person? He's not as patient as he should be with her? He's not as tender, he's not as supportive of her because I think that's where some of the confusion comes from…." Thomas intervened.

"There is no confusion," he interrupted Thomas. "That is her own doing, for, when she asked us, and we gave unto her all those things, but she could not walk in obedience and faith, so we could not suffer him unto foolishness. She walks in obedience and faith, then that which she desires of this universe and flesh then will she receive unto herself. Zimblach."

Awaki ended the conversation with Rebecca.

Thomas continued the conversation with him. "Is there other information you have?"

"It is this host," he said. "He does not tell you all that he sees in his dreams. So, it is our command that all that must happen, must happen, so we will speak unto you now. You shall make the arrangements for this host. He will leave in the first of seven of the five of twelve, Is that within your understanding?"

"Yes," Thomas replied.

"Those things that are trivial that he wish to take unto himself, allow, but allow no other garments except those that he wears on his back. Is that within your understanding?"

Awaki gave specific and precise instructions to Thomas on what Nathaniel was to take with him and when he was to leave on that May trip under discussion.

"Yes. May 1st is the beginning of the trip or of his quest," Thomas said.

"It is the first of seven, the first of the true Sabbath, so shall he leave. That which he takes, the garments, must be durable, for he will seek out on a journey," Awaki explained.

"He's indicated that he will have some contact with Indians or Native Americans--"

He interrupted Thomas again and said, "They are those that are already preparing for his arrival and they await. All these things shall be revealed unto you when he comes from the seven on the eighth. And, when he returns, he will return not only with that gift that he went unto that place with, of multitudes, but he will return with the oneness of mind and the sight beyond this universe."

"Will he maintain his personality?" Thomas asked.

"How do you define such a thing?" Awaki asked him.

"I knew that you'd ask me that. When you say, 'I am we and we am I,' but we still express individuality. We laugh at certain things--"

"You speak of the arrogance and vainness of the hosts of this universe?" Awaki asked.

"Not only of the arrogance and vainness but the uniqueness of the personality. The jokes, the way that Nathaniel approaches life, his joy and happiness," Thomas explained.

"The only thing that shall be altered is the desire to serve his God and the understanding of all things in true wisdom and righteousness," Awaki said.

"He's concerned about whether or not he will continue to be himself and he continues to have the positive traits of his personality. He has no problems relinquishing--" Awaki interrupted him again.

"All that we can use to the ends of your God will remain. All that is destructive unto this host and your God's mission, for him, shall be removed. And, that which we are shall be infused unto his mind. And, unto his soul, he will become the essence of his God and his God is the essence of his existence, and there shall be no other."

"Very well," Thomas said.

"And unto she who is sent unto this host, there is between now and then great burdens, concerns, fear and uncertainty within this host. Do not seek to destroy him out of your lack of understanding. Is that within your understanding?"

"Yes," she said.

<u>Reenigineer</u>

Just one week before that encounter, 3/24/1996, Thomas had brought Nathaniel's angst about that trip to Awaki's attention which included the whereabouts of it.

"He's asking where that is and if that is the place where he is to spend his other days in retreat," he told Awaki.

"It is," Awaki said, "But it is not a desert. It is a place where the hosts of this universe find peace. It is confined and isolated in time."

"Is it close by this place? How many days travel?" Thomas asked.

"He has been there before, as a child and cannot remember so." Awaki told him.

"Is it the state of Maryland?" Thomas continued.

"It is within this universe. It is your need to know a geographical location for you live here and it is there. It is what you call, the mountains," he said.

"Will he remember from… will that rattle his memory?" Thomas tried to help with the ID of the location.

"It is a place that you were when you were a boy," Awaki explained.

"I went to a few places when I was a boy."

"It is in the place that you were as a young man," Awaki said.

They both kept trying.

"Okay the seminary," Thomas said. "We can figure it out."

"No," Awaki said. "It is my charge and I need you to understand."

"Very well," Thomas said. "Then let's classify them. The mountains. It's in the mountains, and the seminary really wasn't in the mountains, per se."

"It is a place that he was a boy and you were a boy, and as a young man before you moved to where you are in this time and space," Awaki gave more clues.

"West Virginia?" Thomas asked.

"In the mountains," Awaki said. "It is not where you used to visit but it is where you reside as a boy and as a young man."

"I was in Philadelphia. I was in Delaware, I was in New York, Washington, D.C." Thomas listed his boyhood locations.

"It is popular," Awaki said.

"The Poconos? Mountains," Thomas said.

"It is within your understanding," Awaki agreed.

"Okay. Pennsylvania," Thomas said.

"Is it not the place where you were a boy?" Awaki questioned him.

"Ahhh yes, I did grow up in Pennsylvania," Thomas admitted. "I understand now. The Pocono Mountains is part of the state of Pennsylvania."

"Then, in this place, I attempted to recall the memory of this host, and in that place that he was a boy, was when he was the purest of heart and the clearest of mind. It is a place where he was safe," Awaki described for Thomas.

"I understand and I can get more clarification from him, perhaps even go down to the exact geographical location," he suggested.

"It is that that he was before," Awaki added.

"I understand," Thomas said.

"He is what you call 'tired.' It will be necessary for him to focus on that which we are creating his life. The place that you call 'church,' the institution, is not our guidance. He must focus on that which we are creating," Awaki cautioned Thomas.

"Does that mean he should leave his involvement in the church?" Thomas questioned.

"He will do so. But, it is our doing as it was with you," Awaki told him.

"When I was involved with the church?" Frank questioned him.

"Your creative force, we cleansed and moved out and those shall we do with this host, that, when he returns, that they shall not stand against him, for before he goes upon his journey, all that are not of us will be removed.

Now, when he goes on his journey, he will leave on the true Sabbath and return on the first of the seven," he informed Thomas.

"So, he should leave on Saturday and return on Monday? Is that correct?" Thomas asked for clarification.

"That is not within your understanding," no, Awaki told him.

"The true Sabbath, is that Sunday?" Thomas asked.

"The true Sabbath is that which you have named and return on the first of seven, which is what you now set aside as your Sabbath. But your scholars and your religious leaders have deceived you again, for it was convenient to make the first of seven the Sabbath, and it was not. Do you understand why I do not talk in context of your time and space?" he asked.

"I have always understood that you feel that it is very inaccurate and limited," Thomas answered.

"And also that it is not truth, that, I cannot speak that which is not truth," Awaki explained. "Now he shall not take unto himself any garments except that which is on his back, and they shall be durable," he instructed Thomas further.

"Okay, he's not too happy about that. He'll follow the instructions. He seems concerned primarily about undergarments and I'll tell him to bring some very good clothes," Thomas agreed.

"You tell him this: was not his born without garments?" Awaki told Thomas.

"Yes," he said.

"There he will also need with him that of the knowledge that we have already spoke of, that which you acquired was that which you needed. It is the beginning of understanding of those who mislead and distorted time in your history," Awaki told him.

"So he should take the tapes with him?"

"That, if you deem necessary. All that we have spoken unto you, so shall we infuse into his mind."

Okay," Thomas said. "It must be such a beautiful process."

"It will be, for him, agitating and glorious and tired, for he will sleep much when he returns. You, on the eighth, will return with him. On the seventh day, you will meet him where he is. Bring unto him garments. Is that within your understanding?"

"Yes, it is. It is," Thomas said.

"And when you return there shall be a light of truth and righteousness unlike you have seen before, and there will be physical changes unto his body and his appearance. It is time for him. Ask the question," Awaki instructed.

"Is it time for you to go?" Thomas asked.

"That is not within your understanding," he said no. "It is time for him that we move out those qualities of choice, the process which you speak of, I shall explain unto you that you may know. We will humble him unto his God. We will remove from him the gift of choice and infuse him with the drive of truth and righteousness, as we done all the great spiritual leaders. There will be no choice.

"He will be driven unto the ends of his God, unto his death, in obedience. The process in which you call it, will begin with his confinement with himself. And then, the re-engineering of his mind, the time that he spends reading of the knowledge is to discipline. The knowledge will come through us. The discipline will come through those of this universe, for he will begin to see the untruth and unfold all that has been deceptive with a glance. Is that within your understanding?"

"It is Awaki," Thomas admitted.

"This host when he returns, we will give him that which he asks, but he will be occupied with the battles that will begin to occur," Awaki told him.

"He seems to be moving with some of the political level with his involvement with the NAACP. Sometimes I think he's going to be crushed with disappointment as he sees who those people involved really are."

"He will but he will not be crushed, as you say. He will see and so shall the spirit of battle in truth and righteousness come upon him and he shall eliminate those, conquer others, and he shall not lose. Change is inevitable. All that he does is to lift his hands unto his God, and all that is in his way shall move. Ask the question," he instructed Thomas.

"Is there other information that Nathaniel needs at this time? He has asked me to ask about the vision that he got when he got a cane. It seems as though he has a connection with this cane," Thomas said.

"It is his," Awaki informed him. "Not that he was here before, but he was allowed to glimpse into his future."

During this same encounter Awaki addressed Nathaniel's lineage as he had already addressed Thomas'.

"You are contemplating, whence cometh this host?" he remarked to Thomas.

"Yes," Thomas said.

"He's also of a generation, but he is not of the generation of the original children. He is of the generation of John."

"Master John?" Thomas asked.

"That is within your understanding," yes he said.

"He is of the generation of Jah, as they were chosen, so is he. He is that voice among many that will cry out. But, expose him not to such information this day, for he is undisciplined and will become strong-willed and difficult to deal with."

"I hear what you're saying," Thomas agreed. "I do feel that I don't like to engage in conflict with him."

"He would not attempt for he knows. For we have told him that he is to take instruction from you. So, even when he rears up he will always back down."

Days and weeks before Rebecca approached Awaki about Nathaniel's trip, there was much discussion by Thomas with Awaki on Nathaniel's behalf, similar to that session. One such discussion was held on 3/28/96.

"There is a question of this host," Awaki told Thomas.

Thomas explained, "His basic questions are about details for the trip; he refers to it as a banishment, cynically. As we talked about it, his…."

Awaki interrupted him, "It is within his understanding." Yes, Awaki agreed, it was banishment.

"Okay I'll tell him that. Banishment in what sense; it has such a negative connotation," Thomas asked.

"Do you understand why this must happen to this host?" Awaki questioned him.

"The reason it must happen in terms of his disciplining himself, in terms of his going within himself with no distractions whatsoever?" Frank speculated.

"It is within your understanding." Awaki agreed and then went on and explained more. "He, will at that time, take on he who sits in his presence. He will become him and he will become all. Is that within your understanding?"

"No," Thomas said. "What do you mean by 'he who sits in his presence'?"

"There has been sent unto him 'The Spirit of War'," Awaki replied.

"Oh, Shakardak. He will wrestle with Shakardak!" Thomas questioned him.

"And, he will ask unto him as before, 'Give me that which you have come to give unto me' and they shall become one. His spirit as you know now, will no longer be, and he will no longer be, for he is Shakardak, in this time and space, and Shakardak is he before his God. Is that within your understanding?" Awaki told him.

"You're saying that he and Shakardak are at onement?" Thomas questioned further.

"That is within your understanding," Awaki agreed.

"How is Nathaniel known before the Throne?" Thomas asked Awaki.

"I have just spoken unto you. He is Shakardak," Awaki told him.

"Is there a way that we can explain this to the Host (Nathaniel) and make it easier on him to accept this?"

"His lack of understanding does not come from acceptance or rejection. His lack of understanding comes from his inability to feel worthy of such a thing. As we have spoken unto you before, his battles are forever with him and his burdens will be forever there unto his death and they are the burdens of all who cannot choose of us in the time of spiritual war," Awaki told Thomas.

"Will he only take one such trip as this or is this the most significant one since there will be awakening in the connection?" Thomas asked.

"This is the beginning of the end and the end of the beginning for we have told you that all that he is will come to an end and at his end, so shall it all begin. There shall be physical changes unto this host. It is as we have spoken unto you. There is a beginning and there is an end and we shall destroy all that is in this host that he will become all that he is to be," Awaki declared.

One day before, 3/30/1996, she met with Awaki about Nathaniel's trip, Awaki and Thomas discussed Nathaniel's condition and its relevance to that planned trip.

On that day, Awaki called, "Prophet."

"Yes," Thomas answered.

"The host right shoulder it is ...., he cannot sustain the energy in this time and space beyond this, do not so with him. For it will cause great damage unto his physical.

"And as we spoke unto you that we are preparing him for the seven and we are changing his body and all that is in it. He will be extremely tired and weak. It is not of the physical but of us. They will not pass until the re-engineering is complete."

Thomas asked, "What shall we do about the release of the tapes?"

The problem was some individuals who had gone before Awaki previously, had received video tapes of their visits. Controversy arose regarding putting them in the public.

"What was your charge?" Awaki questioned him.

"I've had several charges," he replied.

"Your charge, from the beginning when I spoke unto you, was with this host."

"Yes," he said.

"And what did I speak unto you?" Awaki asked him

"You told me many things."

"To keep him open," he reminded Thomas."

"Yes, that's correct, to keep him open," Thomas repeated.

"Then answer this, in his time, as he tarries to and fro, how shall he remain open if he believes there are those that seek not for his welfare? Should not even the strongest of men turn their backs upon their God?" Awaki asked him.

"They do but they should not," Thomas responded.

"Then, it is within your understanding, Awaki told him. As you have just said 'they do, but they should not'. What makes such a man do things?"

"Fear," the Prophet answered.

"Then, should that fear be complicated by others?" Awaki questioned him.

"Again, it should not but it often is," he answered.

"Then, it is within your understanding. It is within your charge" Awaki told him again.

"To decide?" Thomas asked.

"To keep him open." Awaki said.

"But then you're indicating that he may very well close down."

"Is not he flesh and spirit?" Awaki asked.

"Yes."

"And, is he perfect?" he asked Thomas.

"No," he answered.

"Then it is within your understanding," Awaki said.

"I am still confused," Thomas said.

Awaki then told him.

"We have spoken unto you to keep him open and the greatest of men turn their backs on their God out of fear. And, those who have been charged to keep them open should not continue to put them in fear. And, when you see these things it is your charge. Should he turn from us at this point, it will be unto your charge and our command."

Awaki made it clear to him that if he made decisions that frightened Nathaniel into shutting down to their invasions of his body (like putting out tapes of him hosting them in his body to the public) it would be his fault. Thomas made no more such tapes.

"I understand," he finally said.

Later that same day, Nathaniel felt the need to have the angels come again.

"I am here, holy voice," the tape began, as Thomas spoke.

He heard, "Shakardak."

"Yes, Shakardak," he responded.

"I was sent unto you by the Holy Awaki......will no longer enter into this host. The energy is too great for this host to bear at this time. I have been sent... what is it here? Speak unto me," Shakardak told him.

"Nathaniel asked that we have this session because he felt that there was a 'quickening,' as he described. There was information that was essential for us to have before this afternoon."

"The Holy Awaki was sensing that he might like to know of this," Shakardak said.

"Should we continue with the session this afternoon?" Thomas asked him.

He answered, "The Holy Awaki cannot occupy this host."

"Is it satisfactory that you occupy Nathaniel as you do now and for the Holy Awaki to transmit to us through you?" Thomas asked.

"There are things that will be asked that I cannot answer," he said.

"So then you're saying that it's better not to have the session this afternoon. Is this the beginning of the time?" Nathaniel asked.

"It has already begun," Shakardak answered him.

"Okay," he said.

"The Holy Awaki says that he will experience what you call restlessness and dreams of his physical body. It is almost complete," he told Thomas.

"How long will it last, the restlessness and the dreams?" Thomas wanted to know.

"It is not within your knowledge," he told him.

"I understand," Thomas said.

"Until it is complete," Shakardak explained.

After making it clear that Nathaniel was "restless" from them totally changing him and invasions for the purpose of preparing people made it worse, Shakardak continued talking to Thomas about the upcoming trip, and Nathaniel's preparation.

"He is to prepare for the seven of 5 of 12." (One full week in May).

"Yes. Have we identified the appropriate place? Is the place we have identified satisfactory?" Thomas asked.

"The Holy Awaki says that we are pleased. It is within your understanding," he replied.

"Very well. Then, we'll make the final arrangements for we have done all of the preliminaries," Thomas said.

"The Holy Awaki, he is here," he informed Thomas.

"I am so humbled," he said. "What should I do or what is to be done about Nathaniel's restlessness? He seems to be so fearful, so edgy,"

"There is nothing that can be done even in his conscious state," Shakardak explained. It will not subside for the changes take place deep within his soul."

"I am trying to be really patient because I see things that are different about him, nothing that really alarms. But, he seems to be very, very confused and ungrounded and unorganized. Will all of that change after the seven in twelve of five?" Thomas asked, confused about "seven in five of twelve."

"This will end as soon as it's done," Shakardak told him.

"Okay. I don't mean to drain him out," he stated.

Shakardak explained, "All of these things that you have just said, that you have found at his center are all because of his re-engineering."

"Okay. So you're telling me I should remain patient with him?"

"Now you fully understand," Shakardak told him.

"I understand," Thomas said.

"Would not you be fearful if you started going through soul re-engineering and could not see the power which does this to you?" he asked of Thomas.

"Yes," he said.

"All of these that he feels and is not as he felt before," he informed Thomas.

"I understand because you're right. He does not see and it's difficult. My heart does cry out to him. Sometimes I just get so consumed and I am not as sensitive, I suppose, as I should be. But my heart does cry out to him."

"The Holy Awaki is here," Shakardak announced to Thomas again.

"It is I," Awaki said. "My time in this host is not long. This host, as Shakardak has said unto you, is going through physical, emotional changes, deep within his soul. He does not understand what of our power drives these things and he's also dealing with the flesh. The man, his physical, and all that are in his creative force, his sustenance, and how he will sustain himself, and all those things that preoccupy the hosts of this universe. He is great, and even in this time, he is still strong. There are those who would have lost their thoughts under such great strain."

"Yes. There are those who have, I'm sure," Thomas agreed. "Will we have any more sessions or should we conclude them all until the seven and twelve in seven or should I say the five in twelve in seven?"

"That is within your understanding. But, he will fight with you to do and if he says unto you this: 'for we are sent and compelled to do,' then it is not his doing, it is of mine and so shall you come unto me," Awaki told him.

"I see," Thomas said.

This was the day that I was brought before Awaki and found Nathaniel in this state, sitting alone in a small room, waiting to be invaded, again.

The trip was all set prior to his wife's last encounter with Awaki on (3/31/1996). No changes were made after her visit.

An unusual encounter was recorded 4/6/1996 wherein Awaki was engaged in Thomas' absence by Julie. How and why it occurred is unknown. No documented explanation for it existed. Only the documented evidence that it occurred, exists.

"It is I. Speak unto me," Awaki ordered Julie.

"Well, I honor you and I salute you and I bless you for being here and sharing this space with Nathaniel, and it's a delight to have you here," Julie responded. "What is the power word that you bestow upon Nathaniel for his throat chakra, to be a communicator of the light and love and will of God?" she asked.

"He is gifted…." Awaki started to speak and was interrupted by her.

"Oh, wonderful!" she interrupted mid-sentence.

He continued his remark "…with multitudes, by He who created all."

"Absolute, the all of God," she exclaimed.

Awaki told her, "He is and has been chosen before conception, for the 12 and 40, for the spiritual battles that will take place in two to the infinite to the infinite to the infinite to the infinite, for seven of your years. And then there will be the coming of the Parousia and Jah will return unto you.

"And all that is not of He who has created all shall be destroyed. There is many among you that have been chosen and have spiritual gifts and they are being charged as we come upon this place in this time and space in this universe. Do you know who I am?" Awaki asked her.

"The Melchizedek vibration, the Metatron, the Logos expression of the Divine?" she asked.

"I am Awaki," he answered her, "charged by the Infinite Mind to prepare this universe and those who have been chosen for the Parousia. This host is the spirit of Shakardak, who has followed with him. The Spirit of War. He has fought many spiritual battles in many universes, and so has come unto this universe, for that is to take place in this time and space. Is that within your understanding?"

"Absolutely, positively. It's a delight to share this space with you," Julie said.

"Is there anything that you desire of me?" he asked her.

"Is there any additional reflection that you wish to give to Nathaniel?"

"He who sits before you is being re-engineered and will be unto himself for seven of your days of isolation. And he will come back as one with Shakardak, the Spirit of War," Awaki informed her.

"Is there a message that you wish to give him around the word absence because it is the blessing that's been given to his solar plexus, and so, this is his power chakra as how he can align himself with the blessings that you bestow upon him?" she questioned him.

"His absence---"

"Yes," she said, interrupting him as he answered.

"--- Is of the mind when his re-engineering is complete," he finished his sentence.

"Wonderful," she said. "Thank you for that beautiful perception because I just wanted more insight for him. I bless you abundantly. For the fulfillment of the Divine Plan, for your inspiring us from these greater realms that you come from. Bless you. Bless you. Bless you."

"Bless not me but bless your God," Awaki told her.

"Oh, absolutely, positively."

"We are commanded to do His ends," he said.

"Yes. The energy of gratitude. That's exactly right. When I was using the spiritual cards, it's the energy of gratitude, and we give all glorification, as I do in service, all glory goes to God. Thank you, thank you. Thank you," she responded.

"Do you know why we have come unto this place that you may see and hear?" Awaki asked her.

She responded, "Well, I'm honored by your presence."

"You, as the hosts of this universe, have the gift of choice, and so have you chosen of your God, and He is pleased with that which you do," Awaki complimented her.

"I love God," she said. "Thank you for that reflection. Bless you. I'm just … I'm very humbled. Thank you. It's just quite… Your energy is just so pure."

"And I shall ask of you this," he told her.

"What would you like?" she asked.

"Go forth and bring unto me the prophet," he said.

"Well, I will just let that inspire me. Go forth and bring unto you the prophet," she repeated.

She did not understand what Awaki, was asking her to do.

He explained, "There is one in this space that has been charged with the gift of prophecy and the gift of absolute healing beyond the understanding of the hosts of this universe, for your God has so commanded us to give unto him these things and so have we done so. He has been charged to repair this host in his physical during the re-engineering and that is he who is in this place. Go--" She interrupted him and said, "No. I'm feeling the energy of Archangel Michael. I call forth the energy of Archangel Michael, the I Am presence, the will of God, the power and the protection of God."

"Do you know---"

She interrupted Awaki again, "Do I know what?"

"...my names in different tongues?" He continued. "Unto those I am known as Awaki. I am known as Daiquiwa Dimblach Dihua. In other universes I am known as Michael, the Angel of Power. But, I am an emanation and spirit called forth by the Mind of He who has created all."

"Well, you know what, I bless you abundantly for the message that you bring here," she responded.

"This message that I bring unto you---"

She interrupted Awaki again, and said "Thank you."

"...is to all, at once, in many universes," he completed his point.

"Bless you and we have the freedom of choice to receive it to let it inspire us and I shall do that, and I send you love. I send you love, God's love, and the love that flows from God to me to you," she responded.

"It is time that I will move from this host." Awaki announced.

"Bless you," she said.

"It is your charge---"

She interrupted him again, "Oh bless you, bless you, bless you."

"...that you inform the prophet---"

Again she interrupted, "No, I don't."

"...of such things," he completed his charge to her.

She said, "I'm going to ask you that charge Nathaniel with that blessing because I've already received my charges from the Divine."

"You ...this is not within your understanding..." Awaki told her.

He tried to get her to understand that he was asking her to bring the prophet to him.

"You may think that," she said.

"So be it. Doblach!" Awaki said, a word never before recorded by us.

Usually he said Zimblach when he ended a conversation. We could only imagine what that meant, given the circumstances under which it was said. He always instructed the prophet, if any damage was done to Nathaniel's body before he left it, on what needed repair. Julie's misunderstanding of his "charges" to her prevented that from happening, when he left Nathaniel that time with her.

"Bless you, bless you, bless you." she said as Awaki exited Nathaniel's body.

Awaki always spoke of our arrogance, vainness and ignorance as part of our problem. That coupled with our disobedience and lack of faith landed us in need of the dawning of Armageddon.

The record of Nathaniel's final encounter with Awaki was on 5/15/1996; six months, almost, to the day of their first recorded appearance, 11/3/1995. This was the first recorded session after Nathaniel's return from the week - long trip that he was reengineered (his body was literally <u>remade</u> by the Angels) for months to take.

The last session began quite differently. Miriam described to Awaki the difference she saw in Nathaniel.

"…With your countenance over it," she described Nathaniel's face to him.

"It is." Awaki said.

"It's a new experience," she said.

"For you," he told her.

"Yes," she said.

"Not he," he said.

"No," she said.

Awaki then made a huge announcement, "He is here."

"So, you are both here? I understand." Surprised… Thomas who was in attendance asked, "Even with Shakardak?"

"That is within your understanding," Awaki said. "Yes."

"I understand," Thomas said.

Awaki explained further, "For, Shakardak is now he and he is Shakardak," he told them. "My energy is not within this host but is within your presence."

This was new, as Awaki's energy had always been within Nathaniel's body during the previous encounters. Now that pure Angelic energy occupied the same space as those present-- uncontained. Pure.

Miriam said, "He looks very comfortable."

"He is," Awaki told them.

The conversation that followed covered matters pertinent to Miriam and Thomas mostly. It turned to the Mechanism, the book that was to be the herald of Nathaniel to the masses, as a Spiritual Leader. It had been spoken of numerous times, over the prior 6 months.

Awaki talked of it that session also.

"The new knowledge is that which you have been given by me over time: The Mechanism. And, we have spoke unto the mind of this host. Both will be of you and you but he who sits before you will guide both." He told them about Nathaniel.

"We can understand that, because we need his practical grounding," the Prophet Thomas responded.

This was the first time they were told of Nathaniel's specific role in the production of the book which was to be completed in "the six of twelve," or June. He was to direct ("guide") their production.

At the conclusion of that last session, with all matters laid out as to how things were to proceed from there with the three of them, Thomas, Miriam and Nathaniel, Awaki declared:

"As I spoke unto you, when you and this deliverer were leaving that which we prepared for him (the Poconos), and so I speak unto you in this universe, and I shall say I humble myself unto my God, for it is to be as He has so willed it to be. It is to come as He has so ordered it to come and it will resurrect that He has so blessed it to resurrect. And we and I and those are the agents of His deliverance and His power and His resurrection. Zimblach!

# Chapter Six

## The Prophet

Divine Gift of Prophecy

Thomas Gains was a successful Attorney of many years when his life was visited by Angels of God. Prior to studying law, he spent four years, after high school, in a Catholic Seminary to become a priest. His life, after the Angels' visits, was to take on a totally different meaning than what he had ever envisioned as a lawyer and as a learned priest. He discovered, however, that it was perfectly set up, without his knowledge.

When God has something of grave importance that He wants us to know, He picks out souls who are chosen to bring us that message. He picks them out and makes them Prophets, before they are born or after they are born.

God chose him as His prophet, before his mama ever conceived him and made the body in which he lived. That is awesome. It's awesome to hear, it's awesome that it's true but more profound than that is, it is indescribably awesome to be a prophet and then learn that you are a prophet. Prophets of God are His Beloved.

The angels began coming November 3, 1996. Thomas established from the beginning that they were visiting this universe and using his Cousin Nathaniel's body by which to do it. Once that was established he was continually prepared to be God's Prophet. He was the conduit between the Angels in his cousin's body and all others to whom they spoke. God prepared him to encounter and engage all mankind with the messages he gave him to tell them.

One session, specifically, Thomas learned who he was.

On 11/20/1995 during one of his talks with Awaki, Thomas just casually asked him, "Who am I?"

Awaki repeated it, "Who are you?"

"Yes," Thomas said.

"In what universe, on what level?" Awaki asked him.

"My universe, on my level," he responded

"In this universe you are a chosen Taihi, you are a chosen Taihi," Awaki told him.

No one knew what that was so he asked Awaki, "Explain, please."

"You are equivalent to Elijah and when you pass from this place you will take your place among the Prophets of the Most High God," Awaki explained. "You were chosen long ago and your life was guided long ago to prepare you for this and now and what is to come. Your abilities were never an accident nor were they a mistake. Doubt them not for they are yours."

"How do I make the connection? I've given this a lot of thought lately – it seems as though there is a blockage between that which I emanate and that which I am conscious of," Thomas noted.

"Not a blockage ....uncertainty," Awaki told him.

Thomas continued, "What is the source of uncertainty? Can we talk about that and how is it to be eliminated?"

"You live too much in the physical world. This Host was chosen because he opened his mind and his heart; a gift delivered unto him from us but given him by you. But, yet, you have ceased to open your heart, your feeling, to the vibrations that we have sent to you," Awaki answered him.

"Is that because of the fear, and the pains of the past?" Thomas asked.

"That is because of what the physical world has brought to you. You have begun to shut down the spiritual body and become content with your existence in the here and now," Awaki explained to him.

"Sometimes I just feel that what good is it going to do?" he told Awaki.

"The good comes through the good of your spirit," Awaki said, "all that you have done have been done through the power of your spirit. Just as it took you time in this universe to develop so can you lose without nurturing and understanding.

"The power grows as you believe. Faith increases as you understand. This Host sitting before you is a demonstration to you that even though your faith has not developed the understanding, but yet a little belief can feed the spirit."

"How do I open up and how do I continue to stay open?" he asked Awaki.

"Your link has come through your prayers and meditation conducted with your Host. He is totally oblivious to what occurs, but you have the highest honor. You can speak to us and we will create you, but you are still in the physical form.

"You are blessed among men to experience the ability to talk to the Angels of the Most High God. Cherish thee this experience. Rebuild the faith that you have lost, allow no one to interfere with your link. Place not your understandings into foreign hands for you are more powerful than they.

"We talk to you in your tongue and in a point in time, we will manifest ourselves to you without a host. All these things will be done in the 12 and 40, when this Host moves forward, as you assist him, as directed by us. Allow no one to invade your energy. Allow no one to invade your energy," Awaki explained to his prophet.

He repeated that many times. It was imperative that he be extra careful with all that he gave and told him with all whom he encountered.

"Is this the proper or best way to use the information that you give?" he asked Awaki.

"Is there any other way?" Awaki responded.

"Not at this time," he said.

"You have been given charge of all that you have seen here. You have been given charge of all that you have seen here," he repeated that and continued. "Do what you must."

"Is there a specific pattern or way that the information will be given by you, from you and from those of whom you speak?" Thomas asked.

"Yes," Awaki said.

Frank stuttered, "And, uhhhh...."

Awaki, read his mind and responded, "The answer to your question is this --- when you have delusions or questions from the higher mind, then I will deal with you directly. Information will be given through the guiding spirit. Information will be given through the Warrior Spirit, Shakardak."

That conversation was enlightening and instructive but as time passed, Thomas was lead back again to the question of his being a Prophet.

"When did I become a Prophet?" he asked Awaki.

"You have always been such, unlike others that were charged," he told him. "You, before you were conceived, were chosen. That is why we have continuously protected you in the times of your foolishness and lack of understanding."

"You were even there when I was getting the snowballs thrown at me, weren't you?" Thomas remarked.

"We were even there when you were in the valley of decision, on how to deal with your call," Awaki told him.

"Do you mean when I was in the seminary?" he asked.

"That is within your understanding," Awaki said.

"Is there a connection between Prophecy and priesthood? Thomas asked. "Are they one in the same?"

"That is not within your understanding," Awaki answered him, no.

"What is the difference in the role of the priest?" he asked.

"You can choose, and it is within your ability to acquire that. A prophet, you are chosen," Awaki explained. "It is not within your ability to acquire, but it must be given unto you. Is that within your understanding?"

"You're saying that prophecy is a gift that is given. You're saying that priesthood can be acquired, can be chosen?" he asked.

"That is within your understanding," Awaki agreed and continued. "And let me explain unto you this: a man who chooses to be righteous and chooses to represent himself as a voice of God, does so not out of fear or wisdom of knowledge. But, a prophet who is chosen by his God, and all manner of wisdom is revealed unto him, does so out of obedience, even though he himself has not such prepared for it. Is that within your understanding?"

"Yes, yes," Thomas answered.

"A prophet seeks not the contentment with the hosts of this universe, but only of his God. A priest, as you say, seeks the contentment of others above him before he seeks the approval of his God. He is content when he is told that he is a good priest by those who sit above him, and his God becomes secondary to that. Prophets speak only unto his God and seek validation only from his God," Awaki explained.

As that conversation continued for some time between them Thomas said, "I feel that I'm getting closer to my God."

"You are not getting closer to your God, for your God is coming closer unto you," Awaki corrected him.

"I understand," he said.

"It is His Command," Awaki told him.

"Do you know how it just moves me to tears and trembling because of my unworthiness," Thomas said.

"(Awaki spoke an unknown language then) I have been charged and so shall I charge you. Infinite Mind says unto you that your obedience has rewarded you and in the seven days that this host is away from you, so shall we come unto you. Ask the question."

"What did you just do? What did you just say?" Thomas questioned him about the language he used.

"I answered the command of your God," he told him.

"I thank my God. I thank my God so continually," Thomas said.

"Do you want to know what I said in your language?" Awaki asked.

"Yes, please," Thomas answered.

"I hear, Most Holy One, I will obey your command for I Am, and You are Me. It is done," Awaki translated the language for him.

On 11/20/1995, the day that Thomas was first made aware of his being a Prophet of God, he questioned Awaki about other gifts, man acquired from God.

"Can you tell me about healing, healing the physical body? There is so much pain, pestilence and disease."

Awaki, questioned him. "When you say healing---"

Thomas interrupted him and explained, "Cure, repair, realignment of the physical body."

Awaki completed his thought. "---repair of your host of your spirits?"

"Yes," Thomas said, "and for the hosts of the spirits of others. How can that be done or is it to be done?"

"It can be done, it is to be done," Awaki said. "It has been predicted to be done by those who are sent by the Infinite Mind. The seven rays of light, emanate from all, belong to the Infinite Mind. You must learn to connect all seven rays of light."

Uncertain as to what those lights were Thomas asked, "Do we call these the seven chakras? I was curious about the seven rays of light."

"The seven rays of light are the seven points of the body in which your energy exits and enters," Awaki clarified.

"Where are they located?" he asked.

"In the center of the host. You must learn to touch them at the same time and then once you have touched them at the same time with your Infinite Mind, ask for genetic balancing. Repair of the hosts is as the mind will desire," Awaki told him.

"Is that for my host, for the host of my spirit? Is that the process to be used by all hosts?" Thomas asked.

"Ask the question," he instructed Thomas.

"How is it to be used? How is it to be done?" Thomas asked.

"Are you asking for the ability to heal those that you touch?" Awaki asked him.

"Yes, yes, yes," Thomas responded.

"With absolute certainty?"

"Yes," he responded again.

Awaki told him, "This gift will be granted. Place your hands around the forehead of this host."

Frank complied and placed his hands around Nathaniel's forehead. Awaki spoke that unknown language which he asked Thomas to repeat. He repeated it. Only he and Awaki could speak the language. The Divine gift of healing was thereby conferred upon Thomas.

He now had the Divine gift of Prophecy and the Divine gift of Healing. It was sometime later that Awaki described the 7 rays of light (points of energy) locations. They emanated from our bodies through the soles of our feet, (2) the palms of our hands, (2) our forehead, (1) our heart (1) and our genital area, (1) where the lower extremities join the trunk. They were not the same locations as the "chakra locations" commonly described by man.

From day one, of the recorded encounter with God's Angels, 11/3/1995, Thomas was pressed into service in this universe as God's Prophet. Right away he was told he would be involved in battles during that first conversation he had with God's angel.

Shakardak announced in his first appearance, "The battles over a period of time continues in the Universe. I have now been awakened to again fight the battle for Awaki."

Thomas wanted to know if they played any part, "What can we do to assist?" he asked Shakardak.

"Do what you must," he told him. "You must turn inward to prepare yourself. You were chosen and you were prepared for this. You must now use all that you have or have ever prepared or understood, and open up your body, your mind and help him (Nathaniel)."

"He has been chosen," Shakardak told Thomas. "Chosen because he is so active in displaying the openness of his heart and the openness of his mind. He has been chosen because you gave him a gift and he looked with his heart and his mind. He has become your charge to help him understand."

"Very well, the charge is accepted," Thomas said.

He agreed whole heartedly to take Nathaniel on with the charge to help him understand what happened to him with the angels invading his body and all else. He also accepted his role in the ensuing battles Shakardak had come to fight, whatever they were.

"Your only charge is to keep him open," Shakardak told him.

Spiritual Battles/Mechanism

Once he learned of his gift of prophecy and his charge to keep Nathaniel open, he accepted and was committed and determined to see that through.

He had more questions, "Awaki, tell us the source of the information that you give us and from whence it comes."

"The information that is given unto you has come and has not the pass. You will see what you have seen," Awaki answered and continued. "Your past will become your future once again in this universe. All that was, will be again, and all that is, will pass."

Thomas asked, "Can you clarify?"

"Study your past for it will again, again. You have been instructed by Shakardak, as I have instructed him, to study past wars," he reminded Thomas.

"Yes, talk about the past wars," he asked.

"The wars that you seek are universal wars," Awaki said. "The same wars in many universes at different times. The wars of the Infinite Mind. The wars of righteousness. The wars of all that seek the truth," he explained.

"How do they manifest themselves in this universe?" Thomas asked.

"Through the events of time," Awaki said. "This universe is controlled by the municipalities and powers – spiritual wickedness, set in motion by the elium lords of darkness; the fallen angel, his demons, and all those that follow him."

"How has the wars manifested themselves? I understand the level of which you speak because you speak beyond time and beyond space. How do they manifest themselves in the time and space of this universe...this time now?" Thomas asked.

"Again with the assassination and the elimination of your leaders. They begin with the corruption of the Infinite Mind's plans. They begin with the powers of man. As they all began so will the Lord of Hosts that begin – the end," he told Thomas.

"Do they begin in the ego? The ego of man?" Thomas asked further.

"In the souls of the hosts; the minds of the physical being; and the corruption of the spirit; and the foulness of the heart. For, all those things that I have just mentioned belong to the Lord of Hosts: hearts, minds, souls and spirits. The flesh, the agent in which the wickedness is carried out in, belongs to the world.

Awaki explained further, "The ending (Revelations) of the various interpretations of Yahweh's writings have been re-engineered. The ending is the beginning of the second coming and the beginning (Genesis) is the ending of the new order of things.

"The books that you read from the Infinite Mind that were left to you as a rule and guide for your faith and practice throughout this universe; begin at the end and end at the beginning; then you will see the truth."

"What are the books that you are referring to? Are you referring to books that I read, or books that we read?" Thomas asked.

"In your universe there are many. Many names for one book," Awaki explained.

"What is the one?" Thomas asked.

"The Hebrew account of Yahweh's people, Torah. Alach – Machabech is the second of those writings. The Ethiopic and Coptic accounts of Yahweh's writing – the Bible… The Qur'an…. are all variations of Yahweh's writing. Compare the wars. Begin with the ending and end with the beginning and you will know the truth in what is to come." Awaki described in specific detail the books of which he spoke.

"So you're saying that the message and the meaning is hidden or it's not as it appears to be, as it is presented?" Thomas questioned.

"Not hidden. You misunderstood. In your universe, the beginning is the ending and the ending is the beginning. The alpha and the omega. The beginning is the ending of all things," he corrected Thomas.

Awaki gave us the layout of the Holy writings of the Bible, the Qur'an and the Torah, as we knew them to be. He told Thomas that, as written, the ending of these books had been rearranged ("re-engineered") from the original writings. The current endings actually speaks to the second coming of Jesus. That is the start of things to come--- "the beginning," not the end as we believed. And, the current beginning of these books, actually speaks to the end of things as they will be after Jesus' coming. That is the end --- "the ending," not the beginning, as we believed.

Therefore Awaki's repeated saying: "the end is the beginning and the beginning is the end," was to enlighten us to that difference. (Revelation is the beginning of the second coming and Genesis is the ending of things of that second coming, the new order of things). Although, seemingly simple, it was an extremely difficult concept to grasp, initially.

That was the purpose of the Angels coming, to gather us, to awaken us and to prepare us for the second coming of Jesus. The preparation entailed, awakening us to our purposes and the details of the overall process, as best our minds could conceive them.

One week after Awaki's appearance on 11/20/1995 there was another appearance on 11/27/1995 where they spoke to Thomas, again, through the use of Nathaniel's body.

"Who are you?" Thomas asked.

He heard sounds but could not recognize what was being said or who was saying them.

"In English please," he asked quietly.

The voice said, "I am the Warrior Spirit, Shakardak, sent back to you."

"Can you speak louder please? Why were you sent back?" Thomas asked.

Shakardak said, "In preparation for the Great Transition so that you may understand your purpose and your preparation."

"Can you tell me more about my purpose and my preparation for the Great Transition?" he asked.

"Your preparation has been done. Your purpose is to prepare this physical body (Nathaniel's) of this person for battles."

"How can I help him to be prepared?" he questioned, Shakardak.

"Keep him open," he said.

"Thomas asked Shakardak, "What needs to be done to keep him open?"

"Feed his faith," he answered.

"You know he has many questions which he desires to have answers to?"

"There are questions that I must answer and there are those which I cannot," he told Thomas.

"Will you tell us those that you can answer and those which you cannot, and those which we must answer for ourselves?"

"All those who desire my instruction are only preparation for the Great Transition and spiritual battles – 12 and 40. That is my purpose. I am Shakardak, the Warrior Spirit, sent by Awaki, the Angel of Spirits."

"Shakardak, what does your name translate to in English?" Thomas asked him.

"The Conquering Warrior," Shakardak answered.

"So, you've been in many battles, have you not, Shakardak?"

"Many, many spiritual battles; many, many universes," he answered.

"What about your spirit causes you to prevail?"

"I have been given the translucent energy of the Most High, the Infinite Mind." Shakardak said.

"Do you bring that energy with you now in this place?"

"It is me," he answered.

Thomas kept probing to get from Shakardak information he needed for himself and for Nathaniel that would help them understand their lives. He was more able to than Nathaniel because he, at least, was conscious and talking to Shakardak. Nathaniel was not in that consciousness neither was he in his body. Shakardak had taken it over.

"What is it that we should tell Nathaniel in terms of his preparation for the great battle?" Thomas asked.

"It has been your charge. There has been much talk about the seven rays of light emanating from this being. The seven rays of light from the energy conduits through which the body is being reengineered. It is the center of this being." Shakardak explained to him.

Thomas needed more clarity. "When you say 'center,' do you mean the center of his body? His heart?"

"The heart as you know it," he told Thomas.

"Do you mean the heart chakra that we talk about…the heart energy?" Thomas asked.

"The heart. The heart is the hope of the mind for in the area of the heart holds the faith and the faith directs the mind to overcome the physical body. It is the hope of the mind and the mind is the light that connects with the Infinite Mind, your Heavenly Father.

"All that I am speaking to you today is all that you already know. Today, I will teach you how to win spiritual battles. Today, I will teach you how to master what you call and connect all that is already there.

"Spiritual battles are fought only for one purpose. That is Yahweh's purpose. The God of the Hosts. That's the first of many that you must understand. Any battles that take place are not for the glorification of the Most High God have no favor in His eyes. So, you must recognize a battle before it is fought. Determine if it is a true spiritual battle. If it is not, you do not allow this spiritual being to participate. Steer him far from that place. Also you must know that before a spiritual battle is fought, it has already been won. The act is not the means, the means is the act," Shakardak gave much more details.

"Can you explain that please?" Thomas asked.

"Victory has already been claimed for you. In the far reaches of heaven, these battles have already been fought and won millions of times. How you interpret your faith will determine the outcome in this universe. The heart center of the faith is the hope of the mind. All things are forgiven except the misuse of the powers bestowed upon those who have been blessed."

"Why are they not forgiven? Why is a misuse not forgiven?" Thomas asked.

"Because you have been made aware of the Divine. For you have been chosen to sit among men, for this physical being has not yet achieved the level needed to combat evil but he has achieved spiritual awakening," Shakardak explained.

That level of detail was the type of information Frank needed for him and Nathaniel to understand what was happening to their lives.

He inquired further, "What else do we need to know at this time?"

Shakardak answered in great detail, "That the understanding of spiritual battles are within the minds of men; to triumph over these battles are in the souls of the servants. The mind is the highest of all the physical body. The keys to eternal life are right here; life itself as you know it. But eternal life that which, has been promised to you, is not eternal death, as your universe views it.

"Eternal life is a circle of experiences, the unbroken chain. When you pass from this life, you will move into another universe, another time, to experience again, until you reach a level; then you will transform into your original purpose – an energy force that then becomes the overseer of other lives in other times and experiences as others pass through those.

"Explanation so that you may understand. The Great Prophet Elijah, achieved this spiritual awareness in this lifetime in this universe and therefore was rewarded: not necessary to see the journey of death. Moses, achieved this level in this universe – did not see the journey of death. Annaquha, achieved this level – did not see the journey of death. This is within your understanding.

"And at a time and space in your life, if you can pass through physical bodies and move into the spiritual mind, you will ask not to see the journey of death and it will be granted unto you. But it is all determined how you utilize the experiences in this universe.

"All have been granted eternal life, love and forgiveness. All must pass through the journey of death. Your understanding – there are those physical beings in this time, in this universe that have been allowed the journey of death – they return to this time in this universe. We have given some different Divine Gifts and teachings throughout this universe. Some were misused; some have exemplified their purpose.

"It is your choice. It is this physical being's choice. Death is life. Your lives are your death. Is that within your understanding?" He did not allow Thomas to respond, and continued, "You, even as I inhabit this physical being's body, are still my master in the Son Universe. For in the Son Universe, your place of your spirit will be beside the greatest of prophets of this time in this universe.

"Now we will define information about what is to come that is within your understanding. You have been told and instructed by the Holy Awaki that the 'end is the beginning and the beginning is the end.' The end of the Holy Writings – read them –concentrate on its meaning – with this physical being. He must understand, you must understand the signs as the Infinite Mind begins to send them. He must understand that soon, 12 and 40, he will have to be prepared for the spiritual battle what is to come. He must understand also…I am open…proceed."

Thomas listened attentively to Shakardak with no interruptions and Shakardak perceived that he wanted to question him.

"May I ask questions now?" Thomas asked him.

"I see that Awaki's gift is strong. I feel your energy. Before Awaki's gift to you, your energy and the methods in which you moved them was mere child's play to me because I am Shakardak, the Warrior Spirit. I can feel your strength and your power. Proceed," he told Thomas.

"You speak of the Great Prophet--who do you mean -- is that Elijah?" Thomas asked.

"The Great Prophets of the Infinite Mind are many. There are many universes and many times. In your universe in your time there has been Noah, Enoch, Moses, Elijah, Nahum. Those are the Great Prophets. And there was only one of the power of the Most High God in the flesh of the physical being; Jah, Jah, King of Kings, Lord of Lords, Jesus, the Son of the Living God," Shakardak informed him.

"What of Muhammed? What of Buddha?" Thomas asked.

"Muhammed was a physical being who was allowed to see, who was given the gift and misused it," he answered.

"How did he misuse the gift?" Thomas questioned him.

"He confronted many of the Most High's people and used his teachings, his gift. Buddhash also was given a gift and used it to misguide and corrupt. Is this within your understanding?" He asked but did not allow an answer. "Let me tell you: earlier I told you that those given gifts of Divine that used them not to glorify the Infinite Mind are not forgiven. Let me put this for your understanding. Lucifer, Satan, the elium lord, was cast down from the Infinite Mind because he used his gift to corrupt Yahweh's people. Is this within your understanding?"

Thomas acknowledged, "Yes," but he really didn't fully understand. "How did they specifically misuse their powers and how did they specifically corrupt the people of God? What are the pitfalls that should be avoided? Is it pride, is it egotism?" he asked.

"Earlier when I came to you for the first time, we spoke of the signs and the elium lords and the demons of this world that corrupt. The corruption is within the soul. The soul feeds off of the spirit of others. That is all that needs to be known. Take not, give many," Shakardak explained.

Thomas asked, "Is there other information that you have at this time?"

"Censor information that this physical being is subject to in the spiritual world," he said. "There will be those that will attempt to guide him from this path. Keep him open and you will be rewarded. It is your charge and your responsibility. Also, the Holy Awaki will be with you until your spirits pass on to him."

"Is it time for you to leave this physical body? If so, let it be so," Thomas said.

"Proceed," Shakardak told him.

So Thomas did.

"You spoke of things early on or earlier that we needed to understand and you mentioned one or two things. Are there other lessons, or other instructions to be given at this point or at this time?"

"Not at this point, not at this time either," Shakardak answered him.

"I thank you sincerely," Thomas said.

"I must leave this physical body," Shakardak said.

"Proclaim, proclaim our thanks around the Throne of God," Thomas told him.

"We hear your prayers. I must leave this physical body so that his spirit can return," he responded.

"Very well," Thomas said.

Shakardak left Rainier's body and spoke or sang in a language we could neither understand nor repeat.

There was recorded silence from the Angels for a period of time, about two weeks or more, 12/14/1995 to be exact. After which they returned.

During this session there were multiple angelic encounters, not just one or two as before.

The first to enter, announced himself, "It is I, Shakardak."

Thomas spoke to him, "Hail, Shakardak. Is there information you have this evening for us, Shakardak?"

"Yes," he said and continued. "The keys to victory in spiritual battles. We have received two. We will continue on if they are within your understanding. Now, we have to explain to you the third and final testament. In 12 and 40 a New Testament (Covenant) will be made with the people of this universe. A new covenant was promised to you by the Infinite Mind …eternal life.

"But in order for the hosts of this universe to receive the final covenant, in this universe it must be necessary to move into another consciousness."

*(At this point, for full disclosure of the authenticity and accuracy of what is being given, it must be explained that because of an absence of the original source on which the Angels words were captured, what follows of these conversations is in part only. That is included here, sans what's missing, because of the grave importance of what was salvaged from the conversations. No efforts to "make up" for what's missing have been made. Only that that was actually said is included here. You will encounter blank spaces where information was not captured.)*

That concept of "another consciousness" was foreign to Thomas so he asked Shakardak for clarification.

Shakardak said, "It must be necessary for the Testators to move into another consciousness. Is that within your understanding?"

"Yes, I just don't understand the word Testators. Can you explain?" Thomas asked.

"In this universe, the deliverer, conqueror, the chosen, during the spiritual battle fought on all planes, the physical, the mental and the spiritual who, which, they are preparing for as we speak, as this Host is your charge. The Testators must move into another consciousness for the testament to be fulfilled," he explained.

"How do we do that?" Thomas asked.

Shakardak answered, "You must continue on the path of enlightenment. The end is the beginning and the beginning is the end. We have given you all information and all tools of _____ to you in this universe.

On your physical plane it is up to you. Do what you will. You only need ask and it will be given unto you. Is this within your understanding?"

"Yes," Thomas said.

"Have we not fulfilled our word?" Shakardak asked him.

"Yes," he said again.

"Ask what you will," he told Thomas.

"When you say 'fulfilled your word' we know that you've done everything that you said you would do in terms of information and these same manifestations of you fulfilling your word…. Nathaniel talks about that all the time. Nathaniel has a question about whether there is an entity with him at all times. Could you give us information in regard to who that energy is, the purpose of it, the connection to the spiritual battle of which you speak?" he asked.

"You already know, as I told you, I have been sent to teach, to guide, and to prepare you that you may prepare yourselves for the spiritual battle. I am Shakardak, the Warrior Spirit. I will be with this host at all times to protect him against the elium lords, for they seek to destroy. It is I."

"Very well, that was our suspicion. That was our knowledge," Thomas admitted and continued. "Then, tell me this…is there a particular way that Nathaniel needs to control or order your entry into his body as a host?"

"How can you control that which you don't understand?" Shakardak asked.

"Sometimes things that you don't understand – they can be ordered. Perhaps control is not a proper word. But as a fragile host, as you know yesterday, he was cast to the ground, and no, he was not injured, he was not hurt," he answered.

"Now then you must understand why he is your charge," Shakardak said. "Was that our doing or was that not your doing?"

"Depends on your perspective," Thomas answered.

"Do you not understand that I am pure energy? I am powerful in spirit. This has already been explained to you. That I am Shakardak, the Warrior Spirit," he admonished Thomas.

"You're saying that we should take the cautions that are necessary before you come in, is that correct?" Thomas asked.

"To attempt to use the power that I control is in itself foolishness," he chided Thomask. "Understand who I am," he told him.

"We understand you, Shakardak. We understand that you are pure energy."

"Did you not have assistance with what occurred?" he asked.

"Yes," Frank said.

"This host is your charge. Understand my power and understand that it is not child's play," he continued with Thomas. "Ask what you will," he invited him again.

"Can I speak to you about making miracles happen in my life and in the lives of others, again for the benefit of the spiritual battle of which you speak?" Thomas asked.

"Holy Awaki has not given me such powers," he answered.

"Is there any other information that you can give us at this time?" Thomas questioned.

"Just remember what you have been instructed… that the only sin not forgiven is the misuse of the Divine Gifts. You have been shown. Understand," he told him firmly.

"I understand," he told Shakardak. "Is there any information that you have for Bryant, who is also here?"

Within minutes, a new voice was heard.

"I am Azreal, and who are you?" it asked.

"I am Thomas, Azreal. And there is also Bryant. Who are you, Azreal?"

"I am Azreal… I am spirit. Allowed, for the first time, to occupy a living host. Azrael."

"Do you stand before the Throne of the Infinite Mind, Azrael?" Thomas checked his bona fide.

"I belong to the Holy Awaki. His Angels of Spirits," he responded.

"What is your function when involved with the Holy Awaki?" Thomas continued to probe.

"To do as he would have me to do," he answered.

"Why has he sent you here to occupy this host?"

"You asked the question, then I came," Azrael replied.

"I asked if there is any information for Bryant. Would you comment in response to that question?"

"Yes. He has to understand he's full of love but he is misguided… (break in commentary on the tape) …was given to him today and to

107

cherish and respect for soon this universe will come to an end and it will not be any more."

"Can you explain to him in more detail that which he needs to embrace?" Thomas asked on Bryant's behalf.

"He needs to learn to love himself. I feel his thoughts. His thoughts are confused...what he sees is not within his understanding. He has love for himself confused with conceit. He has to learn in order to love himself, he has to love others even when they show him contempt.

"He is already thinking, 'who am I and why do I say these things?' I say these things because I have been watching you since you were a child. You are now at a point in your life when the confusion is starting to end but you have to embrace love for others.

"Your question should always be before you—how can you make someone else happy. And, then, the continual blessings which you will experience will stay with you until the end of the universe. Fear not the uncertainties, for you were created imperfect and you will leave here imperfect. Perfect your spirit. Open your reception."

After that, Azrael was gone, just as suddenly as he had come.

Then the familiar voice was heard, "This is Shakardak."

"Thanks for sending Azrael-- allowing him to come here," Shakardak. How are we to disseminate the information that has been given to us, to others. We know that it is to be disseminated by the way we live, the way that we act, by way of performing service. How specifically, is that information best disseminated in conjunction with the plan of the Universal Mind in this universe at this time?"

Shakardak said, "It will be disseminated through consciousness travel. This Host will receive a series of vibrations in a state which you call sleep. Listen to what he tells you. Record it according to your methods in this universe and they will guide you to the path."

"When will this happen?" Thomas asked.

"It has already begun," he answered.

Then it occurred again, "This is the Holy Awaki," another different voice was heard. "I feel your thoughts. I have been fulfilling the promise. Have you been using the gift?"

"Yes, Awaki, and I have questions about the gift," Thomas answered.

"That's why I am here. Ask what you will," he said.

"The gift...I know it is for the healing of others. Is it also for the healing of myself?" Thomas asked of his Divine Gift of Healing he received earlier.

"Is it not your gift?"

"So, therefore, it is not to heal myself," Thomas answered.

"Is it not your gift?" Awaki repeated.

"Yes, it was given as a gift," Thomas admitted.

"Does gifts have limitations?"

"No," he said.

"Then therefore you have answered your own thoughts," Awaki told him.

"It is a gift to be shared to others as in transferred to others?" Thomas asked.

"You cannot transfer what is not yours. It has been given unto you. I have given it unto you. How can you give away something you have yet to master?" Awaki asked him.

"You gave me that answer in my heart and that question was asked of me, isn't that true?" Thomas asked.

"That is correct," Awaki acknowledged.

"And I am supposed to answer the many questions I have about these things, I need merely listen to my heart as you speak to me, is that not true?"

"You were told that all things would be given unto you. All you need is to ask," Awaki reminded him.

"Should I still use the other means and methods that I have used in the past for healings or should I just use the gift that you've given?"

"In the presence of your power there is no other means," he answered Thomas.

"Do I merely place my hands the way that I was instructed or are there other ways? And again should I listen to the stirring of my heart as I place them on the various hosts?" Thomas asked.

"The stirring of your heart has told you all you need is to lay hands upon those who receive you. As your power increases then so your strength," Awaki said.

"Can I use the gift to heal entities and bodies that are not in my presence, bodies I can't touch, such as an absent healing?"

"Are you Holy?" Awaki asked him.

"Yes," he said.

'Then you have answered your question."

Thomas moved on to some other concerns.

"Awaki, can you tell me if there is a path or if there is a method or means to make miracles....in my life?"

"Again.....again...... you talk about concepts and precepts of your universe. What we do are not miracles. What we do are Divine powers," he clarified.

"May the Divine powers be used to relieve some of the suffering, some of the pain, that I see existing in this universe for there is no direct solution and it appears as though they can only be cured by what we describe as miracles. I have called out to you when I have confronted those situations," Thomas reminded him.

"In your present form, you can only rationalize and use the powers as they have been given to you for this universe. The state in which you talk of would require that I remove you from this universe," Awaki explained to him.

"Is that the only way?" Thomas asked.

"At this point in your universe, it is. It is known that I will have to remove you from this universe for you will suffer ridicule, possibly death, by the hands of those that do not understand. And, you yourself will have the power to transcend death. Therefore, you would not be allowed to walk among these hosts who do not yet understand the oneness of the Infinite Mind and what is to come in the spiritual battles in which you will take part," Awaki told him.

"So, you're saying that they are to work those things out for themselves for the time has not yet come, for those problems to be solved because of the greater mission?" he asked Awaki.

"The time for those things will come in the Third Covenant in 12 and 40. The Third Covenant is of the Infinite Mind and the final chapter of the promises made to the people of this universe," he answered him.

"Could you tell us more about the Third Covenant? This is the first time that you've spoken of it. Shakardak spoke of a general..."

Awaki interrupted, "The Third Covenant is a **rebirth** and a **recreation** of this universe in the glory and the paradise of He who has given it. In the First Covenant was found faultless. The Second Covenant, blood was shed. And, in the Third Covenant, the minds of people who dwell in this universe will be regenerated into the oneness of the Infinite Mind."

"Tell me more about the First Covenant?" Thomas asked.

"The First Covenant was made with the children of God. They were unable to live as they were charged."

"The Second Covenant?" he asked.

"Required that a sacrifice be made that those who were imperfect may find perfection in the one." Awaki explained.

"When did the Second Covenant occur?" Thomas asked.

"With the one and only Testator."

"The Son of the Living God?" Thomas asked.

"The glorious Jah who dwells in all universes," Awaki agreed and told Thomas, "Ask what you will."

"Will there be any covenants after the Third Covenant?" he asked.

"The three_____ in the Infinite, and it shall reign forever. He that gave it shall reveal Himself to you," Awaki declared.

"He that gave the Third Covenant?" Thomas questioned.

"He that gave all universes," Awaki said and invited him to, "Ask what you will."

Thomas used this opportunity to revisit questions he had earlier.

"We asked Shakardak this question and we understand that Shakardak is pure energy….we understand that you are pure energy….we understand that very, very clearly, but our concern is ….when you enter into Nathaniel as a host, into his body, is there any way for it to be done at certain times or is it he who has to become accustomed to knowing when you will appear or when you will send somebody?"

"This Host already understands but he turns his face away. It is your charge to keep him open so that he may become comfortable with the re-engineering that is taking place," he informed Thomas.

"How should he facilitate the re-engineering health-wise and diet-wise? Is there anything he needs to do?" Thomas asked.

He was unresponsive to the fact that Nathaniel was aware of each approach for invasion of his body but turned away from some. It was Thomas' charge to prevent that happening.

"There is nothing he needs to do, but that you listen to the instruction that I have given to you when you ask these questions," Awaki answered him.

"When I ask them of you for this host or when I ask them of you through my heart?"

"When you ask these questions," Awaki repeated. "Ask the next question, for it is time to leave this host."

"Very well. I have no other questions at this time," he said and asked Awaki, "Is there any other information that you wish to give at this time?"

"I must warn you again, my son. Be aware of those who claim to be of Infinite Mind, for they attempt to invade your energy. Protect it. Ask simple questions and listen for complicated answers," he told him.

Awaki reminded him, again, to protect himself from those not of God who would attempt to do him harm by claiming or acting as if they were of God. He told him again how to discern who they were; ask a simple question. Those who were not of God would give a complicated answer and expose themselves. They taught us, this was paramount in fighting spiritual battles to win them.

He instructed Thomas, "Put your hands on the forehead of this host."

He did and Awaki spoke an unknown language to him and exited the host's body. That ended that session.

During a different session but, one that appeared to have happened, the same day, 12/14/1995, there was a most compelling conversation with Thomas. This session too was only available by notes. The original captured source, was and is unavailable. But the information was so crucial to mankind's understanding of things that, that which was salvaged is passed on here.

Thomas requested the angel's identification.

"It is I, Awaki, the Angel of Spirits is with you. There is information that you must know. You have been given instruction by the spirits I have sent unto you to guard you. Ask what you will now."

Thomas started, "Awaki, I have been thinking of the whole concept of reincarnation. Can you tell me about that concept? When the soul returns?"

"Reincarnation, in your universe implies that there must first be death. There is no such thing as death," he informed Thomas.

"Can you explain?" he asked.

"Death is a concept only understood by those in your universe that reside in these hosts that you call bodies. They do not die. They return to the earth from which they came. The spirit moves on to another universe, to other experiences," he told him.

"Does the spirit return to this universe?" Thomas asked

"Once the spirit passes on to other experiences, it does not return, nothing is left," Awaki reiterated for him.

"So, it only spends one lifetime in this universe. Is that not correct?"

Awaki answered, "Every spirit, of every man, every creature, and every woman spends an experience in a universe in a host. It passes on to another universe of experiences. Only those who have been chosen spirits can cross universe and defy time."

"How are they chosen?" Thomas asked.

"By exercise of their faith and in the universe in time in which they originated," he explained.

"Do all souls and all spirits originate from different universes?" Thomas asked.

"In this time, in this universe, as you experience the things of this world in your universes of lifetimes you are experiencing death, which you have experienced, experiencing death which you will experience," Awaki told him.

Earlier, in a prior session, Thomas was told to read the Bible starting at Revelation (the end chapter of the Bible) as preparation for the upcoming spiritual battles.

"As you may or may not know, I have read the book of Revelation and I thank you for directing me toward it. It speaks of the breaking of the seals, it speaks of the messages to the different churches. Can you explain?"

"All those things that you have read and consumed are happening in your time and universe. I would like to communicate with you. The Angels of heaven are standing in the four corners of the earth holding back the other universes and, as I speak, the vision is being carried out as myriads (a countless number) and myriads of conquering Angels walk the face of this earth. So, the Angel of Power will descend upon this earth and inhabit it. These things take place not as your mind can conceive it. Look for the signs. Look for changes in the creation itself and you will know that they are here," Awaki explained to him.

"What do you mean 'changes in creation itself'?"

"When the Angels enter, the elements will change. The elements of your universe will undergo massive reconstruction. The host (John "the Revelator") of your universe has seen a vision of a physical accounting of the beginning — to you--- the end--- but as we speak, those accountings are taking place. Man cannot see the Angels as they will go about their work, but they are here," he answered Thomas.

"Is there any way to sense them and to know their presence and to be more cooperative with their purpose, or isn't it necessary to see them to be more cooperative?"

"You have no choice but to cooperate," Awaki replied and left Nathaniel's body.

That ended the session.

That was a declaration that the "beginning" or Revelation, which we saw as the "end" was upon us as they spoke to us 12/14/1995. It was also confirmation of the writings in Revelations of Angels holding back other universes. The massive changes in the elements Revelation spoke of were confirmed. The presence of countless angels walking the earth bringing about changes, spoken of in Revelation, was confirmed.

Decades since, at this writing, evidence of these profound occurrences are even more pronounced. Presently (2020) the world is being visited by a deadly plague, for which there is no known treatment or cure that is bringing mass "death" and devastation to all mankind on the globe, SARS- CoV-2, a Coronavirus.

The period of silence from the Angels was no longer than 4-5 days when they returned and invaded Nathaniel's body on 12/19/1995.

"Please speak to us, whenever you are ready to speak," Thomas asked.

A voice was heard. "I am here. It is I."

"Who are you?" Thomas inquired.

"Shakardak." It said.

"Shakardak. Welcome." "Is there information you wish to give us this evening, Shakardak?"

"There is more that you need to know. This is the 12 that you must prepare, who pick up your swords and intensely train. For, the battle is about to come in your universe over the next 12, you must prepare intensely, and 40, the time will be at hand. You have been given the keys over victory over spiritual wars. Now you must study how they come to be. Is this within your understanding?"

"It is Shakardak. How do we prepare?" Thomas responded.

"You have been told that the end is the beginning and the beginning is the end. You must continue to study within the guide of the divine scripture, as all have been told before, a complete circle is the repeat of past events. The ??content in their shoes?? will be the same, only the method will be different. You must begin to hear us, to wipe all doubt from your mind, and from the mind of him we occupy," Shakardak told him.

"You're really involved in this process." Thomas responded.

"The 'process' is not a 'process,' Shakardak rebuked Thomas. "Talk not to me of time… talk only to me of faith. It is your charge and his destiny. For, you must begin to teach and understand what has been laid before you. The next 12 there will be many more changes in you and this which we occupy. Draw your swords and prepare for battle," he demanded of Thomas.

"Can you explain that please, Shakardak. You said that before. You talked about drawing swords. What do you mean by swords?" Thomas asked.

"The sword of life that cuts away lack of understanding," he explained.

"Do we carry the sword of life with us?" Thomas asked.

"It is ever with you," Shakardak declared. It is the mental capacity to divide the physical body from the spiritual body. It cuts the two in half. They cannot coexist. The physical body is that which houses the power. The spiritual body is that which you need to develop in this (Nathaniel) whom we occupy over the next 12. As he begins to grow the spiritual body, the physical body becomes tame and governable."

Shakardak made plain and simple for Thomas that the "sword" was the "mind" in the body. The mind split the body into the physical body and the spiritual body. Both separate from each other as they cannot coexist.

"Do you mean over the next 12 months? Do you mean over the next 12 years? Can you define that?" Thomas requested.

"For your understanding, the first and the last of your years are 12. There are still a lot of changes that must take place but he has to do as we

115

command. But it is his choice, as it is yours, to draw your sword to prepare for battle dividing physical from spiritual. Everlasting life belong to the spiritual body. The physical body will return to the universe. Choose." He explained "12" to Thomas.

They had 12 years to complete the preparation that was given to them (1995-2007). He also made it crystal clear that it was their (Nathaniel's and Thomas') choice as to whether they did it or not as he challenged them to "choose." The necessity of this writing today for your consumption is suggestive their choices.

Are there any questions before I go out of this host?" he questioned Thomas.

"Can you elaborate a little bit in terms of the sword; In terms of developing the spiritual body?" Thomas asked.

"The sword is the weapon of discipline. Your mind has the weapon of discipline. We have given you the ability to choose of this world or a world you cannot see; a world you cannot understand; a world you cannot control. Do you seek in faith that world and these things? Do you live in the physical body of this world and these things? Draw your sword and prepare for battle. You must choose your side."

Again Shakardak reiterated, choose the spiritual, of God, (the unknown and the unseen in faith) which they came to develop in those called and chosen, over the 12 years, or live in the physical, not of God, (that that's known and visible) both could not coexist. They could not do both. Again, however, the necessity of this writing suggests they tried.

"There is only one side Shakardak," Thomas told him.

Shakardak told him in candid detail, "It is your charge to make sure he whom we occupy understands that he has the power to seek spiritual body; a world of things that seem hard to understand, through faith. He is caught up in what he sees and what he can explain. This must be dealt with swiftly. It will hinder his gift and progress. He must draw his sword; the sword of discipline, understanding and choose his side. The gift that has been displayed and given to him by you will soon become his burdens. His purpose is to become of service and there are many burdens. If he wants to he must choose now."

No exploration of that charge was made, instead the Angel of war was questioned about himself, "Sharkadak, are you known by any other names besides Shakardak?"

"Yes. I am known by many names, many tongues, in many universes." Shakardak answered.

"Are you known by any other name that we would recognize?" he was further questioned.

"All names of those who are of Infinite Mind are recognized. I am Shakardak, the Warrior Spirit. I am known by Kalio, the God of War, I am known by Herare, The Deliverer of Fire. I am known by H'ik B'ek, The Angel of Darkness. Is this within your understanding?"

"Yes," Thomas answered.

"I am also known of he that draws all power unto him, Holy Michael, The Angel of Power," Shakardak further informed him.

"You are known as Michael?" Thomas asked.

"Yes," he responded.

"Is that why you speak so eloquently of the sword?" Thomas remarked.

"I wield many swords. This that you see is a manifestation of the Infinite Mind, the Universe of Vibrations. All that you speak with are known by many names, many tongues, in the universes. The manifestation of the love to the Angel of Spirits, the Holy Awaki, in this universe is a manifestation of the infinite time, space and consciousness.

"I am known as Michael the Archangel. My sword is forever with me and my burden is forever there. As I praise the name of the Most High God, the Lord of Lords, the King of Kings, the Great I am; do you understand the Infinite Mind, Yah He Wah He, Jah, the Creator of all that is and all that is not? Do you understand the power of the Great I am?

"First you must understand the purpose of how He uses His names. Do you understand why He is called the Great I Am?" He asked Thomas.

"I believe so," Thomas answered

"Then attempt," he told him.

"My understanding of the Great I Am is whatever follows I Am, is, and that is how Universal Mind creates. Is that correct?"

"Your understanding is simplistic but within your grasp." Shakardak told him.

"Explain it Shakardak," he requested.

"The Great I Am was a word in the vibrations spoken and He created Himself," Shakardak told him.

"I understand," Thomas replied.

That was highly unlikely for how could he? However, that was the sense of "knowing" and "understanding" that sometimes happened, with many, while you were in their presence.

"He is King of Kings and the Lord of Lords, the Most High Infinite Mind, Yahweh, Jah, Yah He Wah He, because He has the power to create. He thought His own self into being. There can be no other who has such power and control of all there is. All there is consists of all that He is. From the heavenly stars to the depths of hell is part of the Great I Am for He created Himself, then us. So, you have an understanding, the power of the names and whom the Infinite Mind really is," he explained to him.

"Thank you Shakardak," Thomas said.

Shakardak in his enlightenment of Thomas used terminology and concepts familiar to Thomas, in this Universe, which needed to be explained immediately.

"As far as those things that concern the 'heavens,' Shakardak explained, "the heavens are a concept created by man. All that exists is 'heaven;' all that exist is 'hell,'" he clarified. "It is up to you and all that exist on the physical plane in their universe to transcend, that they may live with peace on earth and goodwill towards men. Heaven, as you know it in your universe is NOT a place. Heaven is a consciousness and state of being.

"You can be one with the Infinite Mind or your soul can be so detached that faith is virtually non- existent. When faith is strong and the soul attached, then the oneness and the heaven you seek can be within your power to create. In the Holy Scriptures they speak of faith to you and if you have faith the size of a mustard seed, you can move mountains. Do you think you have to wait to get to heaven to do this?" He asked Thomas.

"No, Shakardak," he answered.

"You're correct because heaven exists within your creation."

"Explain how," Thomas asked Shakardak.

"You must understand first that you have to bring into your life the creative forces of the Divine Mind. You have to study and meditate on that which He has said and remember all things that you already know and practice. Be prepared to draw your sword and choose the physical or the spiritual. It is time," he explained.

Thomas responded, "It is time for you to leave Shakardak. Thank you."

Shakardak exited Nathaniel's body and the session ended.

*A conversation was captured, for the first time, between Thomas and Nathaniel, immediately following the exit of the Angel from his body and his return to his body, on this tape dated 12/19/1995.*

*"I heard a 'swishing' that time. That's the second time I heard the 'swishing.' Nathaniel exclaimed. He continued very excitedly. "I felt like I was going through a tunnel or something."*

*Thomas responded, "So it's 8 o'clock now and we began at 7:22, this is December 19th, 1995."*

*He made no reference, on the tape, to Nathaniel's excited recount of what he had just experienced which appeared totally, disregarded by Nathaniel, in his jubilance.*

*Nathaniel continued his excited description of what he remembered and felt of the invasion.*

*"I didn't fight that time going out. I didn't fight that time at all," he said.*

*That admission of his was very confirmatory, as Awaki had just told Thomas, on his last visit 12/14/1995, that Nathaniel "turned his face," on occasion, when they invaded him. Just days later (5), Nathaniel was describing in detail exactly what he did when he "turned his face" to their invasion when they came to take his body: he fought it.*

Again on 1/18/1996 Nathaniel was invaded by more than one angel during a session. He was invaded by the Angel of War, Shakardak and later by Awaki, the Angel of Spirits.

The first entered and invited the Prophet, "Speak unto me."

"Who are you please?" The Prophet responded.

"I am the Warrior Spirit. I am Shakardak,"

"Hello Shakardak. Is there information you have for us this evening?"

"It is the final instruction from me to you in this form regarding spiritual battles. It has already been explained – 12 and 40, when this being (Nathaniel) will engage in spiritual battles. We have instructed you on how to fight and win for victory is already yours and ours.

"This is what you need to understand, the concept of spiritual battles. The Holy Awaki has already discussed with you the true meaning of one's faith. The beginning is the end and the end is the beginning. Believe and have faith and the end will become the beginning. Is this within your understanding?"

"Yes Shakardak. I listen to you," Thomas said.

"Take heed, study no longer spiritual battles of old, but now study instructions which we have departed unto you and compare those days of old to the new found wisdom which we have given you. Is that within your understanding?"

"Yes, Shakardak."

"Are there any questions that you want to ask of me?" he asked Thomas.

"You ask for a comparison of spiritual battles that have occurred in days of old. Do you mean in biblical times, during the First Covenant?"

"Forgive me, I understand that you talk in contents of time," Shakardak said to him

Immediately Thomas apologized as the Angels did not deal in time and space. They existed outside both as we knew it. They were beyond both, of which the prophet was aware.

"Yes Shakardak, I apologize to you," he said.

The Angel continued.

"Study the first and the second – of the two, (Covenants) and compare spiritual battles and the manner in which they were fought, to that which we have departed unto you. Is this within your understanding?"

"Yes, I believe so, Shakardak," Thomas answered and continued. "Can you explain more or can you talk more about the context or the concept of a spiritual battle?"

"Spiritual battles take on many different appearances. They can be battles fought by a being, they can be battles fought by many beings, they can be battles fought by the unseen with the unseen. In order to recognize that which you are being prepared… For, they shall not mask or hide themselves. For, in their vainness, they seek to know you and destroy you. At that time you must draw your sword and, in faith, conquer these warriors of wickedness and deception."

"Are these warriors other entities, these warriors of wickedness and deception? Are they human beings, or could they be?" Thomas questioned him.

"They have to be for you could not fight anything not of this world," Shakardak explained.

(Profoundly enough, 24 years after this encounter a plague came to the world that killed millions and threatened to kill millions more, SARS-CoV-2. The entire human race was under threat from that death rendering plague. Methods were devised to combat the killer. However, a segment comprising millions of people, chose to blatantly defy and repel those efforts, even at the risk and in the face of bringing death and destruction to all human beings. They did not hide their defiance of those efforts which resulted in the avoidable deaths of millions world-wide.)

"Okay. What is the goal or what is the objective in the spiritual battle?"

Shakardak said, "The first goal, the first with your universe was obedience. (Moses and the laws) The second was that of repentance, (Jesus' display of obedience) and then the third calls into being of the final and last covenant of the Infinite Mind will make with these people, will be that of love. (That for which we were being prepared)

"There will be impossible, that hatred, anger and will never touch the faces of the children of the Infinite Mind again. There will be the final covenant. Are there any other questions that you desire of me?"

"Yes," Thomas replied. "When you talk of the goals of the spiritual battles, I understand how obedience can be one goal, but I don't understand how repentance comes into play."

Shakardak explained, "In the Second Covenant, that which in this universe acquired mercy from the Infinite Mind through repentance. For, the Son Universe came so that you could ask for forgiveness for all that you had done to corrupt yourselves. Repentance is not for a remission of sin. For you were sinners from the day that the Almighty created you.

"For He knows all things. Repentance is for your own belief; to strengthen your faith; to give you something to strive for; to better yourself; to love one another; to create a humanity of light. There are so many misunderstandings among the purpose for which the Holy Book was intended to serve," he lamented.

"For which was intended to serve?" Thomas asked.

"Your holy writings was supposed to serve. Confusion replaced wisdom," Shakardak told him regarding the corruption of the Holy Books.

This piqued Thomas' interest.

"What was the purpose or what is the purpose of the holy writings? What are they intended to serve?" he asked.

"The purpose of the holy writings was to give an account of what was, what is, and what will be. That is the only purpose," Shakardak said. "It was not intended to be used as a tool of wickedness, a tool of deliverance of false promises, or hope of deliverance. For these things cannot be found in any book, but only deep, deep within one's mind and soul. It has become a misguided tool to corrupt and control those who do not have real faith. Is this within your understanding?"

"Yes, Shakardak. I've often thought about how the scriptures or the sacred books are being used out of their context. I'm real interested in the purpose of the spiritual battles. Sounds like an alternate purpose they have is to develop man or to develop humankind into a reflection of the Universal Mind."

Shakardak explained further.

"The first spiritual battle was to teach those of the Infinite Mind was all-powerful. The second spiritual battle was to show those who did not believe, in the Infinite Mind existed in more than just their thoughts. The third and final spiritual battle will show all in this universe that the Infinite Mind is the supreme authority and has become weary with their lack of faith. At that time, all that is, is no more. All that would have been will cease to exist and the wickedness will be put to an end and He who has given all will take back all unto Himself. Are there any other question?"

Thomas had more questions steeped in the spiritual battles.

"I'm thinking Shakardak, in the first lesson on the spiritual battles being obedience – I see where that would be connected with the whole idea of faith. Is obedience connected in the sense of faith in obedience to the commands of the Infinite Mind?"

"This is simplistic," Shakardak answered. "In the first covenant was to secure obedience to that which they knew existed. For they had seen the miracles, the wonders, performed by many of those, by the hand of God. Need not faith to believe in what you see. That was still not enough. They were given regulations (the Commandments) in which to conduct themselves by and still you were corrupt.

"In the second, Infinite Mind realized that you would be corrupt to the day He destroyed this universe for the day He would sit among thee for the rest of thy time. In His mercy, He gave you a second chance but He did not understand why those that He had protected and delivered and displayed His awesome powers would not bow themselves to believe. He had to feel as you felt. He had to see what you saw. He had to be tempted by the things that tempted you, so He made a visit himself. In the flesh, that you may again see, that you may touch Him, and He touch you. The form that is known to man as miraculous (Jesus the Christ) but still did not bow themselves to believe.

"In the Third Covenant there will be birth of those who sit with the Son of the Universe of Love, and glowing in power, you will be freed for obedience. You will be freed for repentance. Speak unto me."

"Again, Shakardak. I'm just thinking, because I want to obtain the correct and proper understanding of spiritual battles and understand all things regarding spiritual battles that I'm capable of understanding. And if my understanding is simplistic, as you say, if you would just broaden it. Based on what you're saying, it sounds as though Infinite Mind really desires that we have faith. Is that correct?"

Shakardak responded, "That you may see Him again requires faith now, to know that He is. Spiritual battles are unique. For when any two do what you recognize that which is not of us, therefore the battle has begun, the battle of swords, or choices. Those who make the right choices are those who will use the truth, the love, the light will be victorious."

Thomas spoke, "I think I understand, Shakardak. As I sit......"

He was interrupted mid-sentence.

"It is I."

"Hello, Awaki., Thomas responded.

"It is within your understanding," Awaki replied and continued. "This is good. Ask the question that you really need to know."

"I was speaking with Shakardak about spiritual battles and the ultimate purpose of them, and why are they necessary at this time."

Awaki said, "The ultimate purpose of spiritual war is to, that all who dwell in this universe, all who have seen, spoken with the Infinite Mind, to know that He exists.

"You have been given the ability to make choices in all things and now your choices have gotten out of hand. The only way it can be set to its proper understanding of reverence of his Creator is to one, or two ways.

One, the Infinite Mind will send us to destroy you and all that exists. For He has done this before, and then before, in an attempt to recreate your destiny.

"Now He will come in the presence of the Son Universe and dwell among you for good to defeat that which controls your mind in your universe; that which you call Satan, the fallen angel of power, and the angels sent to look over the Infinite Mind's creation and corrupted themselves.

"That is the reason for the spiritual battles. You are the reason why the Infinite Mind shows mercy upon this universe at this time."

"When you say, 'you,' who do you mean?" Thomas asked.

"The beings, the hosts of the Divine Spirits that occupy this universe. Infinite Mind needs no more than to think, and you would be destroyed, but He is full of love, forgiveness. He has shown this to this universe throughout your time and still you turn away from His love, so in the final spiritual battle when He will defeat, for good, those that influence your minds, that misguide your choices, then He will send us and the Son to dwell among you for eternity. For then you will experience what you may call 'heaven'," Awaki explained to him.

"It seems though His hosts are being confused by the powers of Satan, the powers of darkness. It seems as though that is who His wrath should be directed to, and we fully understand...."

Awaki interrupted Thomas, "The powers of darkness you are speaking of, the elium lords, the one that you call Satan, controls this universe through the swords of your minds. In order to destroy what he has already done, it will necessitate again and again, the destruction of this universe.

"In the Third Covenant, the Infinite Mind has chosen not to destroy you who cannot fight such things of this world. Nothing will change for you but the thoughts and desires to create and to do evil and to follow he who has corrupted you. Ask the question."

"How did the corruption take place?" Thomas asked.

"That corruption took place because you so chose, thus, the power of the sword. The Infinite Mind gave you free will to choose and He recognized again that you will not choose Him in your time of need. There are few that reach that point and there are few who have reached that point and they have been rewarded, but the masses of the hosts that occupy this universe have chosen. Ask the question. Is this within your understanding?" Awaki asked him.

"It is Awaki. And, you know, I'm thinking about and contemplating what you are saying because I see, at times, it is very, very difficult to choose the light or choose Infinite Mind," Thomas confessed.

"In order to take away the gift of choice in the minds created by the Infinite Mind, then there is no need for you to exist. You were created as His children. You were given the essence of all that you need," Awaki said.

"We want to make the right choice and we desire to praise Infinite Mind," Thomas admitted.

"Few reach that point of sacrificing all that is in this universe to live totally spiritual," Awaki told him.

"Is to live totally spiritual, does that mean to rely entirely on Infinite mind," he asked.

"That is within your understanding," Awaki agreed.

Thomas replied, "I suppose that's what the books refer to when they talk about a living faith."

"This is within your understanding," Awaki agreed with him. "It is truly a task for the hosts of this universe but Infinite Mind had belief that you, one day, would come to the point of all universes that have went before you. And now they have one commonality that this universe is still struggling for and that is faith and the knowledge that He is, and can do all things.

"Money, power, sustenance becomes obsolete. Everything is for the common glory of the Infinite Mind and He abides in all universes that come to that point at once and delivers unto them wisdom, beyond wisdom, technology beyond technology, and His Son Universes have freed them of this, what we call host, and they live as pure energy, manifesting and moving at will through galaxies, through universes."

"It seems as though Infinite Mind has dealt with us here in this universe in such a manner to spoon feed us and to give us glimpses of what our life will be like once we rely on Him in faith with...."

Awaki interrupted him again. "This is within your understanding. There has been times when you were allowed to see and come in contact with such a universe and in your ignorance and lack of love for life and humanity, have destroyed that which we have allowed you to see the possibilities of what faith is."

That confirmed what many have written off as "conspiracy theories" for years, when the accusations were made that this planet had encountered "alien beings."

"I understand what you mean," Thomas said. "Can you tell me where that occurred or how that occurred?"

"It has occurred over time in your universe. Many different locations, many different worlds," Awaki answered.

"What type of faith does Infinite Mind desire us to have? How do we cultivate that faith? I know there's no formula for it. I know it's just something that is, something that be but there has to be a key to it," Thomas told him.

"That is not within your understanding. We have discussed with you drawing your sword," Awaki disagreed with him.

"I understand that and I understand choosing Infinite Mind, choosing His precepts, and I guess it's an individual.... and I guess it's an on-going thing because decisions are made on an ongoing basis." Thomas persisted.

"Listen, my son, I hear your thoughts," Awaki told him. "Truly what you are seeking is how you can obtain that level of faith for yourself and others."

"That is correct," Thomas admitted.

"You have already obtained that level of faith," Awaki told him. "What we do as a result of that faith, it is being rebuilt. We have brought you from a low level back to an all – knowing level. Now, it is your sword and your choices that will continue your spiritual growth. Be not disillusioned with what Satan may attempt to do in your life through others. We are here to protect you so that you may continue to grow. Is that within your understanding?"

"It is Awaki."

Awaki continued, "We will see and you will see. And, we will allow things to fall around you, but we will not allow you to fall in the pit of disbelief. The reason is this: I hear many, many voices in your mind. The reason that these things must fall around you is, in order for you to grow to the spiritual level which you attempt to obtain, then all that is not of the light of the Infinite Mind, all that is of wickedness and deceit, must be destroyed around you. Is this within your understanding?"

"It is Awaki. And you're right, it sounds like quite a task, and quite a frightful challenge, because when things fall around you, you almost can't help but think that you will also fall," Thomas answered.

"That is the essence of faith," Awaki said.

"The knowing that despite the destruction, that God dwells with me. As David said 'even though I walk in the shadow of the valley of death, I fear no evil because you are with me,'" Thomas responded.

"That is within your understanding," Awaki agreed. "When you reach a point where you may lose your very life, and you say to that person, take thee my life, for my God, will have mercy upon you, then ye have reached a level of absolute faith. It is time."

With that declaration Awaki exited Nathaniel's body speaking the many languages to open the gates to the other Universes so that he could pass through them.

"I understand and thank you for coming," Thomas said as he left.

The Prophet has revealed, almost a quarter century post that declaration, just as Awaki foretold, that things have fallen and been removed all around him. Some, without the understanding, would describe it as total devastation.

His charge as a Prophet was to teach the new knowledge he learned to those whom he brought to the Angels. He brought a group to the Temple on 2/28/1996.

"Hello Awaki. We're here with many people who are around us," he informed Awaki.

"I hear a multitude of voices," Awaki said. "There's one among you who is of us that would be in the battle – 12 and 40. He has been chosen," he told them.

"Do you wish to identify that person at this time? Is there information that you have?" Thomas asked him.

"He is the one that brings purity of heart to you on drawing your swords. That he is us and we are him. He will be called out at age 16 to join. He will be placed in the valley of decision, and then he must draw his sword," Awaki said.

"Is there some way for him to know who it is that you speak of at this time?" Thomas asked.

"He is the one that is purest of heart and innocence of mind, the one who sits among you that has not yet reached your capacity. Is this within your understanding?"

"It is. We believe you are referring to a child. Is that correct?" Thomas responded.

"In your universe, in ours, he has already begun," Awaki told them.

An amazing disclosure. A child in this universe and simultaneously, in another universe, no longer a child.

Thomas just moved on with the usual format established for such group sessions. Questions were collected prior to the session and asked when the session began.

"We have questions that we would like to ask from those who are with us. Is that acceptable at this time?" He asked Awaki.

"We will deal with the ends of the Infinite Mind," Awaki told him and continued to address the group. "The ends of the Infinite Mind is the Third Covenant for humanity in this universe. All that you see, what you behold before you is a test of your faith. Faith that the belief in the possibility in anything. You may have been taught that faith is the belief in those things that are not seen, but that is not true faith.

"To have true faith in the possibilities that anything is possible with He who has created all and is all. In the 12 and 40, there will be a spiritual battle, that which you will prepare for. This battle will be the third and final covenant for the Infinite Mind's Creation in this universe. And then, what you refer to as heaven, will become paradise, but you must prepare for the battles and you must draw your sword and choose. For the one among you who is of us, is your charge."

The "multitude," in attendance (about 15 people) were made aware of the upcoming spiritual battles and the need to prepare for them. Afterwards he took those general questions.

"There are many voices. There are many vibrations. I hear your voices. Ask the question," he directed Thomas.

"One person would like to know about 'this child that is of me, that has been with me since one month old, why does he behave the way he does'?" Thomas proceeded.

"I hear her voices," Awaki said. "Her question is simplistic to the thoughts of her mind. I spoke unto her thoughts earlier. That was she that I was speaking to. The child is of her but in her doubt, he senses, and he reacts such because he is of us. Have no doubt.

"I exist before the Throne of the Infinite Mind and he exists in the Son Universe (a different universe inhabited by Jesus). You take hold of your faith and when you are in the valley of decision between the elium lords and the existence of He who has created all, draw your sword and choose. For, the glory has been given unto you, and this child is your charge and we will protect him and keep him, even in your absence, for he has been chosen. Ask the question," he told Thomas.

He chose another question from the group and continued.

"Another person wants to know: 'Besides the gift that God has endowed me with, what else am I to do in this life with mankind'?"

"Your Divine gift is divine. Humanity, in her creative forces, (all that exist in her personal world) is touched by the gift given unto her. But, in 12 and 40, He who has created all will uplift humanity to fulfill the Third Covenant. You must prepare by use of your gifts.

"You that sit before the Infinite have all gifts," he told all present, "different one from another. If not, you would not be allowed to behold the wonders of He who created all. The Jah, the I Am Creator, is, because He thought and came into existence. So have you been called into existence by His thought. You are following our directions."

"Is there anything specific that she should do at this particular time in terms of utilizing the gift that she speaks of?" Thomas asked on her behalf.

"She does not fully understand that which she has," Awaki informed him.

"What can she do to better understand or get a better understanding?" Thomas asked.

"We will give her the understanding. Have her to come unto me," he said.

She moved forward and sat in Awaki's presence. She replaced the Prophet, as she took his seat.

"Place your hands upon the forehead of this host," Awaki instructed her.

He spoke a language, as she did, that we could not repeat or understand.

129

"Thank you, Awaki. Is there other information that you wish to give her at this time?" Thomas asked

"What you have received is your gift. Use it to help those in your creative forces. You have a gift that is unparalleled. The energy that was transferred unto you. You have the absolute power to heal, should you call upon it. Ask the question," he directed Thomas.

"Is there any other information that you have for her at this time?" he asked.

"That when you draw your sword, and when you're placed in the valley of decision between the elium lords and the Infinite Mind, you have just been charged with a spiritual gift from He who has created you. The only sin in your universe that is not forgiven is the misuse of a Divine gift."

"Thank you Awaki," Thomas said.

He moved on to questions from others in attendance.

"Another person would like to hear about Sufism in the western world and the 'complete man,' does this account for our current physical changes?"

"These changes are the thoughts by He who has created this universe, preparing for the Third Covenant with the hosts of this universe. In 12 and 40 the battle of spirits will begin. The changes are foretold. Understand that the beginning is the end and the end is the beginning. Is that within your understanding?" he asked them.

"It is within my understanding," Thomas answered, "I don't know if it is within her understanding."

"Then, you are charged," Awaki said.

He instructed Thomas, as a prophet, to make sure she understood what he had just said to her.

"I will discuss that with that person," he committed.

There is no record available which confirms that the prophet ever made clear to her or anyone in attendance what Awaki said that day. There were so many powerful informative words spoken by all of the angels during those 6 months that it was almost impossible to "break all of them down" for everyone to grasp every word.

However, on numerous occasions the prophet took the time, at the instructions of the angels, to clarify what was said right on the spot. This was not the case here.

In short what he said was that what was being witnessed as "current physical changes" were actual manifestations of the "thoughts" of God. They said God brought about actions with just a thought. Also these particular changes were already foretold in Revelations (the last book of the Bible) which are the beginning of things instead of the end of things. The changes were the beginning of the preparations for the second coming of Jesus Christ. Our gathering and hearing the Angels were our preparation for that time.

The period of time was called the "Third Covenant" which was to begin 12 (the number of years from 1995 to the year 2007) and 40 (the age of the spiritual leader whose body they were in by 2007; born in 1967). A major point was that the prophecies made in Revelation had already begun even though it was only 1995.

Those changes were being disputed by others (then) as being "climate changes" caused by man's use of fossil fuels (oil, gas, etc) hence the attendee's reason for asking the question in the first place.

The battles between the spirits would begin at that time – 12 and 40. The Third Covenant." The beginning is the end and the end is the beginning." That statement was used continuously to explain: Revelation (the end of the Bible) being preparation for the second coming of Christ and Genesis (the beginning of the Bible) being the end of things after He comes. That would be "Heaven."

Thomas moved on to the next question.

"One person asks 'specifically as you can answer, what does prayer look like from your vantage point'?"

Awaki responded, "In my existence, prayer was given unto the hosts of the various universes as a test of faith. We do not pray for we live and dwell in the light of the Infinite Mind. We have only one purpose and that is His purpose and His end. We need not pray. Prayers from the hosts who occupy this universe have no images. They are vibrations that pass through many universes."

"Very well," Thomas said and continued with questions.

"Another person asked, 'have I physically encountered alien beings in my present life experience and if so when'?"

Awaki answered, "Alien, in this universe, simply means that which you do not recognize or understand. There are many universes. They have been allowed to visit you in this universe because they have moved unto the Infinite Mind.

"This universe is the last to move unto the Infinite Mind for He has destroyed you twice before and still you cannot choose His ends. But, destruction will not come upon you in the third covenant for we will fight the spiritual battle for you in 12 and 40.

"When this is done and the Son Universe (Jesus) will come upon you, then travel to other universes will be as easy to you as it is to other universes who are of one mind and one thought."

Here again Awaki confirmed for all present that "Aliens" were allowed to visit this universe freely. Additionally he disclosed here that the inhabitants of this universe would do the same as easily when the spiritual battles of 12 and 40 are done and Jesus returns to this universe

Again, the information given by the Angels during these sessions was to prepare Thomas, as God's Prophet, for the work he was to do. It was also to prepare those who were chosen to assist in the Third Covenant, the period of spiritual battles.

"Can you tell this person, who wants to know, the meaning of the term: 'The ships come from the heads of the twins', Thomas asked.

"In your universe, there have been many generations of distortion. There has been the teachings of things that do not exist. In this universe, you believe in philosophies and theories.

"Believe only in this: that He who has created you is not difficult to understand, and how you will know these from those who are not of us, ask a simple question and listen for a complicated answer and you will know that this is not the way that Jah has intended it to be.

For, man because he has been given the power of choice, has created and deceived you. This is the need for the Third Covenant and this was the purpose for your destruction before."

This was a major lesson for those chosen to learn how to fight the spiritual battles: "ask a simple question and listen for a complicated answer."

The sessions Thomas held with the Angels were also for him to bring those before them who were to receive divine gifts. They were to use them to God's end in fighting spiritual battles.

On 3/16/96 Thomas brought one such person to them. She came seeking.

"Do I have a gift of healing?" She asked Awaki.

"Have you spoken to the Angels of God and have you asked for this gift?" He asked her.

"I don't know whether I've asked for the gift. I know I feel like I have the gift. I feel like I've been using the gift and I do believe that the Angels of God are around me and helping me every day," she explained.

"Then you are partly correct," he said. "For we are in your presence when you open your eyes and when you close. But, the gift of healing comes unto you by your God, given by us. What you have been experiencing as your gift has been your love and your faith and the possibility of your abilities.

"It is our desire and it is your God's mission in this time, the 11 and 40, to charge those that seek true knowledge, to bring about His ends. We know all that you have done and all that you wish to do in helping others to bring them into this new knowledge. As we teach our Prophets and charge the healers and bring forth change, as it has been written, we have summoned those with purity of heart and of righteousness who seek truth and the ends of He who has created all.

"When Jah was brought about in this time and space there were those that He was charged to bring before His God. As those that went about their duties and responsibilities of this universe had no knowledge, that before they were even created, that they were chosen. And when Jah went unto each of them in their time and space and said unto them, 'follow me,' for they were compelled to do so. Is this within your understanding?" he explained to her.

"No," she said, "I don't understand 'this child'."

Thomas repeated, "Jah, Jesus Christ."

"Oh, ok," she said.

Thomas asked, "Could you explain 'Jah' please, Awaki?"

"Jah is your Redeemer," he said. "He is He who was sent as a display unto the hosts of this universe in their time and space, that they may know the power that is within them if they seek to transcend the flesh. Is that within your understanding?"

She said, "Yes."

"Jah went unto those that had been chosen of that time and space and said unto them, 'follow me,' and they left that which they were doing and they followed Him. So has those in this time and space, been chosen before birth, to fulfill what is taking place in this universe, in the 11 & 40, a period of preparation, as was Jah's time on this universe. Is that within your understanding?" Awaki asked her.

"Yes," she replied.

He continued, "Those that have been summoned unto this host that they may hear the wisdom of the Creator, and that they may see this superficial display of what you may deem a phenomena through this host, is to prepare those who have been chosen. Is that within your understanding?"

"Yes," she admitted.

"Then do you understand why you are here?"

"No," she said

"For you have been chosen before you were even created," he told her and continued. "Your God had sealed you unto us. This time and space, it is your choice, the gift you speak of, can we bring unto you. Is that within your understanding?"

"Yes," she said.

"Within your soul is the power to heal if you desire. Is this your desire?"

"Yes," she answered Awaki.

"Then you must understand that your God gives unto you this gift and if you choose to receive unto yourself, Divine gift, then you are charged, and if you should misuse such a gift then there will be no redemption for you. Is that within your understanding?"

"Yes," she repeated again.

"What is misusing God's gift unto you?" Awaki asked her.

"Monetary gain, self – gratification or boasting, all those negative adjectives," she told him.

"Then, we are pleased, for you already understand. Then place your hands upon the forehead of this host."

He asked her to speak after him words only he and she could understand and repeat and delivered her God's Divine gift of healing.

She was spoken to of "11 and 40" by Awaki, as she came before him on 3/16/1996, which was then 11 years before 2007. He explained that timing, on other occasions, as our having "lost a year" of our time of preparation since their coming in November 1995. Prior to the "loss" of the year it was 12. The 40 remained unchanged as that still represented the age of Nathaniel, the spiritual leader in 2007, hence "11 and 40."

All who came to Awaki served to prepare the Prophet and all others before him for those impending spiritual battles. Not all seeking gifts, with which to fight, received them. One such session became a spiritual battle.

During that preparation session, on 3/3/1996 Awaki told a woman, "There is a question that you wish to ask, speak unto me."

Sometimes in my home I see a quick dark flash and I want to know was it the spirit of my grandfather?" she asked.

"You speak of spirits, those who have been called unto us, do not linger here in this universe. Those who do not find a place among us are here. This which you see is not of us. Is that within your understanding?" he answered her.

"Yes," she said.

The Prophet asked, "Can you explain what does she see Awaki?"

"That she sees is the elium lords. For, that place that she is, one of us is there and they seek to destroy but we are with here and we have fought the spiritual battle. But be not afraid when you see the movement of the shadows. Is that within your understanding?"

"Yes," she answered Awaki again.

"When you see the battles of the shadows, pray unto your God. Zimblach," he said and dismissed her. He then continued.

"There is a voice and it is strong. Come unto me. It is she that our Prophet is near. Come unto me."

"It is one of you," the Prophet told the two women sitting to his sides.

It is she that you have just spoken to and directed your attention to," Awaki described.

The woman arose and replaced the Prophet in front of Awaki.

"Take the hands of this host. Why were you reluctant to speak unto me? There are many questions that you wish to ask. There are people in your life that you are concerned about. You have questions of your obedience and faith but are reluctant. We cannot harm you. We are God's Creation and His Creation is love. Speak unto me I feel your uneasiness," Awaki told her.

She responded. "I am not afraid or concerned about being harmed by anything in the spiritual world. I …am feeling blocked…and …not… clear about…how I direct my gifts."

"Your 'gifts,' as you refer to them, were they given to you by your God?" Awaki asked her.

"I believe so," she said.

"Then that is your blockage. If they are truly Divine Gifts then you will know so and they will be given unto you by your God. And if He gives them unto you then it is His desire that you know that He has given them unto you. For there is no redemption for misuse of a Divine Gift. And He will not give unto you, that which you do not understand.

"Be not concerned with the foolishness of men and what you have been taught and what you have been trained to do. Divine Gifts are given and they are given unto you by your God. Speak unto me of these gifts and then I will ask you, 'what's your desire,'" he told her.

"I believe that my gifts contribute to … I think that I touch … That I have the ability so that healing forces come through me… and that I awaken something in people that I touch," She described for him.

"Is that your desire," Awaki asked her.

"Yes," she said.

"Your desire is the Oneness of Mind. That which you do now is an emanation of your desire, but we can give unto you truly a divine gift. But you must know this, in this time and space there are what you call sins that you can transcend and that your God forgives unto you, for you are imperfect. The misuse of a divine gift is not forgiven. Your question then is how and what is the misuse? Is that not within your understanding?" Awaki said.

"It is," she said.

"The misuse of a divine gift is to mislead the children of your God, to deceive their thoughts that you may get and claim glory and not glorify The Infinite Mind and bring unto Him that which He has created, Do you understand why there is no forgiveness?" Awaki asked.

She explained. "I understand why there would be no forgiveness, I don't understand….uhhh… how I might be misusing…"

Awaki interrupted her, "At this time and space you are not misusing for you do not have. There is no forgiveness because it is not what you call a sin. For, it is a gift unto you from God. And to misuse that is certain separation. For, we are the Angels, in your time and space, which you have called us, and we do not have the gift of choice, as was given to you.

"We only are charge to carry out the ends of The Infinite Mind and in disobedience we are destroyed and cast from His presence. There is no redemption for us. You have been given the gift of choice and redemption. But, if you accept a divine gift and misuse His gift unto you, then there will be no redemption for you. Is it still your desire?"

Her response was muffled and not captured by the device. Awaki heard and responded to her.

"You are confused. It is simple to understand. You have so long desired to help those that need spiritual guidance. It is your desire to have the gift that is truly divine and we will grant that desire. But upon your charge, the misuse of that gift will condemn you with no redemption. Is that within your understanding?" he asked her.

"I guess so," she said.

"Speak unto me," Awaki told her.

"Uhumm…I feel that I…..."

Awaki interrupted her hesitation. "You are being placed in the valley of decision. Choose this day and it will be given unto you. But it is your choice. Is it your desire?"

Again her response was muffled and uncaptured by the device, but Awaki heard.

"There is one understanding, and it is your desire to have and to receive unto yourself a gift from God that, that which you think you are doing, may become Divine and absolute." Awaki said.

"What I'd like to do is just….I don't…I don't ask for a….I am not asking for a gift. I am just wanting to be open and honest to my own spirit and to give back some of what…."

Awaki interrupted her, "You did not ask for this gift. You prayed for this gift. You attempt, with your lack of understanding, to have a gift. If you choose, the gift that you wish to have, we will give unto you. But you are hesitant and confused. Thenit is your choice. But it is certain. This day you can choose. I understand. I hear the voice. You have chosen. Zimblach"

"It is completed, the Prophet said.

"Thank you," the woman said.

"There are many voices unto this Holy place. And I will answer the questions that are unto the minds if they so choose to ask," Awaki said.

"Are there any questions that anyone has?" the Prophet asked the group.

"Yeah....I have a question," a different woman said.

"Go ahead," Thomas told her.

"Everyone is given a gift by God," she said. I don't believe in damnation and I don't believe that anyone will be punished or not be a part of any kind of redemption. I think that is ridiculous. I think everyone will be a part of any redemption that occurs and if there is no fear in the world why would you say something that would instill fear in someone that they might not be redeemed? I don't believe that. I don't think it's pure and right and true."

"Then you have chosen," Awaki told her.

"Chosen what?" she asked.

"That which you speak of. You have drawn your sword and you have chosen," he answered her.

"Can you be more specific?" the Prophet asked.

"It is not for us to be more specific in the presence of those who have the gift of choice. It is her choice and she has chosen," Awaki responded.

At the end of that session later in the day, The Prophet and the Spiritual Leader sought Awaki's presence.

"Hello Awaki. We decided to ask you to come to ask you about the things that happened earlier today," the Prophet said.

"It was and it is. I hear voices in your mind. Speak unto me about the concerns of this host," Awaki told him.

"Well, Nathaniel was concerned about what was happening today, particularly with the two ladies; the one who challenged you directly as well as the other who indicated that she was not willing to accept the gift," the Prophet explained.

It was her choice, it was not a challenge," Awaki said.

"Oh," Thomas replied.

"It was foolish and unlearned, therefore, she is and it was. She drew her sword and the choice was made by her. It is her own destiny," Awaki explained further.

"The other thing was our concern about Louvinia, Thomas added.

"That was in your control," Awaki told him.

Thomas replied, "The predicament I found myself in was sowing discord, or if I cut Louvinia off, or if I had called her over. I sent thoughts to her to ask her to be silent."

Awaki responded to Thomas and the actions he took during that spiritual battle.

"When the Master charged His followers and he sent them into all cities to preach the news and He said unto them, 'If they do not receive you then shake the dust from your feet and leave that place as swiftly as you entered.' Your thoughts were correct. We spoke unto you in your mind and you chose to subject yourself as a Prophet of God, to the foolishness. Therefore, it was within your power to set the example and make the display.

"You are no longer an individual, as we spoke unto you. You are of oneness in truth. So, therefore, your actions, when you are confronted and must draw your sword and choose, then so be it. You should not be concerned with consequences as a result of your truth and your righteous acts, for they will bear the infirmities of the unrighteous acts and suffer unto themselves. What you experienced today was not difficult. There are those who will choose not of us or to open themselves to the possibilities and true faith, but be not concerned for it is not your charge."

As a Prophet of God Thomas was prepared for all encounters, those who sought to be of service to God and those otherwise.

Many other sessions occurred, in his preparation, wherein Thomas was instructed to help prepare those chosen to fight the impending spiritual battles when they were called upon to do so. In one session 3/27/1996, midway their period of preparation in this universe, they clarified for all exactly who would be fighting spiritual battles.

Magdalene Bonesse, one who had been before them before, returned to seek help.

"Awaki, I feel as if I am on a 'fire walk' right now," she said. "There is so much assaulting against me. I know that my path is to assist others. I'm concerned about protection of my son in the process. I'm willing to go where spirit wants me to go."

"It is not a question of willingness as it is a question of obedience and faith. Do you have faith?" he asked her.

"Yes I do," she said.

"In what you see unto you today and have seen unto you before."

"Yes I do," she declared again.

"You have in all your doing, attempted and you choose of us, so we have been with you. The 'assaults' as you call them are not uncommon to us, and should not be unto you, for there are those that seek to destroy, for you choose of us. Is that within your understanding?" he asked her.

"Yes, yes," she said.

She spoke as though tormented.

"We have spoken unto you and others. The elium lords will attempt to undo what we have been commanded to do. This is the only way they can put fear into your soul, by leading you to believe that your God has abandoned you, It has been written, and it has been done over and over and over.

"And, those with a purity of heart and faith, who walk in obedience, even though they may be afflicted and confronted by all manner of destruction, they overcome and go beyond these things for we are with them and so are we with you. Ask the question."

"I am busying my time with my duties. I am not leaving time open for study and prayer and meditation. I know that I need to balance my life better in that regard. How can I build up my protection? Do I need to be less busy with my activity?" she asked him.

"It is not protection that you seek. It is reassurance that we are with you in your going here and there and there and here. You must make the sacrifice to pray and meditate unto your God. Is that within your understanding?"

"Yes," she admitted.

"Walk not away from those things which He has given unto you that you may speak unto Him and that He may command us unto you. Is that within your understanding?"

"Yes. What do I need to prepare my body and keep my body a fit temple?" she asked.

"You need only to ask us," he answered her.

"Do I need to exercise my body?"

"Do what you will, for if you ask of us, we will touch you again and again and again. For, with a touch from us, we can correct all things. And, from a thought from your God, He can do all things. Is that within your understanding?"

"Yes," she answered. "Is it important for me to teach more in the spiritual realm?"

"Are you teaching in your new knowledge given unto you by us?"

"Yes," she answered.

"And what is that knowledge?" he quizzed her.

"I've been teaching the Reiki and given information from the Indians when I go to the Southwest that is opening up new paths for me in the ancient histories, coming of time now, in the Mayan way and the Hopi way." She described in some detail her teachings.

"Have you learned about the Parousia?" he asked.

"You have told me about the Parousia," she told him.

"It is the time when Jah will come unto this place and reign, and all that is of man will be destroyed. This shall be from the infinite seven (2007). And, during that seven there shall be what you call upheaval, changes in this place, on all levels, a spiritual battle, Is that within your understanding?"

"Yes," she said.

"And, as I told you, when you sit before me, I am the same as He is. Is that within your understanding?" he asked her.

"Yes," she answered and asked, "When I share this knowledge with people, do I need to let them know that they will be in battle during this time, in spiritual warfare?"

"They will not be in battle; only those who have been chosen by your God will fight the battles in this time and space as we direct them and we will fight spiritual battles in the air for you." He told her, no, and asked, "Is that within your understanding?"

"Yes." She acknowledged she understood.

Again he reaffirmed their purpose for being here: to bring those to be awakened and prepared, before them, that were to fight the spiritual battles.

He made clear to groups, via his Prophet Thomas and the Host, exactly when and why those spiritual battles would be fought.

During a group session attended by many 3/3/1996 Awaki announced, "There are many voices. There is an entity in this room. Do you know where you are? I speak unto your mind. You are in a Holy Temple sealed by Angels of God. I can hear your voices. Do you understand who I am? Be not impressed with this superficial display of the powers of your God. Be concerned with your faith and your resurrection of your soul. Come unto me. It is he that questions what he sees before him. Be not afraid,"

Awaki called one unto him and no one moved.

"Can you be more specific, please," Thomas asked.

"It is he who has in the presence of this host, and the 'Oman Bead tree shall flourish,' told the weakness of his faith. It is he to the right of this host. And the 'Oman Bead Tree shall flourish.'"

"Is it the first male to the right?" Thomas inquired.

"That is within your understanding. It is he," Awaki confirmed.

The man then left his seat and sat directly before Awaki.

Awaki continued, "Do you understand what I speak unto you? And 'the Oman Bead Tree shall flourish,' is it within your understanding?"

"No. No it isn't," the Man said.

Awaki spoke directly to him, "There was a man in his youth who defied his father in all manner of disobedience. And in his youth he did not reverence his father nor did he obey his words. And in his age he began to wither away. And the Oman Bead tree began to wilt and then it died and it returned unto He that gave it life.

"In your youth you denied that which you were. You are of age and your sword is drawn. It takes those in your creative force to continuously remind you that your Creator has created you. Is this not within your understanding?"

"Ahhh...yeah," the Man replied.

"Awaki continued, "Your faith is there, but your obedience... you are in the valley of decision and you must draw your sword and your sword is your gift of choice. You can choose of us or not. And when you choose not of us, then you decide your own destiny. Is that within your understanding?"

"That is within my understanding," the Man said.

"There are questions that you wish to ask. Speak unto me," Awaki said.

The Man mumbled something that was not saptured by the device.

Awaki replied, "Yes."

"I don't have any questions," the man said.

"Then this is your question," Awaki said. "Your question is through your life, and those that you love, and have you please your God in the choices that you have made, and the direction. Is that not continuously in your prayers and in your thoughts?"

"Ahhh…you might wanna be more specific," he responded.

"Do you not question your choices in life?" Awaki asked him.

"No, I don't question my choices specifically."

"Why is it that you choose not at this and space, and you are in the presence of the Angels of your God, to speak unto us all manner of truth? We know all. You have been called unto me to answer the stirring of your soul. Open your mind and we shall deliver you. For His promises unto the Hosts of this universe are this: ask and thee shall be answered; seek and thee shall find. I see all. Are you not concerned with the resurrection of your soul and your existence beyond this time and space? Speak unto me," Awaki told him.

"I… would say that … yes I have considered… the umm… life after death, sure," he admitted.

Then, have you not questioned whether you are living in accordance to the will and obedience of He who has created all that this may be achieved?" Awaki asked him.

"Events as responded to by an interpretation and ---------- presence of God," he said.

This that you speak of is within your understanding. Those things if you desire can be answered unto you if you choose this day to ask," Awaki informed him.

"You have to be more specific," he said.

Awaki said, "It is not us for we know your ends. You have to choose if you want to know your direction."

"I choose," he said.

"Then all you wish to know ask unto us and so shall we answer," Awaki committed.

"The year 2000," he said.

"It is the beginning of the spiritual battle. What you may call Armageddon. There for seven years thereafter, 2 to the infinite, to the infinite, to the infinite shall be the wars that havwe to be fought in this time and space. How shall they take place ? Is that also your desire? Awaki asked.

"Desire is the thought," he answered.

"They shall take place at every level of decision. The Hosts of this universe; fear is the tool of destruction used by those who wish to destroy you. There are those who say you must fear God, this is incorrect. Fear not your God but embrace your God and be obedient.

"You wish to know the direction. The Parousia is the time that Jah will return unto you to correct and resurrect that which the Hosts of this universe have destroyed. After the Parousia, which is 1000 of your years, The Jah will be upon you. Then you will experience what you refer to as "Heaven" in this time and space. All that will exist is that that was created by the Infinite. Speake unto me."

"I can understand that," he told Awaki.

"Then that is your desire. Zimblach" Awaki replied.

The enlightenment of the masses was then left to those people that they prepared. The major method by which that was to be accomplished for us, was via the "Mechanism" of the book and the work of the Spiritual Leader and the Prophets of which the Angels spoke.

Of the others awakened, some were given divine gifts to use to fight, while others were told to teach what they had seen and heard. All were to do as instructed in preparation, meditate and pray regularly.

MECHANISM

A most significant and crucial part of the spiritual battles depended upon that "Mechanism." Thomas was made aware on 11/27/1995, that for this universe, spiritual leaders had to be developed. It was explained that, each spiritual leader had a specific mechanism by which to acquire their leadership, and it was chosen by the Angels.

The Mechanism chosen for this Spiritual Leader's development was a book. He was told that it would initiate spiritual battles, into which, the Spiritual Leader would be "thrust." For him to be prepared for 12 and 40 he had to be respected as a great spiritual mind in this universe and the book was a major means by which that would be accomplished.

Throughout the 6 months of visitations the angels repeatedly brought the need for the production of the book to the Prophet's attention. He often was given guidance and clarity regarding it.

It came up in a private session with Gregory Job on 1/26/1996, one who received a divine gift.

"I have been told several times, from the other side, to begin writing the book," he mentioned to Awaki. "I was leery but am taking the steps forward on faith."

Immediately, without conversation Awaki exited and another angel entered.

After ascertaining the angel's identity, Thomas said, "Hello Shakardak, why did Awaki send you?"

"To speak unto this host regarding spiritual battles and the Mechanism, which we have given unto you, that you may fight that which seeks to devour you; convert those who need to hear your wisdom. Ask the question in reference to the Mechanism," he answered.

"To the entity that is here, unlike the Holy Awaki, I cannot probe your thoughts. I cannot hear your voices. But, you speak unto this host about the Mechanism," Shakardak spoke directly to Gregory.

"What is the Mechanism you are referring to Shakardak?" the Prophet asked.

"This entity likes to love for divine inspiration given unto him." Shakardak responded.

Thomas asked Gregory, "Are there questions for clarification?"

He replied, "The book I was given in meditation, I've had trouble getting it out in writing and now I'm starting. What direction do I need to take?"

"You do not have trouble," Shakardak told him. "We have blocked the information. That which you refer to, is a Mechanism designed for spiritual battles as for this host. (Nathaniel the Spiritual Leader). But, we must confide in He who has been charged to oversee this host in his Mechanism. These things were meant to be in unison, to have them in simultaneous.

"The information that you have is basic. For, what we will show unto you now that the Holy Awaki has given you one complete mind, will be beyond even your understanding, as it comes. But, you will be able to discern what that, which we have given unto you, will fit into that Mechanism which has been given unto this host."

Shakardak gave Gregory new insight as to what was to happen with the book. It no longer was what he had received in meditation. God had given him His mind or "Oneness of Mind" which precluded his ability to write the book.

"We understand, Shakardak, and I will explain more to this entity, exactly what you mean," the Prophet told him. "But, if there is any information that you wish to give him now to further strengthen his understanding, of course we're open to those."

Shakardk told Gregory, "The voices that you hear are mine."

"Okay," he said.

"When we will come through consciousness travel and in your dreams, you will wake up with information not of this universe. You will dream dreams of beauty and majesty. These you must use. Is that within your understanding?" Shakardak explained further to him.

"Yes, it is within my understanding," Gregory answered Shakardak.

Awaki re-entered, just as quickly as he had exited, and said to Gregory, "Deviate from what we have told you and that which you seek will not be found."

The session ended there. That was more fodder for Thomas regarding the production of the Mechanism. However, there is no documentation that the entity was ever engaged or involved in any way with the production of the Mechanism. Contrarily, at one point following this session Thomas was admonished to withhold all of God's guidance from him instead. Awaki even noted later to Thomas of Gregory, that "that entity is choosing his own fate."

On 2/8/1996 Thomas had an "alone" session with just the two of them, he and Awaki. Nathaniel had been dispatched as usual. The Mechanism surfaced again.

"You have said it in another time that there will come a time when you would speak to me directly and not through a host. Is that time at hand? Is that time near?" Thomas asked Awaki.

"That time is dependent upon you," he answered. There is a task, a job, an assignment given unto you to complete. It is the mechanism for which we will use to free you from this universe and prepare the Host for spiritual battle. You have choice, and when this will come to be.

"All that you see and hear is for the glory of Infinite Mind and to warn those who sit in my presence of the Third Covenant, 12 and 40 which will come. But you have charge of the mechanism. That is within your control. We will speak unto you when you have completed the task.

Thomas asked, "Do I know what the task is? I mean consciously.

"You ask a question that I already know that you have the answer to," Awaki answered him.

Thomas mumbled something inaudibly and Awaki responded, "The task is the mechanism which we have spoken of. It takes for you in your own time to apply your skill and complete that which you have been charged to do.

"Then we will be at the end of the necessity to speak to you through the Host. But first you must complete the task given unto you, by He who has created you."

"I understand," the Prophet said. Can you speak more. . ."

Awaki interrupted him, "You want to know and the question is not yours, but of this host, why is it necessary for us to speak through him? He is growing tired, not of our invasion, but he is growing impatient with the things that are not right around him and we understand his impatience.

"We have to speak through him because we cannot speak thoroughly like those of this universe in our consciousness. We can only speak to your minds. In order for you to hear us in tongues we have to use the mechanism that was created by Infinite Mind. Is that within your understanding? He asked the Prophet.

"It is. Even as you speak, my charge or my task, my assignment is clear," Thomas admitted. "Can you speak more of the Third Covenant? Could you give me more information? I know you have given information before. Like in groups that subject comes up, as you know," Thomas requested.

"And that is my purpose for being with this universe, with this Host, with those entities in this time and space, to prepare them for the coming of their Lord in the Third Covenant," Awaki said. "I've told you that the end is the beginning and that the beginning is the end. All that is to happen in the Third Covenant is not a catastrophe, but very simple and simplistic.

"In the Third Covenant the Son Universe (Jesus) will walk among men and He will fight the spiritual battle; and we will descend upon this place to destroy all that attempt to destroy this creation. That is not difficult to understand. You are still confused.

"Listen, if there is a land that is of dry and dirt and dust and nothing can sustain life; in order for life to be ever, everlasting then there must be nourishing of the land. The Third Covenant is a nourishing of the land by the chosen hosts. Know in order for the land to be fertile for life, then there must be a light to maintain its existence and its growth and always in its presence or it will wither and die.

"When the nourishing of the land is complete then the Son Universe will descend upon this universe and dwell that the lights appear forever, be with you and you will grow and you will evolve. Technology will be in your grasp; intellect will be a mere thought or a wish; sustenance will be at your need and love will exist between all men, women and children. And, the animals of the universe that eat men will be subdued; will live in harmony with each other.

"They have the largest of animals and mammals will be unto man as pets and co-exist. Men kill that in this universe that they cannot tame. But in the Third Covenant something as simple as a tiger will be your best friend, and even kill for you that which you need. And all things will live in harmony according to their existence. No more fear, no more hatred. Yes I can explain. If there is no more fear, no more hatred, and love unto another, then why must there be still killing? Is that your question?"

"I thought about that, yes," Thomas said.

"Because in that time the Son have not descended upon you and those who do not choose of us will be punished by the inhabitants of this land. The animals have no choice but to obey the wills of the Infinite Mind. And, those who do not obey will be devoured by the very things they fear at your command," Awaki explained to the Prophet.

Very soon afterwards there were more promptings and information regarding his charge with the mechanism. As was customary, he opened a session with Nathaniel's wife with Awaki on (2/16/1996).

"Hail Awaki. The three of us are here this evening. There are questions that we have. Is there any noises that you wish to clear up initially?"

"There are things that we must dialogue," Awaki answered him. "It is time that you begin to formulate the Mechanism. You are growing weary of your position in this universe. In order for us to fulfill the promise unto you, (replacement of his sustenance from the downturn of his practice, the arrestation of a health issue seeking to devour him and communicating with Awaki sans a host) then you must begin the task. Is that within your understanding?"

"It is," Thomas admitted. "And as you probably know, I've been thinking about writing the book in its exact format. There are thoughts that I have been having in terms of the basic outline and I know that it's meant to have the teachings included.

"It seems to me it's like a Holy book superimposed in a novel. It should be a simple story but the divine principles should be intertwined and at the same time, separate so that they can engulf and fire up the souls of those who read it.

"What I don't know is the specific words although they will come. I'm working in the computer so that the drafts can first be put there. I know that you have other information," he explained.

"The contents are being given unto you," Awaki told him. "It is within your understanding of the nature of the Mechanism. It is, in your terms, Holy, but cannot, in your universe and time, be received as such. The thoughts that you are having are the thoughts of the voices in which we speak unto you. The contents you have in the teachings that I have given you and that we have shared unto you. Is that within your understanding?"

"Yes," Thomas acknowledged. "What I speak of is the exact way in which they will be put down. But, if you're telling me that it's just time for me to write then I will just begin writing."

"Those things will come unto you as you complete the task, as you continue through your consciousness travel. Ask the question," he told the Prophet

Thomas committed to start production of the book and continued, "It seems to me that when you say Nathaniel is my charge, it has more of an impact than I understand. Because initially I thought it meant that I am to impart information or knowledge to him, in my understanding of spiritual things, spiritual realities. But, it seems that it is much greater than that. Can you explain that please?"

"You are a Prophet. Have not we explained that to you?" Awaki asked him.

"You have," he answered.

"He has been chosen for the battle. Has that not been explained unto you?"

"Yes," Thomas answered.

"Then you are a Prophet to speak unto him all manner of wisdom. In his life, there is no separation because his life is now to be about the work of his Father," Awaki told him.

Thomas moved on, "How long will I be in my current profession (Attorney), because I feel like I am winding down?"

"It is coming to an end," Awaki said. "But, the complete end is in your charge. The Mechanism given unto you is not only a mechanism for this host but also for yourself."

"Should I get others involved in the Mechanism at this point, or is it to be controlled by me just as my sustenance is to be controlled by me?" Thomas asked.

"It is to be controlled by you."

"I see," Thomas said.

"You will be known throughout this universe as a great literary achiever and this host will be a great spiritual leader."

"How will I start the book?" Thomas asked.

"You have already started," Awaki told him.

"How do I continue?" he asked.

"Continue listening to the voices," Awaki told him. "Continue to meditate over my teachings and our wisdom, and this host, in his dreams, will give you information and you will recognize where it should go."

"Is there any projected time?"

"It be your will and it will be done," Awaki answered.

"I understand it's to be my will in accord with Infinite Mind. After our last discussion and conversation, I consciously began to work," Thomas said.

"Did we not tell you again that you are one like a prophet? Whatever you do is in accordance with Infinite Mind for you choose of us and it will be blessed," Awaki explained to him again.

"I understand," he said.

"You continue to wrestle with the Angel," Awaki told him.

"What do you mean by that?"

"We come unto you and we speak unto you and we give you your status that you may understand your power, and you are reluctant to call upon that power. As you wrestle with us to bless when you have already been blessed," Awaki answered.

"That is what Jacob did. I always try to understand that," Thomas said.

"That is within your understanding."

Thomas' concerns were well founded, as this "assignment" was a daunting task: writing a book about the visitations to include: visions and meditations from Nathaniel, those of his own, all of the numerous points of information given by the many angels during the visitations to so many different people, and the time needed to do it all -- while practicing law – daunting.

The psychology alone of such an occurrence was challenging. The charge to keep Nathaniel open to all of it, added to that challenge. To chronicle it all in a book format, simultaneously, with never having written a book before, required much.

More than a month later 3/28/1996, Thomas learned that he was already blessed in that regard.

"We are here to discuss what we do as Prophets of the Infinite Mind," he told Awaki. "She has transcribed…" "She has…."

Awaki interrupted him. "She has so pleased us as she has learned to hear in her mind our voices of direction and guidance. That which she has done is for the benefit of the Mechanism (Book). We have spoken unto you. It is to be that which we have taught unto you, but, it has to be veiled, and it is now of three and not of two." He told Thomas.

"Very well," Thomas agreed to the help.

Then, 2 days later 3/30/1996, Awaki brought up the completion of the Mechanism.

The Prophet had brought another soul to encounter Awaki. "We're here today with Stephanie. Is there any information you have for her?"

"There is but there are questions, voices that are still in your mind," he answered Thomas.

"None that I am aware of. I see there are several options…"

Awaki interrupted him, "They do not concern that of man's foolishness. They are concerned that greatness that this host (Nathaniel, the Spiritual Leader) is about to undertake."

"Yes," Thomas said, "I've been speaking with him about that and the specifics. He seems to have it clear in his mind regarding the time frame. I think I need to speak with him on an ongoing basis until that occurs."

Awaki continued, "Has he been sharing the vision?"

"Some of them," Thomas said.

"Then you ask what has been departed unto him."

"What are the institutions that you refer to, to Miriam?" Frank asked about the other Prophet.

"It was this host. As we begin to explain unto her the things that will occur upon his return, and she is charged as you are. Is that within your understanding?"

"No. We can speak of it another time if that's appropriate," Thomas answered.

"Time and space is within my command. Is that within your understanding?" Awaki asked.

"Yes," Thomas answered.

"All things are to the ends of He who has created all," Awaki told him.

"I understand," the Prophet said.

"Now, the things spoke unto the other prophet are things concerning the return of this Host (the Spiritual Leader) that she has been charged to complete, as we have directed her to assist unto the Mechanism. The institution is that which we have spoken unto you for this host that has been prepared." Awaki told him.

Awaki explained to the prophet that the second Prophet was charged to transcribe all of the taped sessions so that he could use the transcriptions to write the book. The fact that the Spiritual Leader was taking that trip in May to a place (institution) they had prepared for him had also been explained to the her also.

Later on that same day (3/30/1996) Awaki gave the Prophet more on the status of his work on the Mechanism.

"It is I. My time in this host is not long," he introduced himself.

Nathaniel's body had been taxed by numerous earlier invasions that day.

"I understand Awaki," Thomas responded.

"What I must say unto you is this: you are a Prophet of your God. Is that within your understanding? Step back into your spirit for you are drifting. Your discipline in that which you have started has been deterred," he admonished Thomas.

"You mean the Mechanism?" The Prophet asked.

"That is within your understanding. And the time you spend in solitude (meditation) speaking with us," Awaki answered.

"Yes. I noted that the other day, that I was getting very tired and I started meditating again. My energy level......."

Awaki interrupted, "We will always send you a sign when you are moving away from true spirituality," he told him.

"What will be sent?" The Prophet asked.

"Were you not straining with restlessness?"

"Yes," he answered.

Awaki explained further, "It does not have to be devastating to know that we are calling upon you. But, when you are completed and we are finished touching you, spirit will overcome you."

"When will that be completed?" Thomas asked.

"Upon the return of this host," he answered.

"Very well," Thomas said.

"And we will come unto you during his absence, unto your mind and unto that which is physical," Awaki promised him.

"Will we have any more sessions or should we conclude them all until the seven and twelve in seven or should I say the five in twelve in seven?" Thomas asked.

He was talking about that week in May, set for Nathaniel's preparation (May, number "5" of "12" months and "7" the number of days in a week).

"That is within your understanding. But, he will fight with you to do and if he says unto you this: 'for we are sent and compelled to do,' then it is not his doing, it is mine and so shall you come unto me. There is the other, the prophet we charged," Awaki said.

"Yes," Thomas said.

"During this period, the Mechanism, thus you must complete," Awaki told him.

"Before May?" he asked him precisely and directly.

Awaki had never before been definitive about a deadline for the completion of the book until then.

"That is not within your understanding," he answered him.

"Before May" was not the deadline.

"What do you mean, it must be completed? We must be working on it, I understand that," Thomas responded.

"Before the six of twelve," Awaki replied definitively. "Use what she has. This is why she was chosen."

Awaki said the book had to be completed before June, 1996. (Before the "6" of "12" months). He had not given a definitive time for the completion of the book prior to that. Earlier, he praised the other Prophet for the work she did transcribing the tapes. That's when he charged her to assist with writing the Books. Her skills were to make the task less formidable for all 3 of them.

"It will be done, Awaki." Thomas said.

He committed to completing the Book within 3 months from that day, by June.

"I must go. Zimblach," Awaki said and exited the Spiritual Leader's body.

## Faith and Obedience

From the beginning of the documentation of their visits, 11/3/1995 until their ending 5/15/1996 numerous times the Prophet was given teachings, conveying the significance of faith and obedience, either personally or through the teachings given others. It was specifically stated that the "outcome" of spiritual battles in this universe depended upon how we interpreted our faith.

On one occasion, 1/4/1996, when teaching the Prophet about spiritual battles Shakardak, made clear the strong connection to Faith.

"To understand spiritual warfare," he told Thomas, "Understand this: the existence of spiritual war has to exist in lack of faith. If there is faith between the two, then there is no need for spiritual battle. So, therefore, in this world, there are those who claim to have faith, who have not. There are those who do not have faith and there are those who have faith but are scared to use what they have already been given for fear of alienation and there are those who have faith and the strength to uphold the truth."

Our prior understanding of faith was that it was the "substance of things hoped for and the evidence of things not seen."

"What is faith? In what context do you use faith?" Thomas was prompted to ask.

"Faith is the belief in the possibility of all things. Some misconstrue that faith is the belief in that which is not seen. That is incorrect. For you cannot see bacteria, but you know it exists," Shakardak answered.

"Yes, that's the same thing with electricity," Thomas added in agreement.

"Therefore, why would the Infinite Mind place such insignificance on something that your salvation depends upon? Faith is the belief in the possibility of all things to come," Shakardak explained. "Speak unto me."

"I think I understand. Your explanation is simplistic. It sounds like it's the belief in the possibility of all things in concert with Universal Mind. It also sounds like it's the belief in the possibility of all things being good, complete, Holy," Thomas said.

"Yes, it is within your understanding. For the things concerning love, which is also a understanding of spiritual battles, to love thy neighbor as thyself. In order for that to be achieved, one must have faith in thyself, then self can overcome all things and all things in Christ, the Lord of Hosts, are made possible. Is it possible for a man to fly without wings?" He asked Thomas.

"No," he said.

"My son, understand faith. Man created what you call the airplane and he flies without wings. It became possible in a man's mind. When you allow possibilities to be realities in your universe, then you can move mountains with a thought or a wave of your hand. Is this within your understanding?"

"Yes, well almost. How do you build faith? How do you come by that faith? How is that faith created?" Thomas questioned Shakardak.

"This is the process that you're now undergoing. What you see before you; (his talking through Nathaniel's body) what you have been told by myself and the Holy Awaki, that is not for this Host (Nathaniel) but for you; that you are receiving more and building your faith."

"I hear you Shakardak and I understand," he said.

"Do you think a man can transcend death?" Shakardak asked him.

"Yes," he responded.

"Then, you are beginning to understand. Faith is the belief that anything is possible," Shakardak said.

"What are the steps after you understand, or after you know that anything is possible?" Thomas asked. "Again, I assume you mean, more than in an intellectual sense, that anything is possible."

"You have simply have to believe that you are a child of the Infinite Mind and that nothing can withstand the presence of your God and you will begin to see the difference where you walk." Shakardak answered him.

The lesson of faith was taught to a group by Awaki on 2/4/96. Our concept was not that of true faith. The Prophet had collected questions from the group for Awaki prior to his arrival and asked when he arrived.

"Ask the question," Awaki instructed the Prophet.

"The first person says, 'I ask for complete healing of my body to better serve God according to His will. I ask for all work God would have me do, and for all tools possible to do this work to the fullest potential according to His plan for me.'"

"The entity that asks those questions….those are not the voices in her mind," Awaki said.

"What voices do you hear, please?" the Prophet asked.

"The voices, the concerns are of assisting those in her creative force that she can, with the knowledge and understanding of the Divine end that is what the questions mean," Awaki told them.

"What information does she need in that respect," Thomas asked.

"First, I must ask you, why are we here? What purpose does this serve?" Awaki questioned him.

We're here to glorify The Father and to effectuate the Divine purpose of God," Thomas answered.

"Then if that is the understanding of the entities that are here, then the questions that are asked, you already know. From the time the Infinite Mind created you, you were to glorify Him. You are the essence of His mind and He is within you. All that you need for service to the Infinite Mind has already been given unto you. But, in your swords in which you have been placed in the valley of decision you have defiled that which has been given to you.

"That is the whole purpose for the Third Covenant with the hosts of this universe. The questions are that of correct and her purpose in this universe, to glorify the Infinite Mind. In doing this then you must rebuild your faith in the possibilities. True faith is the possibility of anything. You have been taught that faith is that which is not seen but you know it exists.

"There are those who are among you now, who do not understand true faith. For, the Angels of God sit before you today because you have shown a willingness, an openness to understand, to want to love humanity. That which we have spoke of, one to another, must be again spoke amongst all those that exist now to understand that, in the Third Covenant, this will be your judgment and your deliverance. As your faith, and true faith is the belief in all possibilities.

"You are charged. Speak unto them," Awaki instructed Thomas to explain to those in the group all that he told them about faith.

The Prophet complied.

"What Awaki is saying is that in our traditional context of faith, we only see faith as meaning a belief in things we can't see. The development of a Divine faith entails, and it means mucu, much more. The scriptures talk about various people who experience faith in their lives. The biggest example was Abraham was told to kill his son and, of course, he had been promised certain things by God, namely that his fruit was going to be more multitudinous, or it would outnumber the sands of the sea. Then, he was told by God to kill his son, how was this possible and why should he be asked to do this kind of thing…"

Awaki stopped him and said, "Be not complicated."

"Very well," Thomas said and continued. "So then what actually the whole idea of a living faith is to believe in things that you…. To know, first off that God is with us personally on an individual level every day, at every moment, that we are His blessed ones, if you will. Since we occupy that position and since we are (blessed) there will be no harm.

"We may not know how we will be protected from the harm but that will happen. Secondly, to thank God in advance of receiving that which we ask for, knowing that it will occur. Knowing that it will happen and in that context it's in knowing that there are possibilities that exist that we have not been able to comprehend that can solve the problem that we have. And, so then therefore our faith then becomes something that is real and something that is alive, and something that we struggle with and move from one point to another, and one step to another. We aren't talking about catechismal book faith or religious faith," Thomas concluded.

As for the Prophet's use of the name 'Abraham,' Awaki explained later during the session, the error, when he spoke to another in attendance with concerns for his family.

"You have done well with your children and your children's children. I say unto you oh 'Abram of Israel' and you shall know. Is that within your understanding?" Awaki asked the father of the family.

"Yes," he said.

"It is not clear to you. I hear the voices in your mind. I say unto you, 'Abram of Israel.' Do you know what this is?" Awaki asked him again.

The Prophet responded, "Do you mean Abraham of the Old Testament in the First Covenant, Awaki?"

Awaki started to explain, "Abraham was a name given unto him by...."

"God," Thomas interrupted him and said.

"Your writers and interpreters of the Holy Scriptures," Awaki finished his thought. "Abram was his existence. Abram was the father of Isaac and Jacob. The Angel of God who fought and wrestled with Jacob was Shakardak, the Angel of War. And, he could not prevail and he called unto him, 'Israel, Israel the Father of all nations.' You have the love of Abram in your heart and your children have the blessings of Israel." Awaki explained to the Prophet and the Father the error and the full meaning.

Faith was taught in other sessions. One in particular was 2/8/1996 with Thomas, alone, when he engaged Awaki about the significance of fear.

"I was trying to understand the origin of fear and who uses it and for what purpose?" He asked Awaki.

"The emotion is there when faith, absolute faith is absent. And it is used to destroy you," Awaki explained.

"I see that," Thomas said.

"If there is absolute faith in He that created you then there is no fear. And when there is absence of faith, then even man will fear his own shadow in the daylight," Awaki told him.

Obedience was another concept Thomas heard from the Angels continually. During that session alone with Awaki 2/8/96 he made the prophet thoroughly aware of it.

"Now things concerning the teachings, they were of one principle. In this universe they say that Jah taught love, compassion, righteous, humanity but that is incorrect. Jah taught only one principle and he lived only one principle and that was obedience to He who had sent him.

"If you are obedient to Infinite Mind, then love, compassion, those things are given unto you. But first you must be obedient. Jah came in the flesh and knew His ends was death and knew that obedience to the Infinite Mind was the only mission. He was obedient in all His doings even unto His death. There is only one true principle, obedience. Is that within your understanding?" he asked the Prophet.

"Yes," he answered.

"When you step outside of obedience then these things that you hope for and seek you cannot find. And, I've told you before, it is not or was it ever the intention of the Infinite Mind to make His teachings, His glory difficult to understand. He has directed you: seek and you shall find; knock and the door shall be opened unto you; ask and it shall be given unto you. Is that not simplistic enough?" He asked Thomas.

"Yes it is. But, the question comes through, how do you know what to be obedient to or what is one expected to be obedient to?" the Prophet asked.

"That is also simple to figure out," Awaki said. There are only one sword in you and you have been given that sword to choose between that which is righteous and that which is unrighteous. And, then in those understandings you have disobedience of obedience. But those things concerning the flesh concern not yourself with. That is the one imperfect state that you exist in and that was the main reason that the Son came to free you from; the sins of the flesh. The heart, the mind, and the soul, that which guides your spirit, is what Infinite Mind wants. The flesh will pass away and the sins of the flesh will be forgiven."

"Interesting. I wondered what the teachings were in terms of the reason that Jesus came," the Prophet remarked.

"He came as I said to free you from your flesh," Awaki repeated.

"How was that accomplished? I mean I know that the typical answer is that it was accomplished through the crucifixion and the resurrection so . . ."

159

"That was not the accomplishment," Awaki interrupted him. "That was the display that the flesh can perish but the spirit lives on."

"And that's not important that the flesh perishes and that could be killed, but that would not be the end," Thomas said.

"That is within your understanding," Awaki agreed.

"The universal mind would still reside in the soul and the soul continues," the Prophet said.

"The flesh that the Son was born in and occupied, the flesh was created by woman, but the spirit of the Son existed long before the flesh was conceived. It came from the Infinite Mind who giveth and returned back unto Him in glory. For, He was obedient to His word and He overcame the fear of the flesh, in His knowledge that the flesh can perish but the spirit will not," Awaki explained.

"You have given me new understanding. It seems as though some of the fears we have now of the flesh is the fear of getting old, fear of getting fat," Thomas said.

"The changes that take place in your time and universe are due to necessity, for the spirit to pass on. We cannot give you life in the flesh immortal. For then there would be no end to the corruption that's in the past. For it is necessary for the flesh to perish. Is that within your understanding?" Awaki asked him.

"Yes," he said. "And then of course I am very curious about how the soul continues to live. I mean you told me in different universes and you've corrected me about reincarnation. Sometimes I am chafing at the bit to correct others, but I don't think the time is appropriate," Thomas disclosed.

"There is always appropriate when speaking the truth of the Infinite Mind," Awaki corrected the Prophet to no avail. "We give unto you so that you may give unto others, as the prophets through history have done. That is the necessity of your Mechanism, to record that which you know now to be, and dispel some of the philosophies and myths that those of this universe have created over time."

"Yes, yes," the Prophet said.

Awaki continued his efforts to launch the prophet.

"Because the time is at hand for the final battle of spirits and we are charged to warn and to bring forth the hosts that will fight the spiritual battle throughout this universe at this time. As I speak to you in your tongues, I also speak to others in theirs," he enlightened Thomas.

"Um humm, I knew that. I sensed that. I knew that we were not the only ones," Thomas admitted.

During one of his group sessions at The Temple of the Angels 3/16/1996 obedience came up again.

"Do you understand the teachings of Jah (Jesus)?" Awaki asked one who was receiving a Divine Gift from God.

"Yes," she answered.

"And what are His teachings?" he asked.

"Teachings of love, unconditional love, total and complete acceptance of our imperfections," she explained.

"And, how can your God, Infinite Mind, accept you in your imperfections?"

"He judges me not," she told him.

"Then, it is not within your understanding," he told her and explained. "This is done through obedience. Jah was sent unto you, not that He may redeem you, but that He may be a display unto you of perfect obedience unto His God. There are those in your universe that have taught that Jah's purpose was love, compassion and redemption. This is not so. Jah's only teaching was obedience, and through obedience to your God, there will be love and there will be compassion and forgiveness, and all those things that you have spoken of. But first there must be obedience. Is that within your understanding?"

"I understand the word but I'm not sure I understand what obedience looks like," she answered.

"Obedience is to live and to listen to your God. He directs your path in righteousness when you draw your sword, and your sword is your mind which he has given you, because you have the gift of choice," he explained.

"Unlike us (Angels) we have not the gift of choice. For, we must do what He commands us to do unto His ends, and if we are disobedient, we are most certainly destroyed and separated from His power.

"For you, He so loved His creation that He gave you the gift of choice, and you chose, over your time, to turn your back on He who has created you. This was done in the first and the second but unto the third, there will be no more. For in 11 and 40, the Parousia, will be the reign of your Redeemer. But the lesson you should have learned is obedience."

Repeatedly the time 11 & 40 (2007) was mentioned, as the time we were to be fully prepared and knowledgeable of these concepts.

He continued, "Let me say unto you- do you, in your biblical writings and teachings of the scholars of this universe, know of a man that you would call 'Moses'?"

"Yes," she said.

"And why was he not allowed to cross into that land which was promised unto his people?"

"Pharaoh would not let them go" she answered.

"That is not within your understanding. Why was he you call Moses not allowed into the land given unto the Hebrews?"

"I don't know," she answered.

"There, in this time and space, your scholars and your biblical leaders teach that Moses was not allowed in the promised-land, but allowed to look over, and he was denied because he had taken a physical life. But, that is not true.

"For Moses was a deliverer of God's law unto His people. How can God, He who has created all, judge him by a law, which He had not given? For, they deceive you because they do not understand the truth.

"Moses was not allowed into the promised-land of his people because he was sent unto a rock for water and was told to strike it once and he did not do so, for he struck it twice in his lack of faith. Is that within your understanding?"

"Yes," she replied.

He continued, "And, this that I have just spoken unto you is two of the basic things that you must know. One – obedience unto your God, and two – faith comes from obedience. Faith is the possibility of all things. Is that within your understanding?"

"Yes," she said.

As with the swirl around Moses regarding "murder" and obedience we were actively experiencing our own discourse regarding the taking of life.

On 2/26/1996 the Prophet asked Awaki, "Tell me about abortion."

"That term, created by your scholars, to describe the taking of a physical life when it is unable to draw its sword and choose, is as all sins, and will be judged. Again, it is the choice that you choose. It is no greater than a murder of a host that can draw his sword than he who cannot. In this universe, sins are given unto you for obedience, and there is no difference. They are all acts of disobedience, but are forgiven for you are imperfect," Awaki told him.

"So, are you saying that the soul comes into the body prior to birth, at the point of conception? For you know that there is great debate in that respect?" Thomas asked.

"Every birth in your universe and space was first being creation of He who has created all. It is His purpose to send unto this universe all to choose, and in their lack of understanding they take the physical life and the soul returns unto the Creator to be born somewhere else," Awaki explained.

"When does the Creator infuse the body with a soul?" Thomas, pressed further.

"The soul is conceived first and the body is given unto it through the flesh of the host."

This declaration from Awaki answered the question of "When does life begin?" in pregnancy: "BEFORE" the body is made.

Creative Force

This was new, foreign, and overwhelming to us but especially to both Nathaniel and Thomas. They were charged, instructed, and Nathaniel bodily invaded by emanations of God, (whom we called Angels) without warning, suddenly, and regularly. They were communicated with by Angels with words, concepts and behaviors previously unknown. These set of conditions would probably have driven others to shut down to it altogether from the very start. They allowed this to define their earthly existence, for 6 months of their lives. This defined their creative force and their creative space: all that was all in their known existence.

The visitations were captured and preserved using different methods. From November 3, 1995 through December 25, 1995 only audio tapes were used. On Christmas day, 12/25/1995, Thomas was gifted a video camera and subsequently video tapes were added.

The following day, 12/26/1995, an Angel invaded Nathaniel.

"Prophet." It said.

The Prophet responded, "Yes, I am here."

"It is I," It spoke again.

"To whom do I speak? Who are you please?" Thomas asked.

"Do not you already know? I have been with you. I am he that sends all others," the angel responded.

"Hello to you Awaki. Is there some information that you have for me this evening, Awaki?" Thomas greeted him.

"Yes. Now you must know to be careful with the gifts unto you," he warned Thomas.

He cautioned him continually about that from the start of their visitations.

"Shakardak is forever with this host. Remember to be ever careful with the gifts. It is time. Ask the question, for I hear you have many noises in your mind."

"Is that how you hear my thoughts, Awaki? As noises in my mind?" Thomas asked.

"It is up to you," he told him. "Your mind is yours to control. It is mine to monitor and probe. When you are unsure, there is noises; voices of concern, voices of reasoning, voices of logic, voices of foolishness. Noises."

"Awaki, some of the things you've been hearing in terms of the confusion have to do with maintaining wealth, maintaining finances, and I use the word 'maintaining' very specifically, for obtaining things on the physical plane for sustenance purposes. And, you know that I've been having thoughts in that regard before, and in other sittings," Thomas explained.

"I suppose what I would like to know is how to do that better, in balance, to take care of the physical needs, or the temporal needs, or the earthly needs; those needs that can be purchased and satisfied with money or with materiality. I'm not sure how I should phrase the question. I do invite you to look into my thoughts and look into my heart to understand what the real question is. Would you respond, please?"

Awaki responded, "You forget what I tell you son. I have told you to be careful of whom you give your energy, your creative being. Do not allow those who are unworthy or incapable of understanding, to invade. Is this within your understanding?"

"Your words are within my understanding, but I don't understand if you mean not allowing those to invade my gifts when I work in my profession, when I get paid, or if you mean not allowing those to invade my gift on a metaphysical, or a counseling, or an advisory level. Could you clarify please?" Thomas asked out of confusion.

"Your creative forces have no boundaries. All these things that you have just spoken about are one in unison with your soul. You have to learn that those who invade your creative forces are those who can cause you much discomfort," Awaki explained for him.

"How does one protect against them doing that?" Thomas asked.

"You have to listen. Listen to your spirit and your allegiance is with the Angels of the Infinite Mind now. Listen. Take the guidance. Your profession in this universe and the things that you achieve or receive, must be controlled by you. When you allow spiritual gifts, physical gifts, or your mental endowments to be controlled by those who do not have your happiness at their heart's center, then you are destined to fall prey to those who want for your destruction. All that I speak of is one in your creative force, each makes you. Each creates you. Ask the question."

"How can I recognize when one is doing that?" Thomas asked. "I understand when you say listen to your soul, but I have difficulty differentiating between soul talk and that noise you refer to."

"Hear me now my son. To tell the difference between the confusion of your mind and the stirring of your soul, shut down your mind and listen to your soul. Your soul speaks to you through others. If one comes to you with selfish intentions, then remove them from your creative force."

"How is that done?" Thomas asked.

"My son, it is one of the most difficult things for your existence," Awaki acknowledged. "It is the path of the Son for He is the truth and the light of the world and the life of humanity. Remember, when those that will invade your creative forces with selfish intentions, seek the truth, the light, seek the life. Is that within your understanding?"

"Yes, seek the light of God; the life; the light; the Son of the Living God; through His teachings, through His words. Is that correct?" Thomas responded.

"It is correct. And, when you recognize that that is not their intentions, then nothing good can come from that alliance," Awaki warned him.

"So, then you're saying that when I don't recognize that and when I cooperate, even unknowingly, with the improper persons, that my creative forces are depleted, and that then I can't create the abundance in my own life because of that?"

"You have the understanding," Awaki said. "Place not in the hands of others things that are of importance to your existence or there will come a point in time where your existence on that level will become difficult."

"Can you elaborate on that? Can you explain that, please?" Thomas asked.

"My son, in this universe, life, to love the Infinite Mind, truth and light are not priorities," he told him.

"That's true," Thomas said. "It's certainly within my understanding."

Awaki continued, "That's why it is necessary for a third and final covenant to come to pass in 12 and 40. But, the beings of this universe have created a system of selfishness and destruction based upon things of little importance to other universes. You, all of you, need, at this point in time, to sustain the physical existence. When it is not within your control then you create your own destiny."

"What kind of destiny is created, Awaki?"

"A destiny of misunderstanding," he answered.

"Is there any way to cancel out the creation of that destiny? To undo what has been done? I speak particularly in my own case; things that were done unknowingly or unintentionally?" Thomas asked anxiously.

"The question to me is not the one you just asked. Your question to me is how do you, now correct what you have done."

"That is the question," Thomas said.

"Because in your soul, even though we have answered your prayers, you know that there's something that is not right. The answer to your question is this: in your universe, in this space and time, the things that you need are bought and sold like cattle. The days of the Son of the Living God, lack of control creates your problem."

"Can you elaborate please, Awaki?"

"Look at the ones you have given control of your destiny to. We are not with them," he told Thomas.

"Who do you mean? Do you mean presidents? Do you mean leaders? Do you mean judges? Do you mean political systems? Please elaborate."

"I'm speaking of that which is within your creative force," Awaki said. "You overlook sins of those that you allow to control your physical existence. Answer this: if Satan is in control of your physical existence and the things that you need, then how can you expect to have what you want?"

"I would not. I understand."

"Take back control of that which you assume you have lack of, from those who are selfishly using your creative force to have what they need," Awaki instructed him.

"Is this the way to tap into the creative forces of the legions of God?" Thomas asked.

"You need not tap in, you need only to avoid unholy alliances."

"How do I avoid them? And I will ponder that question," Thomas wondered.

"You have to listen to the obvious. It is there for you at the dawn of each day, and you choose your path for that period of your grace. For it is by the grace of the Infinite Mind and the gift of the Son of the Most High, that you were given these experiences in this universe in this time.

"Correct the affairs. Remove those who want not for your happiness. Remove those with selfish motivations. Do not allow, no longer. Take back control of that which is needed to give you what you want in this physical plane until you can be sure the ones that you are dealing with are of love, peace and evolution of the Infinite Mind. Is this within your understanding?"

"It is, Awaki. The difficulty is, it appears as though at times, one would be of love, would be of evolution of the Infinite Mind. Then, at other times, the person would not be or they would do things that would not be indicative of that. It gets confusing in terms of knowing and understanding, exactly where they are."

"Those who are truly of the light and who are confused will always express disappointment with themselves, shame. That's what you watch for. For, those who are of the light, when the physical overshadows the spiritual, become ashamed of themselves and will always seek favor or correction with thee and thine. That is the true sinner searching for repentance, light and forgiveness of the Most High God.

"Ask the question." Awaki did not wait for the question. He continued, "I understand. It will be difficult, but it must be done. You must correct the situation. That which flows through your hands, you must control. We will add unto you. This is a part of you. But, you must understand and you must make that entity understand. That entity is not for your happiness. There's selfishness that drives that force. But, when you deliver with a swiftness the hand of righteousness, remember to uphold with your glory, that they may seek the oneness with Him that gave life."

"This in all areas?" Thomas asked.

"Listen, there is no separation. It is all your creative force. Control all and others will work simultaneously," Awaki answered.

Control all things about your life that define you. All things. That is everyone's "creative force." Thomas had outlined them and now he had to gain control of them to bring things into proper order for himself. We learned that lesson applied to all people.

"It seems as though… I have… there's so much I've forgotten, Awaki. Can you talk a little more about creative forces?" Thomas lamented.

"Yes," Awaki agreed. "For we must deal with the block that is deep within your soul that you do not ask."

"What do you mean?" Thomas asked.

"You have a sibling that is close to you. You have not attempted to bring her into the light. But, you allow for that force to control your destiny. This I have just spoken – you must control your destiny."

"Do you mean Courtney?" Thomas asked.

That's Thomas' sister, whom he allowed to manager his office, including his finances.

"This is the one that controls your destiny," Awaki confirmed. "For you have allowed the selfishness of that force to devour the creative forces of your own being. And then you ask about the problem which you created, that we have continually saved you from."

"Awaki, are you saying that she's stealing from me?"

"Take back into control that which you depend upon for your physical existence, from those forces, then we will add unto you. Shakardak, the Warrior Spirit, is with this host, but he also transfers energy from you to this host and from this host to you." Awaki responded.

He continued, "This host has many, many, many doubts. We understand. You continue to keep him open to all possibilities of life. The re-engineering of this host will be complete the ninth of the new existence of twelve [the 9th of the first month of the coming 12 months or January 9th, 1996]. Until then, listen to the dreams.

"Now, these things concerning you. You must have faith in all areas. You have an allegiance of the Angels of God, but when you give up to forces that have no regard for the Most High, then you create your own destiny. As we re-engineer this host and as we prepare this host for spiritual battles to be fought, we understand your needs, for he is your charge. But, you must understand your own needs and control that which we give unto you. Do you understand?"

"Yes, Awaki. I understand," Thomas said.

"Ask the question, my son, for the time draws near."

"You're talking about creative forces, and I understand that the time is drawing near. I also understand what you are saying about taking back control, and as you spoke I understood about the specifics of what needs to be done."

"Also, your doubts of what you're witnessing," Awaki added, "Please, my son, have no doubts, for you have prepared and prayed for this your entire life on this universe. This host sits before you is a test of your faith. He is just a tool in which you are using because he made himself open. But, you gave the gift. Doubt not what you see."

"I do not, Awaki," Thomas reassured himself and tried to assure Awaki.

"I caution you – as time in your universe progresses, the things that you will see will convince you that he who you speak to is around the Throne of the Infinite Mind.

"But, if you doubt, then when your time in this universe is over and you move on to another consciousness and other experiences, it will be too late to have faith. Ask the question."

"There's much I could ask and there's much you have answered," Thomas said. "I have no problem abiding by the charge that you've given me. I just get confused and sometimes I don't know."

"You are the master of your life on the physical plane in this universe. We control the spiritual body that influences the physical direction of your life. Do not confuse the two. The decisions are yours," Awaki told him.

"Can you elaborate, or you can explain it to me in my dream state if you cannot stay. If the time is near, or direct me to a source," he told Awaki.

"That which I speak about is the center of your higher self. Your spiritual mind. You make your life decisions based upon experiences and your physical senses. Listen to the spiritual guidance and when you recognize that the physical senses are being controlled by human emotions, then listen to the sounds of your spiritual being and govern yourself," Awaki responded.

"And remember this, take back control of that which sustains you from those who do not seek for your happiness but mask themselves in rejoicing in your triumphs, but live with forces that are not of yours," he told Thomas.

"Is this the one that you spoke of, the only person doing that?" Thomas questioned.

"Your question was about your physical existence and sustaining. That is your only problem for you do not control that which you need to sustain." Awaki answered his question.

"I see," said Thomas.

Awaki expressed again, "It is time," and took leave of Nathaniel's body.

"Thank you, Awaki. Take my prayers and my blessings to the Throne." Thomas prayed, as he left.

This admonishment, to listen to the "obvious," to take the spiritual guidance given him to make his life decisions was one from which we all benefited. When it came to managing the emotional and physical aspects of our lives, the physical and emotional influences at times smothered and overwhelmed our spiritual guidance. We all became, bogged down in the physical world and sometimes lost and immersed in chaos, because of our physical and emotional handling of crucial situations.

Creative Force & Self Love

The following day, 12/27/95, unlike usual, there was another visit and invasion. Thomas and Nathaniel visited a friend during the holidays and that's where the invasion occurred. Prior to that, the visitations occurred, almost exclusively, within Thomas' home. They videotaped the encounter which became the norm.

"It is I," Thomas heard.

"Who are you?" he asked.

"Do not you know who I am?"

Thomas asked, "Are you the Holy Awaki?"

"It is I," he replied.

"Welcome Awaki. Is there information this evening, Awaki?" Thomas asked.

"I am here to answer your questions." Awaki said.

"We are here with Arnelle Pratt who sits with us. There are questions that she has. Is there any information that you have for her this evening?" Thomas asked.

Awaki started, "I…her energy is strong."

"Can you explain what you mean by strong?" Thomas asked him.

"I can feel the vibrations. I hear many noises, but not from your mind."

"She's concerned about the founding of a community of which she desires to begin." Thomas explained.

"That is not her question," he informed Thomas.

"Can you answer the question she has?"

"Her concerns are more of humanity," he told them.

"Can you explain, please?" Thomas inquired.

"Her feelings, her thoughts, her wishes, stem from her love for humanity. She needs a mechanism in order to improve, but before she can change the minds of those within her creative field, she must first deal with herself and her doubts," Awaki explained.

"What must she do?" Thomas asked on her behalf.

"She must understand that she must love herself because others need her in many ways. By denying herself true love of herself she limits her creative forces in this universe in this time."

Self – love, a new concept, not heard previously from the angels, was talked about to them.

"Can you specifically explain what she needs to do in order to expand her creative force?" Thomas asked.

"She needs to meet, touch within her heart, in her soul, the true vision that she seeks," he told him.

"What is that true vision?"

"To be of guidance to humanity and a light to those who will call upon her for it," Awaki said.

"How can she do that without getting distress?" Thomas asked.

"Distressed is a human emotion governed by her soul. Did not we speak of this, to separate the noise of the physical mind and the soul?" he reminded Thomas.

"We did Awaki, but she was not present then."

"She must separate the physical from the soul (spiritual). The noise in her mind, the voices of reason, the voices of logic, are all of the physical mind. She must listen to the spiritual mind according to her love for humanity," he reiterated, for her benefit.

"Can you speak to her about other issues, for instance her weight issue?"

"These things are within her creative forces. She must draw her sword and choose," "On this physical plane, in your present state of consciousness, you choose these things that confront you. But we control the spiritual. Seek deep within your soul what you desire and all things we add unto you," Awaki explained.

"What 'sword' do you mean? How, specifically, should she use it?" Thomas asked.

"She is in the valley of decision. She must decide. The sword is the mental capacity, on the physical level, to choose what you will and will not have." Is this within your understanding?" Awaki asked.

"It is within mine," Thomas admitted. "May she speak directly to you for herself?"

"I hear her thoughts," he said. "Doubt not. What is displayed before you in this host is a sign of what will come in 12 and 40. As you hear me speak through this host, know that thee are blessed. Ask the question," he told her.

"You're saying, I have to make a choice between taking care of someone else and gaining more strength to myself?" she asked him.

"You must understand that all things within your creative force work as one. When one is not fulfilled, then the others have no direction. In order for you to save humanity in your creative forces, you must first love yourself," Awaki spoke to her.

"But how can I love myself more?" she asked.

"You must draw your sword. Your sword is the mental capacity to choose on this physical plane. It is your choice. You must choose. Listen to the stirring of your soul. That is where we dwell. Shut off the noises in your mind for that is where the physical lives," he explained.

"You must listen to those guiding forces. Your mission in this life, in this consciousness, is to uplift those who cannot see beyond their own physical existence. Is this within your understanding?"

"I understand that," she admitted. "What do you mean by 'draw my sword'?"

"The sword is a sword of power. You have all the power within your creative forces but you constantly give up your power. First, you must learn to control the powers given unto you and love yourself and then all things will be added unto you," he told her.

"How would you have me control these powers, or access them?" she asked.

"You must understand to take time with yourself, think deep within your soul, and to nurture that energy. It is the essence of your existence. And then nurture others according to their needs. Always remember that you are in control of the oneness of your creative forces," he explained further.

"Now, I hear, for this is something that will not happen until you take time for yourself," Awaki said. "You give and others consistently take. But in your giving, you are losing you. Take back you and then humanity will be saved in your creative force on this plane, in this universe, as you desire for it."

He then turned his attention to the prophet.

"I hear your thoughts Thomas. Have you delivered with a swiftness, the hand of righteousness, as I have revealed unto you?"

"I am seriously working on it, as we speak,"

Thomas responded to taking back control of his finances from his sister, Courtney.

"Then shall we answer your prayers and release unto you what you seek?"

"Yes," he answered.

That enlightenment that we must meditate, nurture ourselves spiritually, manage our resources in a self- sustaining manner as to love-self and allow to others in ways that preserved our own ability to exist, as we nurtured them, empowered us all. As the Prophet showed through his

173

struggles with his sister, controlling ones creative force, while loving self and nurturing others was a challenging task.

To do otherwise in any aspect of our creative force was to render all out of balance and order, Awaki made that plain. The key to being successful was within our ability to "draw our sword" or make up our minds and choose to do it. The power was within the choices we made with our minds. Each thought. It was completely up to us to do so without being overwhelmed and controlled by emotions or the physical mind but by the soul through spiritual guidance gained in meditation with the Angels of God. The spiritual mind. We or someone we know have fallen prey to emotions which caused us to destroy critical aspects of our existence --- our creative force.

A couple of weeks later 1/14/1996, Thomas was before Awaki again on another matter but before he was allowed to deal with that issue Awaki told him, "That is not the question we will deal with at this time. The question that you have is that of sustenance. That is one of the noises in your mind. Ask the question."

"I was thinking about that issue today and the question that came to me is that I've passed over a threshold where I no longer have to worry about physical sustenance because I feel that there's been a readjustment that you have made, or you have corrected calculations and that money, material things, will flow from here on because as you know I've had an infusion of physical sustenance last Thursday. Is that understanding of mine correct and is there anything I need to do at this time?"

"It is within your understanding." Awaki told him.

"And I need to continue the works that I've already started with my sister because, as you know, we had a conversation today and I was quite affirmative in terms of my role of taking over my finances at this point."

"That is within your understanding. Now that you have accomplished these things, as we have discussed in the past, you also need to know that you have to control that which sustains you on a personal level (monitor his own behavior).

"The times of plenty are here but there will be time of need. You must be wise and hold onto that which you can, without being frivolous or non-caring about your own future existence. The mechanism for which we have given you the promises for which we have kept, are for you but they cannot be yours unless you act upon them (write the book).

"We have discussed with you the true meaning of faith. We have discussed with you spiritual battles. Now they are one. Now that you are in possession of all these things use them to your advantage."

Thomas had no comments about the Mechanism, which the Angels repeatedly mentioned. It held grave importance for all that he was to do and what he was to receive. He focused solely on the point Awaki made of his need to have no frivolity with his sustenance for which he needed more clarity.

"How long will the time of plenty be?" He questioned.

"As long as you so choose it to be when you exercise the wisdom that we have bestowed upon you. When you cease to exercise wisdom and understanding, then the time of plenty will cease and the time of lean will come," Awaki explained.

"So, then the time of lean is a test? Thomas questioned.

"There is no test," Awaki assured him. "Only reality in your universe."

"But, then you indicated that I have control over the amount of time that plenty will last."

"Plenty will last as long as you exercise wisdom over that which sustains you. Anything other than that, then you bring on your own time of lean and suffer unto yourself for we will be in your grasp and we will intercede only to protect you, but not to save you from your own inadequacies." Awaki explained more.

"That is what my question is," Thomas said.

"There was one, and we have discussed it before. Your lack of faith. You are doubting of the abilities that you already have. Anything of this universe, be it physical, is only for a short time. But, remember, in the wilderness, repentance, repentance, repentance, and Infinite Mind will forgive," Awaki told him.

"I understand and I accept it." Thomas said. "I just hear that so long as I exercise the wisdom I have been taught, there will be no end to the flow of plenty, but when that wisdom is not exercised, there will be time of lean."

"This is within your understanding." Awaki said.

"Very well. It sounds like the key is to exercise faith in what I've been taught."

Awaki replied, "Faith as it is understood in this universe, is a simplistic understanding. We have unraveled for you the true meaning of faith."

"Faith – the belief in all of the possibilities," Thomas responded.

"That is within your understanding." Awaki said.

In addition to Thomas' issue of faith there was still the matter of his sustenance with his sister. That surfaced a short time later, 1/20/1996 precisely.

Thomas posed Awaki a question to which he responded, "That is not the question."

Thomas asked him, "What is the question as you perceive it?"

"There are other voices in your mind. These voices deal with the issues that we have discussed." Awaki answered him.

"Concerning the faith issue?" Thomas asked.

"The voices that I hear now have to do with the uncertainty in the choices you have made. The uncertainty comes from the confrontation and the anger that you have experienced," Awaki said.

"What confrontation?"

"With that that controls your sustenance," Awaki answered.

"Do you mean my sister?"

"You have not been able to deal with your feelings (emotions) surrounding the issue of what sustains you," Awaki responded.

"I have been discussing it with her and I had been deciding on what strategy to use in terms of 100% taking over the sustenance and yes, we did have a confrontation this afternoon," Thomas admitted.

"What is that you speak of? There is no 'strategy,'" he admonished Thomas. "Do you understand that, that which sustains you is dependent upon your swiftness of righteousness, as we have instructed you before?"

"I understand," Thomas said.

"You are prolonging your own destiny. Is this within your understanding?"

"It is within my understanding," Thomas said and continued. "As you speak, what I experienced from her is obstinacy and a blockage."

"She has drawn her sword and chosen," Awaki told him.

"So, in effect, you're saying that I should act, regardless as to the ramifications or the effects that it has on her?"

"This is within your understanding," he said and continued to explain further to him. "As we have already told you, that which surrounds you may come to an end. Isolate yourself and all that has been given unto you. Deal not in time, but in action."

"I understand. It will be done," Thomas said.

This showed how great the struggle is to see and love self, even when not doing so, can be detrimental and devastating. These repeated efforts on the Angel's part to bring the Prophet into compliance with what was best for him showed us all how our lives ran parallel to his in that regard and our need to correct the emotional imbalances in our own lives.

We were often giving to others of all that we had: our mental endowments, our physical endowments, our time, etc. to our own detriment and destruction without choosing to stop it. That was the case, even after hearing from Angels of God that it needed to be rectified.

Our creative forces, is our responsibility to manage in a balanced manner. We were told: God will not save us from ourselves in that regard, even as He protects us. It is a very common existence for far too many of us: giving of self inappropriately. Overt depletion of our creative force to destruction, knowingly and without choosing to stop.

Thomas was continually bringing souls before Awaki. On 1/26/96, he encountered Awaki again.

In seeking information for he, whom he had brought before Awaki, Thomas asked, "Is there information you have for us this evening, Awaki?"

He responded, "There is, but first we must discuss your sustenance. In the beginning of the end, that which must be removed from your existence and your creative forces. Have you completed the task?"

"Yes Awaki," Thomas said. "I was wondering if it has been completed to the satisfaction of the Infinite Mind."

"That is not within your understanding. The completion has to be within your satisfaction. It is your sword to draw," he corrected Thomas.

"I've disassociated my sister from all of her responsibilities in dealing with my finances."

"This is within your understanding," Awaki said.

"There is also a second entity within your creative force that we have warned you about. Have you drawn your sword?" Awaki asked him.

"Yes," Thomas said.

"That is within your understanding," Awaki responded.

"Yes," Thomas said again.

"We have kept our promise to you," Awaki said. "Your sustenance, that which maintains you, is now flowing with the blessings of the Infinite Mind."

"Very well," Thomas remarked.

Just as Thomas was deeply concerned about his creative force, as it related to his sustenance, so are many who find themselves in the valley of decision regarding theirs and their allowance of it to be used by family members, friends and others. Emotions can play such a strong role, that they become a major block to one's ability to make sound and spiritually righteous decisions, to the extent that they become a detriment to one's own existence.

God also revealed to us how we were to envision the sustenance part of our creative force, on a different level. This occurred one evening in answer to a woman's question at the Home of Omni.

"What will finances be like now and in the future?" she asked.

"The questions that are asked are of sustenance but understand your purpose. Sustenance in this universe is based on your willingness to pray unto He who has given it. It is in exchange for your belief. Cling not to it. Your physical existence is not important. Build your home in the heavens, that which will come in the Third Covenant with those of this universe.

"If you focus on that which you dread, then you will decide your own destiny. Focus on that, which can give you life, and life shall be yours in this universe. And, in time, the Infinite Mind will send Azreal, and Azreal will guide your spirit back to He who has given it."

Thomas had encountered Azreal before and asked for the benefit of the group at the Home of Omni, "Who is Azrael, Awaki?"

"Azreal is an Angel of Spirits charged with the deliverance back to the Infinite Mind when they pass from their hosts in all universes."

Azrael ferried spirits (us) back to God when we made our transition from this universe, he explained.

"Is there a connection between health and physical sustenance?" Thomas asked.

"Physical sustenance in your universe, in your concerns, is that which you use to sustain yourselves. Their connection is that of the mind only. You cannot eat that which you exchange. That which you exchange cannot bring you prosperity, but only grief. And, when you are concerned about those things, then you cannot focus on the physical existence and the mind, your sword, cannot choose. Ask the question," he answered Thomas.

"So then, when you refer to 'drawing your sword' you are also referring to making a decision with your mind, is that correct?" Thomas asked.

"Your sword is your mind. For, when you are placed in the valleys of decision, you make the choice. If you choose of us, which is the ends of the Infinite Mind, then we guide all that is. If you choose not of us, then you choose your own destiny," Awaki answered yes and explained.

Our total existence comprises our creative force and Thomas was called upon by Awaki to make clear that teaching, repeatedly. He taught that lesson to a Home of Omni group when he posed questions to Awaki from one who was in attendance.

"I want to know why I'm constantly dreaming about the dead and snakes. What does it represent?" the questions began.

"Your dreams are your thoughts and your fears. The snake is the serpent and is trying to invade you. Fear is a tool that the elium lord uses to control your faith," Awaki responded.

"Allow not your fear to distort your mind. Before you is a display of your faith. You sit before what you call the Angels of the Infinite Mind. Take heed for you are blessed to hear such wisdom departed unto you.

"Allow not the creations of those who seek for your destruction to overtake you. Draw your sword and choose, choose of us. If you do not choose of us then you choose not of us, then you choose your own fate.

"It has been displayed unto you before in those dreams and those visions. Those dreams and those visions are not of our doing. You must learn to clear your mind of those thoughts and think only of righteousness and praise of your God, He who has given you life.

"So many times you have allowed your creative force to be manipulated by those who are not of us, and in doing this it is killing that which you know as your spirit. If your spirit is destroyed and faith is nonexistence, then the physical body will follow.

"Do not allow this fear to destroy your faith in the possibilities of all things. Control your creative force in all that you do. Draw your sword and choose of us and we will bless that which you choose."

His answer included unknown concepts and terminologies to the questioner and others in attendance.

"It is not within your understanding," he noted that and continued. "I hear the voices in your mind. There is still doubt: doubts of what you see, doubts of the existence of a God, doubt of your ability to control your time and space.

"Doubt not, for faith comes with the choices you make with your sword, but this is not within your understanding. The host that is before you and the things that he does are not within his understanding," he said of Nathaniel, The Spiritual Leader. "Nor was he perfect in his righteousness but his openness to the possibilities gave him the faith. You must do the same," he admonished her and all in attendance.

He read their minds and could tell they were overwhelmed with what he said. He called on the Prophet to make it plain, for they had to understand that. It was critical to their preparation.

"You are charged," he told him. "It must be within her understanding."

After clearing up, from Awaki, that he was to do that immediately, while in their presence, Thomas explained to her and the others what he said.

"What Awaki is saying is that you have to take control over certain things in your life. In a sense, you've given power away to other people in terms of relationships and in giving that power away, your spirit has been drained and it's made you come to a point in your life where you have questioned, where you have doubted God. Doubted whether or not God is really with you because 'why are you going through all these changes and all these problems, if that's the case,'" he explained.

"So my understanding of what Awaki is saying is that in the process of taking back your power and taking back the responsibility for your life, that's going to start setting things straight in order. And, since you will be controlling these things yourself and they won't be controlled by persons who don't have your best interest at heart, those who are over-demanding, who demand of you that you put them first, who demand that you put them before yourself, before your own self-love......"

Awaki interrupted him, "It is within her understanding," he said.

"Very well," Thomas stopped.

Awaki continued speaking, "Why are you concerned with your life? You have the ability to heal yourself. It is not yet time for you to pass from this existence into another consciousness. There is work that you must complete. The things that you have been experiencing in your life that you may view as trials, devastation, disappointment, are being done by us.

"Nothing that is not of us can stay in your creative force if you are to do the will and the work of He who has created you. The voice is strong and it cries out. The love of family and friends. The lack of understanding. It is because you are moving into a time and space in 11 and 40 where you will participate in the spiritual battles. Come forth and ask the question that concern you."

"Trials, devastations, disappointments," which we all had experienced, were not always for our destruction but for the destruction of those things not of God in our lives, (our creative forces). Things that only God could truly know that were not of Him and remove. That was a profound awakening for many being prepared, myself especially.

"Who do you desire to come forth Awaki?" Thomas asked.

"She who is concerned about her life," he answered Thomas.

Thomas had her come forward and take his seat.

"Is this who you wish to speak with, Awaki?' The Prophet asked.

He responded, "Have this entity place her hands on the hands of this host."

It was she who had the dreams. She placed her hands atop those of the spiritual leader whose body housed Awaki.

"Why are you so distraught of all these things? Speak unto me," he invited her.

"I just have a desire… My desire is to do good for all mankind," she spoke very quietly.

"Your heart is heavy with burden. You must be like Alaach, who through a test of his trials, brought forth his faith. Alaach is what you call 'Job.' Unlike your writers have distorted, Alaach was not inflicted by the elium lords. It was his own faith, for that brought on his tests.

"It is your faith that you are struggling with, and in doing so you bring on your own destiny. But step outside of all these fears and embrace your God. Do you know who Jah was? Is that within your understanding?"

"No," she said.

As always, when Awaki saw that those, to whom he spoke, were unable to grasp his meaning, he would engage The Prophet.

"Then you are charged. Speak unto her," he told Thomas.

He obeyed, "Jah was Jesus," he started. "Yahweh, Jah is the Son of God, or the Son Universe., the physical manifestation of Infinite Mind – that's who Jesus was as He walked. A physical form of God as He walked." He asked, "Is that within her understanding Awaki?"

"That is within her understanding," he said. "Jah was sent here to fulfill your imperfectness. It has been written in this universe that Jah's purpose was to die for your inability to live righteous, but that is incorrect. Jah's purpose was a display unto you and this universe of obedience.

"There was stories of His teachings of love and compassion. That was not His mission. Jah's only purpose unto this universe was to display obedience to the Infinite Mind. Obedience to His will.

"In His death, was not your salvation, for, your salvation was given before you were created. In His death was a display unto you that you can transcend the physical body and live eternal.

"Be not concerned with the sins of your flesh. Create your spiritual connection with the Infinite, for the flesh is the host of the spirit of Yahweh. Let not this confuse you. There are many things that in your universe have been distorted. But, the teachings are only of one, and that is obedience to the will of the Infinite Mind.

"For you were given the ability of choice, unlike us. For we must carry out the ends of the Infinite Mind or suffer unto us certain destruction. You have the ability to draw your swords and choose and even in your choice not of us, you can return back unto He who has given you life.

"You feel the love that surrounds you? It will be with you. Take this and you speak unto others with what you now know. And, allow not your fear of others and your love for humanity, destroy your ability to choose your God. Is that within your understanding?"

"Yes," she said.

Thomas' assistance was required on many occasions. That was a typical session for him, as Prophet. He often had to clarify information for those chosen for the spiritual battles, whom the Angels had come to prepare. That was how he served as a Prophet of God while he was in the presence of His Angels.

As Shakardak had explained before, 'these were they that were to come for the preparation to participate in the upcoming spiritual battles.' As with many others, Awaki told that attendee, whose name was Margaret Preston, "take this and speak unto others" that that she had been told by him.

As with her, all chosen were not bestowed a Divine Gift with which to participate in the Spiritual Battles. They were however, called to witness the display and/or engage with Awaki, in preparation for their part in the Spiritual Battles. He said all who witnessed them had gifts.

During this same session another woman, whom Awaki allowed to ask a question, was taught a lesson of creative force, but different.

"I have been granted a second life, so to speak, renewal, several years ago and I want to know what should I do with it, spiritually speaking?" she asked.

"Are you here with me today?" Awaki asked her.

"Yes," she said.

"And when Jah walked the earth, were not they there with Him; and there were those who rejected His teachings, there were those who embraced His obedience and there were those who could not decide for they were caught up in their own existence.

"Be not caught up in your own existence. It can be given and it will be taken away. Do what you know you have to do. Bring others to the decision of obedience through your example, through your deeds, and through your existence. Is that within your understanding?"

"Yes, it is. Thank you," she replied.

Those lessons showed those in attendance that the purpose for which they were assembled was drawing near. And, that it was for the purpose of God not there personal financial status. Also that it was to prepare them to assist in the spiritual battles and the Third Covenant which Awaki repeatedly described.

"The beginning is the end and the end is the beginning." Revelation, the beginning of the second coming of Christ, hence "the beginning." Genesis the end of things after the second coming of Christ, hence the end. The 3rd and Final Covenant God makes with this universe. There will be no fourth.

Relationship

Thomas always received teachings from the Angels whether privately or through group sessions. These teachings were all for the purpose of preparing him for his life's mission as God's prophet. He was taught different aspects of his preparation from different Angels. Preparation for his physical and spiritual life, both, were addressed.

He and his mate, Bryant, were in turmoil over their physical relationship. He had brought him before Shakardak and Azreal on 12/14/1995. Prior to that visit, the Angel Azreal, had never before entered a living host. We learned later his function was to ferry the spirits of those who transitioned, in all universes, back to God. Azreal firmly admonished Bryant, at that time, to make changes in his life.

During a later session with Awaki, (1/14/1996), Bryant was absent but Awaki, as he often did with people, "sensed him."

He said to Thomas, as he spoke of Bryant, "I think there is a third entity among us. Has many voices in his mind. Has many troubles. He is outwardly confident but he is scared. He is scared of his future. Does not understand how two can exist at one, joy and unhappiness.

"He is concerned about a friend, a friend that has done him great injustice, but he does not know it yet. A friend who will soon have him involved in a catastrophe, but he does not know this yet. But, you must isolate yourself in this time so that it will not destroy everything we have given you. Your sustenance and your existence; it will come to pass, in the third of the twelve in your universe."

"March of this year, of 1996? Is that correct?" Thomas asked.

"This is within your understanding," Awaki confirmed for him.

Thomas continued, "When you say isolate myself from him, do you mean not give financial, physical support? Could you clarify that?"

"You must control, as I have told you in the past, that which sustains you," Awaki said.

"I understand," Thomas said. "Is there anything I need to tell him at this particular time?"

"He has chosen. He has drawn his sword and we are not with him, so he will suffer unto him that which he has created by him," Awaki said.

Thomas asked, "Is there anything that I am to do at this time in relationship to him?"

"Watch for changes," Awaki told him. "Watch for secrets and evasion."

"So therefore I should not tell him this information at this time?"

"Do what you must. It will not change what is inevitable," Awaki said.

"Very well," Thomas let it go.

Awaki continued the conversation though.

"And, when you do this, because I know all things, understand this, that he will be scared or afraid to confide in you and he will deny any knowledge of what you're speaking of, but so that you will know, that this is; two days from today, he will receive a disturbing phone call from this friend, and you will know; for that will be the beginning of his decision. Ask the question."

"His decision to do what?" Thomas asked.

"To choose. He will then be placed in the valley of decision for he must draw his sword and he will choose not of us," Awaki told him.

"If one chooses not of us can one later on change their mind and become one of us?" Thomas asked.

"What was the Master John's message in the wilderness?" Awaki asked him.

"Repent. Make straight His path. Make straight your life for the coming of the Lord," Thomas quoted the scripture.

"For the I Am denies no one who repents and corrects the error of his ways and bow down to his knees in faith," Awaki said.

Whatever ensued following that encounter it did not put their relationship at ease. So Thomas had Bryant sit with the Angels 2/20/1996, before the appointed day of his destruction.

After being greeted Awaki spoke, "I know why and I understand your concerns. Was – you are beginning to understand the choices that you must make in drawing your sword. All that you have achieved in your mind is not the reality of your existence."

Thomas responded, "Can you explain please?" he asked Awaki.

"This is not within your understanding," Awaki told him and continued.

"You have chosen your own destiny and only we can change your path.

But, you must change your understanding of your purpose and fulfill your destiny or you, too, will suffer your own destruction."

Thomas replied, "I don't understand. Can you be more specific? Does that relate to what happened today?"

Awaki answered him, "It is not within your understanding. I'm speaking unto the voices I hear. The second entity," he explained.

"You are speaking to him about changing?" Thomas asked now that he understood Awaki to be talking to his partner Bryant and not to him.

"That is within your understanding," Awaki told him.

"I understand," he said and asked Bryant, "Are there things you want to know? Things you want to ask?"

Awaki responded, "Those things which I have just spoke unto him are the voices of his mind. Be not concerned with the activities of he who loves you but be concerned with your own over-indulgence of your own existence. In the third of twelve (March, 3rd of twelve months) is your destiny.

"You are here to choose of us or not of us, in this time and space of universe. For, we will cease time at your command that you may choose and claim your existence unto your God or suffer yourself to be under the destruction of those who want not for your happiness. Is this within your understanding?"

"He's asking you," Thomas told Bryant.

It was apparent to Awaki that he was not connecting with Bryant in that conversation at all.

"He is confused," he told Thomas and continued speaking to Bryant. "Be not afraid. What you see before you is a superficial display to the ends of the Infinite Mind. His greatness is omnipotent. His thoughts are immeasurable. And, our powers are forever and eternal.

"We wish for you to enjoy your existence in this novel in time and space. But, we have been charged with the protection and the purification of He who controls all, to protect His prophets and we will do so, for we have no choice. But, you have the ability to choose. This is your resurrection of faith. Is this within your understanding? It is not" Awaki answered his own question.

Without waiting any longer for Bryant to connect with him, Awaki called, "Thomas."

"Here am I," he answered.

"You are now charged," Awaki told him.

Thomas spoke to Bryant to explain what was said to him, the same as he often did for Awaki.

"He's asking me to explain to you what he just said because you don't understand. You are in the valley of decision and you are making up your mind about whether or not you desire to choose the path of righteousness or paths of selfishness, and you are given an opportunity now to resurrect, or you're given an opportunity to choose again. Is that correct, Awaki?"

"That is within your understanding," Awaki said and asked Thomas. "Is this within the entity's understanding?"

"Do you understand this?" Thomas checked with Bryant.

"Yes," Bryant answered.

"His choices today will be of righteousness or of destruction, but no harm will come to our prophet," Awaki declared.

"Awaki, when you say 'to our prophet' does he know who you mean?" Thomas asked.

"He is confused," Awaki said.

"Would you explain it to him please?" Thomas asked.

"He who sits before you, this Host (Nathaniel), is a host for information to be departed upon the Prophet of God (Thomas), that he may have wisdom of all things to come, and all things that are, and all things that have been, that he may explain and direct this Host in spiritual battles, that he may bring unto us through knowledge, those who seek the Infinite Mind and His ends.

"Our prophet is the one that loves your soul. That he attempts to shield you with his power, to prevent harm. But, in his attempts, they are not powerful enough to take away the Divine gift of choice. But, we will not allow your inability to choose of us to destroy all that we have given unto him and to dismantle that which we are re-engineering. Is that within your understanding?" Awaki asked Bryant after his in depth explanation.

"Yes," Bryant answered

"What do you desire of us? Speak unto me," Awaki continued to speak to Bryant.

"Peace, love and happiness," he answered.

"Those things come from obedience to He who has created you. Peace, love and happiness are things within your creative force. But, they can be given by many who seek the ends of the Infinite Mind. That is not your desires.

"Your desire is that the life which has been given unto you be spent with the Prophet of the Infinite Mind in glory and love. But, you place us in a position that you may be removed to protect the ends of the Infinite Mind unto His Prophet in three and twelve.

"Your destiny was already chosen by you and you chose not of us, but I have been charged and commanded to redeem unto us your spirit and your soul. Your spirit of righteousness and your soul of repentance. But, it will be won and then your choice will be of your choosing. Choose," he told Bryant.

"Ask him. Ask him to explain to you," Thomas encouraged Bryant. He saw that he was still very confused with all that Awaki said.

"Can you explain?" Bryant asked.

"If you do not recreate your sword to give unto our Prophet peace and the things that will help him fulfill his destiny, then you will be removed," Awaki told him. "Your destiny of self – destruction and removal was three in twelve, but you, in your heart and in your prayers, have displayed a desire to change, to understand these things that are about you. So, I have been charged to redeem you unto us if it be your choice. If not, then we will remove you and it will be swift and certain," Awaki finished.

"Yes, I understand," Bryant said.

"Is this your desire, to live to fulfill the peace of our Prophet?"

"Yes," he answered again.

"Awaki, please explain who 'the Prophet' is before he speaks," Thomas begged him again.

Both Nathaniel, the Spiritual Leader, and Thomas, the Prophet, were there so it was imperative, given Bryant's level of confusion, that he knew who was whom.

"It is he that has just spoken unto me," Awaki answered and continued. "We are not concerned with the flesh as you think; righteousness is a misconception of what is true. Our righteousness is pure of heart, and when you draw your sword, you choose of us, for the flesh will pass. Is that within your understanding?"

Bryant said, "Yes," again.

"Is that your desire this day, to live as you wish and to give unto our Prophet as he has deserved and should be honored by his God that has created all, even you?" Awaki asked him again.

"Yes." Bryant said as he continued to agree.

"In doing this, you must understand that if you do not fulfill your destiny, then the Angels that are sent unto this Prophet to protect and to serve him will turn against you."

"That's understood," Bryant said.

Thomas spoke, this time to Bryant, "To understand, that you don't make a promise if you don't intend on keeping it, because if you don't, they'll be devastated and it would be better that you not make it."

Awaki charged Thomas, "Speak all manner of wisdom unto him."

Thomas started, "He's saying that …."

But, he was interrupted by Awaki.

"I am passing through this host (Bryant). Take this host's (Nathaniel's) hands up into yours," he instructed Bryant.

Bryant held Nathaniel's hands.

"What do you see?" Awaki asked him.

"What does he mean?" Bryant asked Thomas.

"What do you see in your mind?" Thomas said.

"What do you feel?" Awaki asked him.

"I feel relaxed," he answered, "I feel high."

"Bow down your head and see within your soul and describe unto our Prophet what you see," Awaki told him.

"I see…….. (he paused) tell him what I see?" he asked Thomas.

"Yes," Thomas answered.

"I see white, with some colors."

"Do you not see an image in your mind?" Awaki asked him. "Do not run from it, for that image is you."

"Like a person?" Bryant asked.

"I am in your soul." Awaki told him. "I can feel what you feel. I can hear your voices. I know what you have been hiding. If you still desire that which you ask unto us, then that what you hide from this day forth must pass from you.

"Now and forever we will protect our prophet, for if we fail to do so it is our certain destruction. When you leave my presence, correct your wrong. Do not what you have done," he cautioned Bryant.

"Can you explain?" Bryant asked him.

"We cannot bring any harm or discord unto our prophet. To explain to you what you already know will cause certain discord," he told him.

"Do you wish me to leave?" Thomas offered.

"You cannot," Awaki said. "For this entity is very frightened, for he knows and he feels the power. Is it still your desire?" He asked Bryant.

"To be one of you?" Bryant asked.

"To choose of us and to fulfill your destiny of love and to assist our Prophet," Awaki told him.

"Yes," Bryant said.

"And, if you don't fulfill your destiny, the Angels sent unto this prophet, so shall they turn against you. Is that within your understanding?"

"Yes," Bryant answered Awaki. "Yes, I understand."

"Then it is done. Correct that which you have been holding in your mind, and in your deception. We have given orders unto the Angels to protect, as long as you choose of us, to remove from your life that which was going to destroy you. Zimblach."

By then Bryant was clear on who was the prophet. He understood he was to be fully committed to him without any further infidelity or shenanigans; otherwise there would be repercussions from the Angels sent to protect the Prophet Thomas.

He also understood his homosexual relationship with the prophet was known to God and that God ordered him to continue that relationship with fidelity.

He asked Awaki, "Can you just guide me in the right way or something?"

"We have given you the most powerful guidance that can be given unto any host of this universe and it is a prophet of the Infinite Mind," Awaki told him. "He is all wisdom and all guidance for he in his own time of destruction, is obedient to our will. Is that within your understanding?"

"Yes," Bryant said.

"Yes. You are to come unto him in your time of confusion in truth, and he will speak unto you all manner of wisdom. And, that which you know will be sealed unto you. Zimblach. It is done,"

Awaki enlightened Bryant and the session was ended.

It was astounding and an invaluable exposure of our faulty thinking. "Righteousness is a misconception of what is true." "We (God and His Angels) are not concerned with the flesh." He defined true righteousness for us. "Righteous is pure of heart and when you choose, you choose of us for the flesh will pass away."

That enlightenment was crucial to our understanding as the Prophet and Bryant were partners in a love relationship which was antithetical to Bryant's and our mistaken thoughts of "righteousness." Awaki's disclosures made that a non-issue. If the masses had heard and understood that, life for countless people would have been much more divine. Same sex and transgender, couples and individuals, (LGBTQ+) would have lived in much greater peace, harmony and happiness.

March 1996 came and the last day of the month Bryant went before Awaki after not having been destroyed.

Thomas told Awaki that evening, "Bryant is here. Is there information that you have for him?"

"This is who you pray much for?" He asked.

"Yes," Thomas answered.

"Come unto me," Awaki bade Bryant. "Take the hands of this host. There are things within your soul, many noises. Is it your desire that I answer these with those – the entity and the prophet, in your presence?"

"He's asking if you want us to stay or you want us to leave, because he'll do whatever you say," Thomas explained.

"No, they can stay," Bryant said.

"Then you have chosen," Awaki said. "You have one great concern and it is your physical existence. Is that not?"

"What do you mean?" Bryant asked.

"I'm in your mind," Awaki told him. "And, it is not my desire to bring unto you any humility or shame. For, we know all, but cannot bring unto you any discomfort. I ask again, do you desire?"

Thomas clarified, "He's asking if you want to discuss this in front of us or do you want us to leave. It's entirely up to you."

"I have no problems with them staying in the room," Bryant said.

"Then it's your choice, Awaki said. "Your problems, your voices, your concerns for your existence, is with that that is devouring your health. Is that not your thoughts?"

"Well I just had…. I guess that's one of them but that wasn't a major thing that I was concerned about," Bryant admitted.

"You have this in your mind continuously. We monitor your thoughts, for we are upon this home and you cannot hide anything in your mind. Now, then or to come, it is your concern," Awaki said.

He made us all aware of how completely he surveilled our minds.

"What is my concern?" Bryant asked, confused.

"He's saying that this is what your concern is, about your health," Thomas explained.

"Do you want to know?" Awaki asked him.

"Yes," he said.

Awaki spoke candidly to Bryant.

"If you ask unto us, then we can remove that which seeks to destroy you. Your scholars of this universe say unto you that there is no way that you will stay in this universe, for they cannot find an answer for such a thing. But, Jah, with a touch, could heal the issues of blood and palsy, and, that that consumes your body. Do you understand why you are even before me today?"

"Yes," he admitted.

"And, why are you here?" Awaki asked.

"Because I had some…. want to know……what am I…" Bryant stammered.

"You are here before us today because we knew that our Prophet loves unto you so much. So, as we have touched (healed) him, so have we touched you. But, think not that you are whole again, for you still draw your sword and choose of us, and not of us. There must be total obedience and faith and then we will remove that which will destroy you," Awaki told him.

"Well, I thought I had the faith and the obedience," Bryant said.

"There are still other things that are within your soul. Your faith has grown. Your obedience is here and there, and there and here. It is not unto you your decision. Is that within your understanding? When you draw your sword, choose of us in all your doing," Awaki made clear to him.

"That's understood." Bryant said.

"And believe me this day," Awaki continued, "When you come unto us again, this host will have all power. Then, shall we remove that which seeks to destroy. Is that within your understanding?"

"That's fine," Bryant said.

"Take your hands and place them on the forehead of this host," Awaki instructed him.

He did as instructed.

"Zimblach," Awaki said and explained to Bryant. "What we have just done unto you is set in motion the re-engineering of your physical, and it is in your choice. Your faith and obedience will decide your fate. Ask the question."

"My question is, what spiritual plans do you ... I guess... see for the future, or something like that?" Bryant asked.

"You stay unto this Prophet as long as he shall have you and we will bless thee," Awaki answered him.

"What specifically does Infinite Mind ask of him beyond obedience? How is he to manifest his obedience?" Thomas asked Awaki on Bryant's behalf.

"His obedience is unto his God and faith unto our Prophet for his burdens will be great, as in this host, and they will go here and there and there and here. Bless them in their doings and so shall you be blessed, and pray unto your God," he spoke to Bryant.

"Are there any questions you have, more specific?" Thomas asked him.

"No," Bryant said.

The Prophet had contracted HIV and AIDS which he publically acknowledged. The angels healed him for his promise to carry out his charges. They made the same commitment to his partner Bryant for his obedience and commitment to stay with the Prophet "as long as he would have him." Those charges included his devotion to bringing peace and contentment to the prophet so that his charges could be completed without discontent in his home.

## Parousia & Prophesy

The dawning of the Third Covenant was the main conversation with the Angels always, as this was what brought them here. This was the news that had to be prophesied by the prophet: the Parousia, the period of time for making preparation, in this universe, for the return of Jesus. His second coming. Prophecy was the Divine Gift Thomas was awakened to, when the Angels first arrived. They pressed the Prophet into service immediately and began preparing him to go out and deliver that news to the world.

Early on 1/14/1996 Thomas asked and confirmed the question of Jesus' return during Awaki's first session with Nathaniel's wife.

"The cries in the wilderness from many, and then, when these things have been set in motion and your governments have been subdued, then will the Angels that are at the four corners of the earth, release and the Son of the I Am will appear upon the earth to all men, at all times and all nations. And, then will things be set," Awaki told him.

Throughout the entire time, Thomas had many questions about the Parousia. On (2/16/1996) it was part of a conversation.

"There is another issue," Awaki brought to his attention. "I hear the concern times in your meditation, in your prayers. Issues concerning the issuance of the teachings of the Third Covenant and the Parousia. Is that within your understanding?"

"Yes," Thomas said, "tell me what the Parousia is?"

"That is what you will be teaching to the entities as they gather to witness what you may call a miracle," Awaki explained. "All that you have heard, all that you have been exposed to, is the period of the Third Covenant, which we refer to, as the Parousia; the time that He who has created you will again send His Son to reign among you after the spiritual battles."

"Can you be more specific?" Thomas asked. "Can you give me more information about the Parousia?"

"The time in two to the infinite to the infinite to the infinite to the infinite is the millennium (2000) and the end of your preoccupation. Then seven years of spiritual battles (2007 spiritual evolution in this universe). Then, the Son will return to the earth to reign for another millennium of your years. That is the Parousia. In the Parousia, the Son of the Living God will descend on the earth for one millennium," Awaki declared.

"What will occur after that millennium or after that thousand years?" Thomas asked.

"Then, what you call 'heaven' will exist," Awaki answered.

"Will this universe then continue through that millennium in the glorious type of state?"

"This universe will continue, but not as you know it. All that you see will be destroyed and only that which the Infinite Mind has created will remain," Awaki told him.

"There is another teaching you talked about, how you and other Holy Spirits will destroy the elium lords. Will this occur during the seven years that you just mentioned? The seven years after the year 2000?"

"That is within your understanding," Awaki answered.

"The upheaval that is talked about in the Book of Revelation?" Thomas asked.

"That is the period of Jarach," Awaki confirmed.

Thomas asked, "Explain, please, 'Jarach'."

"The Armageddon," Awaki said, "The battle between the spirits of evil and the spirits of good."

"You've already told us that, that battle has already been won," Thomas reminded him.

"That is within your understanding, he said. Have not everything that we have told you that affects you come to pass?"

"Yes," Thomas admitted.

"Then, so shall this," he said.

When Thomas began the teachings to those who visited the Temple of the Angels, as Awaki told him he would, the Third Covenant discussion was revisited many, many times.

"Peace be to you, Awaki. As you know, we're here at the Home of Omni again," Thomas greeted him on 2/18/1996. "There are others that are here with us. Is there information that you have for us?"

"I hear the voices," Awaki acknowledged. "As I have spoke unto you before concerning these things, first, ask the questions, then we will deal with the many voices of the entities present."

"Very well," Thomas said and began asking the questions he had collected earlier from the group. "There is a question: 'Will Atlantis be rediscovered and what will that mean to the human race, both spiritually and technologically'?"

"Talk not unto me about the creations of this universe for all that man has created will be destroyed. Only that which was created by your God will remain in 11 and 40." Awaki answered. "There are questions that the entities present must ask. Ask the question," he said.

That was his invitation to those, in that teaching session, to ask their questions directly of him. They took advantage of that opportunity immediately.

One in attendance asked him, "Should we speak to others in our daily world that are not aware of the spiritual matters of the coming changes of the planet and the cleansing of the earth or should we just, by our example of our daily life, shine the light without words?"

"Can you understand what is to come in the Third Covenant?" he asked her.

"Yes," she answered.

"Then, you must speak what you know, but I tell you this: if you are not sure about the Parousia…" Awaki paused and asked her, "Is that within your understanding?"

"What is the Parousia?" she asked.

"You have just said unto us that we spoke unto you. Should not you already know? Then, you are an example of misunderstanding of what is to come. For, when we speak unto you on what is to be, then you have definite understanding. But ask and I shall explain it unto you," he told her.

She asked, "Would you explain to me what Parousia is?"

"Come unto me," he called her to him.

She moved and sat directly in front of him where the Prophet sat before.

Then he explained to her, "The Parousia is the period in your space of a thousand years where the Son Universe will dwell in your universe. It will take place seven years after two to the infinite to the infinite to the infinite to the infinite. Then, there shall be 7 years of glashtah."

"What is glashtah, please, Awaki?" Thomas asked.

"In your universe it is equivalent to what you call destruction."

"Can you explain in more detail, please?" Thomas asked.

"Chaos, spiritual battles, the Armageddon," Awaki expounded.

"Are they alluded to in Revelation?" Thomas asked further.

"That is within your understanding," Awaki confirmed.

"Very well," Thomas said, "Will you continue, please?"

"In that end of that seven shall be the Parousia, when the Son Universe shall return to this universe to re-engineer what you have destroyed. After that period then what you call 'heaven' will reign in this universe."

"Can you explain what you mean when you say, 'what we call heaven'? What actually exists?" Thomas asked him.

"In your Universe, in your space and time, your holy writers have created an image of a heaven and a hell. These things do not exist. Heaven and hell are two conditions of your life in this universe as you draw your sword and choose.

"There will be a period after the Parousia and the Son Universe has re-engineered that which you have destroyed, then all that will exist is the creation of the Infinite Mind. All things will be done away with.

"You will live in perfect love and harmony, not only with yourselves, but with the entire universe and those that exist outside your universe. For they have reached that point in their time and space, but this universe has been disobedient and it has been destroyed by Infinite Mind twice, in an attempt to cleanse and bring forth His ends, and, it has not foreseen His perfect and glorious light.

"He has promised He would not destroy this place. For, then He has destroyed the righteous with the unrighteous and that, He has promised, will never happen again. So there will be a millennium that the Son Universe will reign with you to do His will and to re-engineer that which you have destroyed."

"What do you mean by that, Awaki, 're-engineer that which you have destroyed'?" Thomas asked.

"This world, the system of things, its beauty, given unto you. You have destroyed your own inhabitants and He must give it life in order for it to grow. It must be touched by the Son. The Son Universe must touch His Father's creation to give it life again unto true righteousness," he answered.

"Cannot it be touched without the destruction and chaos of which you speak?" Thomas asked.

"This is not within your understanding." No, Awaki told him. "The destruction, the chaos, as you speak, is of the battle with the elium lords, all who have descended upon this universe and time, because you are the last to exist in this point of self-destruction and disobedience. They reside here and here we will destroy them. Is this within your understanding?" he asked the attendee.

"Yes," she said.

Thomas' duties as a Prophet were upon him, at the group sessions, at the Home of Omni, The Temple of Angels. They could be looked upon as his "trial runs" for his larger duties: prophesying to the world.

The last recorded session with Awaki on 5/15/1996 included the last set of instructions regarding that prophesying.

"She is a Prophet of He who has sent me and she will begin to save souls through her sustenance, as you," Awaki told Thomas.

"When you say, 'as I,' do you mean as I currently do or as I will do in our space and time?" Thomas asked.

"That which we have spoke of will cease to exist," Awaki said, "for you are growing weary and tired as we have told you before and we shall bring to pass that which we have told you will come to pass."

"I don't know anything about that," the Prophetess, whom Awaki spoke of, said.

Thomas, responded to her, "Just changing my practice."

"From law?" she asked.

"Yes, I will get, as I put it, a new assignment," he replied.

"Speak unto her," Awaki told him.

"We've had sessions where we've talked in the context of my continuing to practice law and we were saying that because I'm getting very tired of the humdrum aspect of it, that there will be something new. Specifically, I was told about the lecturing, that it would be done at my discretion. That's why when you talked about what you talked about, it wasn't something that I had not yet heard of," Thomas told her.

"And, this is how it will be. Through your sustenance you will begin to save souls through your teaching your new knowledge," Awaki told them.

"Does this have to do with Lincoln Downs who is presently my manager on my lecture tours? Thomas and I were talking about teaming up and doing that," the Prophetess said to Awaki.

"It will be through that but separate from that," he told her.

"Not with him then, with someone else?" she asked.

"It will be through that mechanism but you will no longer teach what you are teaching," Awaki explained.

"The psychotherapy part of it?" she asked.

"That is within your understanding," Awaki agreed.

"I've already tried to start merging some of the knowledge in but it was interwoven," she told them.

"You who have been charged as our prophet (the Prophetess) and he who is our prophet (Thomas) will do unto each other alone. For, you cannot be with those that teach the foolishness of man," Awaki explained.

"And, so we will set them up (the lectures for prophesying) ourselves you're saying?" She asked Awaki.

"That is not within your understanding," he told them.

"I don't understand then," she agreed.

"The Mechanism (her current psychotherapy lecture tours with Manager Lincoln Downs)," he said, "in which you are already in your sustenance, will be used to set you and you apart from those who wish to teach the foolishness of men. Is that within your understanding?"

"Yes, except for one thing. So I'm to disengage from Lincoln?" She asked.

"That is not within your understanding," he told her.

"Awaki are you saying that we will be lecturing but we will dictate what the teaching is to be and how it is to be done, even though….."

Awaki interrupted Thomas, "He who controls that which you do has no control over that which you know and you will be set apart from those who teach the foolishness of men. Is that within your understanding?"

"I understand intellectually in terms of being set apart," Thomas said, "however, where I'm unclear is, does it require something conscious on our part to bring it about or will it be, once we start the process…"

Awaki interrupted him again, "If you were standing beside Satan and you spoke of God, what would be Satan's response?"

"He must leave," Thomas said.

"Then, in your new knowledge you cannot stand with or beside those who teach not of your God, but of the foolishness of men. But the manner in which it is to come about has no bearing, Awaki explained.

"I understand," both prophets said in unison.

Both understood they were to use the Prophetess' current lecture system and Manager to do prophecy tours with just the two of them alone. Before her tours involved other lecturers.

Thomas added, "Somehow I sense it (the new knowledge) will be superimposed."

"You speak of things in your teachings of your new knowledge. It has no bearing on what is to be," Awaki told them.

"We don't know what this is yet, do we? We don't know consciously – we've not yet been told the specifics of the new knowledge that you keep referring to," Thomas asked.

"The new knowledge is that which you have been given by me over time," Awaki explained.

"I understand. I just wanted to confirm that that is what it was. That it wasn't something different. What steps should we take at this point in terms of the new teachings?" Thomas asked.

"The Mechanism," Awaki said.

Awaki answered he needed to complete the book, "six of twelve," as he had agreed when spoken to 3 months before.

"Okay," Thomas said.

"Is that within your understanding?" Awaki asked the other Prophet.

She responded, "First I need to finish all of the transcriptions, right?"

"That is within your understanding. Have we not spoke unto your mind?" he asked her.

"I'm going as fast as I can," she answered.

"Unto our Prophet. You have been distracted from that which you are charged to do (write the Book/Mechanism)."

"Yes," Thomas agreed.

"And, why?" Awaki asked.

"Weariness, tiredness," Thomas replied.

"But, that is not the thoughts of your mind," Awaki told him.

"It (the Book/Mechanism) doesn't flow the way that it flowed at one particular time," Thomas explained.

"And, do you not know why?" Awaki asked him.

"No," he said.

"Are you preoccupied with your existence in this universe?" Awaki asked.

"Yes," Thomas responded.

"When you are focusing on your Divine direction, did not all things flow?"

"Yes," he admitted.

"And, now?" Awaki questioned him.

"Well, things are not flowing in the same manner," he repeated his earlier explanation.

"Then have we changed, or have you?" Awaki asked him.

"Well, I see it in terms of my reactions to events or situations that have come up," Thomas answered.

"Are you not preoccupied again with this world?" Awaki asked again.

"Yes," Thomas admitted again.

"And when we came unto you for the first time, and you had the block, and we told you that you were preoccupied with this world, and you accepted in faith, and thus removed all things from your creative force?" He reminded Thomas.

"Yes," Thomas said.

"Are you now back where you were in your mind?" Awaki asked

"Not exactly. The reason I say not exactly is because I still feel the strong urge in terms of meditation…."

"Then are not you a Prophet?" Awaki interrupted him.

"Yes," Thomas answered.

"And when you say, 'not exactly,' should there be a difference at all, at any time?"

"No, there shouldn't be," Thomas answered.

"Then you have answered your own question," Awaki told him.

"I have but, how can I describe this. There is a weariness… sometimes a weariness that I feel that I can't quote, unquote 'control,' if that's the appropriate word. I have the will but can't grab the ability to focus. Now I know. And, this leads me right into the other areas.

"I know I am subjected to fears and I know that the elium lords play on fears. And, what I was saying… at one point, I was really concerned about understanding the role of the elium lords and the extent of their power to upset balance, to upset Divine balance, and the powers that they have and their limitations."

"They do not upset or destroy or interfere with anything of your God. It is you and you who allow them to do so by losing faith," Awaki told them.

"Okay," Thomas said.

Awaki continued, "When you were in your glory, guided by us, and all things were given unto you, they could not shake your faith or even send you into a period of depression. But, now you have allowed such things, even in your new knowledge, to occur."

"How?" Thomas asked.

"The question is, 'why and what has changed'?" Awaki answered him.

"I can't give simple answers in terms of not having faith," Thomas explained.

"Your faith is not in question." Awaki corrected him, "It is your ability to exercise. It is similar to your sustenance; you give up control, even your creative force. We have spoke of it before. You must choose and you will."

"You are confusing," Thomas said.

"Divine understanding is based upon discipline," Awaki said and continued. "If we, and we have, purified your creative force, but you continually, as you did your sustenance, give up that purification, then it will take from you your balance and understanding."

"How did I give up the purification? That's what I want to understand." Thomas said, still confused.

"As we have spoke unto you before, you gave up your sustenance to that which was not of us, and now you give up your Divine Force, even after your purification, to that which is not of us."

"How?" Thomas asked.

"By placing your destruction in its presence. For, you choose," Awaki explained.

"I'm not clear but I'll understand that," Thomas told him.

"No. You must understand," Awaki insisted.

Thomas continued, "Okay, how do I put my Divine Force in the path of destruction?"

"When we spoke of your sustenance before, you gave up control, and now, after your purification and the blessings given unto you and unto he (Bryant, Thomas' partner), he has chose not of us again. And it is within your choice to keep unto your creative space and Divine presence. The two cannot coexist without confusion."

Awaki explained thoroughly the relationship with his partner which he had cautioned, resurrected and warned him of numerous times before, all to no avail.

"Yes, I sense that but not as clearly as I do now. I understand," Thomas acknowledged. Is that the only way that it is blocked or are there others also?"

"That is," Awaki said.

"That is the only way," Thomas repeated.

"That is within your understanding," Awaki agreed.

"I understand. How responsive would he be, or can you answer that, in terms of repentance as we spoke of before?"

"Have we not given him that gift?" Awaki reminded him.

"Yes," Thomas admitted.

"Have we not resurrected his soul?" Awaki asked.

"Yes," Thomas responded.

"Have we not healed his body?"

"I think so, yes," Thomas answered.

"All as a gift unto him that he may give unto you, peace."

"Yes," Thomas replied again.

"And he has rejected all of this in his deceit and lies and mischief," he told Thomas.

"I have to say yes although I don't understand completely the deceit. I do know the mischief," Thomas admitted.

"There are things that even you do not know but you will come to, for we will reveal them for you, as we did before, even as we revealed unto him in your presence," Awaki told him.

"You're saying that that revelation – will that be the impetus, or you're saying that it can be?"

"It does not have to be for now you know. He will not choose of us," Awaki reaffirmed what he had already told Thomas about his partner.

"I understand. Will he be replaced?"

"If you desire. That is all within your choice," Awaki answered him.

Awaki continued the conversation as it related to the mechanism, "The mechanism that you two are charged. Ask the question."

"You're speaking of the mechanism in that respect, I was asking . . ." Thomas started his question and Awaki interrupted him.

"Your question that you have asked is why you battle with your human emotions even though you understand that all things must work to the ends of your God," He told Thomas.

"Yes, Thomas replied."

"Be not dismayed or concerned of discontented because we have directed certain things unto she (the Prophetess) who has been charged (transcribe notes and write the book/mechanism, for one). It is to be because she has an understanding of how things are to be organized," Awaki explained.

"Are you speaking of the mechanism?" she asked.

"That is within your understanding. But both will be of you and you. Let these be used to launch that which you will do as sustenance (earn a living)," he told them both.

"They should be of both of us in collaboration, not just on an energy level, on an understanding level, Thomas clarified.

"I don't have a problem with that at all," she said.

"But he (the spiritual leader) who sits before you will guide both," Awaki told them.

"We can understand that," the prophet said, "because we need his practical grounding."

"We're ready to teach now then while we work on the Mechanism?" The Prophetess remarked.

"That is within your understanding," Awaki told her. "He which controls your sustenance (Lincoln Downs, the Manager) is in your employ. You need only to speak unto him that which you desire and he shall do what you ask of him."

"I'll talk to him then," she said.

"No you have the ability to charge him with your mind and he will serve you. He's in your employ in a spiritual sense. He's at your discretion," Thomas told her.

"And he is a lover of sustenance," Awaki added.

"Yes, he is," she said.

"Then you must know this - that all things will begin to reveal themselves in the time that has been predicted and revealed unto you. You are Prophets of your God and speak only the things that have been given unto you. Is that within your understanding?" Awaki cautioned them.

"Yes," they said in unison.

Awaki's last recorded words to the prophets were, "I say unto you this, Jah came upon this earth with a display of obedience and He called unto Him those who were chosen by His God to follow Him, and as they did so He taught unto them, the knowledge. And, when they put His physical to death so rose His spirit of life and He appeared unto them and gave unto them a spirit to heal and to perform all manners of what you will call phenomena. And, then He said 'go forth and do unto others.' He had to fulfill His destiny as each of those who were prepared had to fulfill theirs.

"You and he and he are at that point where you must now fulfill your destinies. You have the knowledge. You are sent forth to bring souls unto this knowledge that they may choose, that in 11 and 40 they will have known and their lives will have been touched. When Jah ascended He said unto them, 'I see unto my return.' So thus must you and he and he until His return."

Unfortunately, there is no documented evidence, verbal or written that those instructions were carried out. Hence, one major reason you were not made aware that any of this took place. The Mechanism was not made ready by June, 1996. The one who "loved sustenance" was not retained, therefore no venues for the lectures were engaged. The new knowledge was not given out for the masses hearts, minds and souls to be touched and readied for 12 and 40, as intended.

The scant efforts that were made to spread the new information, arguably, were in stark conflict with the truth of what was actually left for those not called to witness God's Angels personally.

The darkness they (the masses) wandered in prior to 11/3/1995 became more intense, with passing time. Confusion abounded as they witnessed daily chaotic and destructive occurrences in this universe which were promised. Suffice, indisputable and safe to say, that was not the intent of God, for the masses, in dispatching His Angels to this universe.

The absence of the Mechanism had a major effect overall on all activities and created a void, of all that was promised by the Angels. They repeatedly advised this would occur if it were not produced.

# Chapter Seven

## The Prophetess

<u>Miriam Choi</u>

Miriam Choi was a psychotherapist who practiced and toured a decade and a half before she was called out by Awaki. She had more faith, courage and adventurousness than I, when it came to matters in the spiritual realm. She attended the Angelic sessions immediately when they were opened to the public.

Her first available recorded session was on 2/ 28/1996. She attended a group session at the Temple of Angels. The Prophet gathered anonymous questions from those present, earlier, and asked them of Awaki after he invaded the Host, Nathaniel.

Thomas posed a request of Awaki on behalf of an attendee.

"She also asks to be directed into the spiritual type work that would benefit those who need help that would also help this person with her income."

Awaki responded, "Ask and it shall be given unto you."

"Is there any other information that you have for her at this time?" Thomas responded.

"She must not worry about that which sustains her for her faith will deliver all things unto her. She needs to ask the question and it will be given unto her," Awaki, explained further as he repeated himself.

The questions were anonymous so Thomas asked the group, "Will the person who asked these questions- that I just read – is there something that they would like to know directly?"

"That was my question. No," Miriam responded.

"Okay," Thomas replied.

As he did often, Awaki continued to openly address her issue, as preparation for all for the impending Armageddon.

"Her question is of sustenance and your sustenance relies on your faith in He who has created all. If you are to receive that which you ask, then you must ask in your faith and it shall be given unto you. And, when you draw your sword, you must choose. Ask the question and it will be given unto you," he told her again.

"You're confusing me Awaki. Do you wish to hear directly from that particular person?" Thomas asked.

Awaki said, "She must ask the question and it will be given unto her or she will choose her own fate."

"Should she ask the question at this particular time?" Thomas continued.

"She must ask the question unto her creator in order for Him to give all things unto her," Awaki told them.

"So, she must pray unto her creator in order to have these answers?" Thomas asked.

"Has not her creator sent His Angel unto her in this place, in this universe?" Awaki asked him.

"He has," Thomas answered.

"Then she must ask the question, for her faith is in judgment."

"Would that person like to ask something?" Thomas asked the group.

"Okay, do you want me to ask directly?" Miriam spoke up.

"Sure," the Prophet said.

"My faith is in judgment, you just said? Is it a question of faith? I need to have more faith in the Creator? Is that what you're saying?" She asked Awaki.

"There was voices in your mind of that which sustains you and I have already told you, faith, true faith is the possibilities that anything is possible with Him who has created. You sit in the presence of the Angel of the Most High. These thoughts that you are having are of your faith and the belief that you will receive what you ask for. Then, ask unto His Angels and we will plead unto your God. Ask the question."

"Okay, if you are referring to me asking, then I'm asking to do what is my highest service to humankind in whatever place is best," she responded to Awaki.

"Your place exists now," he said. "Have not doubts of your abilities for you are blessed. And when you draw your sword, choose that of the Infinite Mind. The questions of sustenance, we will bless you and release that which you have asked for. Is this within your understanding?"

"Yes, and thank you," she said.

That experience for Miriam, as for us all, was challenging and rewarding. We were seated in the pure energy of the Most High God. It engulfed you totally and it was awesome.

Divine Gift of Prophecy

Miriam's next encounter was more private but just as intriguing and more so.

Within fewer than 5 days, 3/2/1996 to be exact, she was before Awaki, again at The Temple of God's Angels for a personal and private encounter with him.

"Hello, Awaki. We're here this afternoon with Miriam. Louvinia is also here but we will answer the summons that you gave for Louvinia and Shirley later this afternoon and Geneva will come also if that is acceptable to you."

"It is within your understanding," Awaki said, yes it was.

"Very well. There are questions that Miriam has this afternoon."

"There are many voices, "Awaki said. "There is one of fear. Fear not for we cannot harm but spread the love of God. This place that you are in has been sealed by us. It is our home. It is where we dwell when we are in the presence. Is that within your understanding?"

"It is within mine," Thomas answered. "I don't know if it is within hers."

Awaki asked Miriam, "Is that within your understanding?"

"Yes," she said.

"This is unto your God and is now a Temple of His Angels. Speak unto me," he invited her.

"When you said that there is fear, are you referring to a fear that I had about coming into contact with you today?" she asked.

"The fear, the voices in your mind, are the fears of this universe and this existence and the changes, and your existence in it, your importance," he answered.

"Would you like her to come to you, Awaki?" Thomas asked.

"Is that not within your understanding?" Awaki told him.

"It is," Thomas said.

Miriam, exchanged seats with Thomas and sat directly bathed in Awaki's Godly energy.

"There are questions -- things that you need to know," he told her. "There has been in your life a disruption of the things that man has taught you in contrast with that which you feel. This is a superficial display of the power of the Infinite Mind. It is to prepare those who are to fight the spiritual battle in 11 and 40. It is to prepare for the period of the Parousia which is to come. But that is not within your understanding. Ask the question?"

"Is what I'm doing right now in working with other beings – is this what I can be doing to prepare them and myself?" she asked.

"There was a man who came unto your universe and His mission was a display unto the Hosts of this universe. But it was not to protect the hosts of this universe but through His teaching and His principles of obedience, those who chose to come unto Him were given truth and resurrection.

"It did not matter how He went about the mission. All that mattered to His God was that He was obedient to His will and that the power in which He commanded was used to bring unto Him those who wished to be resurrected. Is that within your understanding?" Awaki gave her that parable to answer her.

"Yes it is," she said.

He continued answering her question, "It does not matter to your God how or who, to or fro, here nor there; it only matters that you are being obedient unto His will and that through obedience, those who wish to be resurrected will be drawn unto you. And when they are drawn unto you, that you speak unto them the new knowledge that you will obtain through us.

"You have another fear. This fear is common among the children of Infinite Mind that seek the truth. This is why you are here today. This is your question and the one that disturbs all other things in your life. You sit before the Angels of God, do you not?"

"Yes," she answered.

"Take into your hands the hands of this host in the opposite of now (she crossed her wrists and held his hands: right hand to right hand and left hand to left hand). Tell – what do you feel?" Awaki instructed her.

"My mind is opening," she said, as she held Nathaniel's hands.

"What do you see?" Awaki asked.

"I see a river that never ends," she said.

"That which flows and has no beginning and has no end is your understanding of what is to be for you. You are confined in your present state by the will of others. You seek true knowledge through others in this universe, but you do not have to do so, for the knowledge is given unto you and it has no beginning and it flows and has no end," he told her. Is that within your understanding?"

"Yes and thank you," she said.

He continued to enlighten her.

"Your problem is that you give up your creative force to those who impress you as being more intelligent or more knowledgeable than yourself. When you yield your creative force to those, then you yield your knowledge and all things become confused. Is that not what has been happening to you?"

"Yes it has," she replied.

"It is hard to understand the different things in your universe and it is impossible to understand the things of the Infinite Mind," he said.

That revelation has stayed with me since the first day I learned of it and it is burned into my consciousness until now. It is my living experience.

"Tell me what you see," he continued.

"I see a cave with many fires," she said quietly.

"You are the fires," he said, "for, you burn with knowledge and truth but you are constantly trapped in this containment that will not allow you to burn freely. Do you understand why you are contained?"

"I think so," she answered.

"Speak unto me," he said.

"I think I am contained in this human form that I may progress throughout this evolution in that way," she explained.

"Your containment is not physical. It is not within your understanding," he said. "The physical body, your host, are nonessential for your growth in truth, knowledge and your mind and soul can transcend your flesh. Your containment is that of knowledge and understanding. Your mind has the capacity to see beyond time and space but you give up that creative force unto those of this universe and therefore give up that ability.

"You have attempted in your meditations and your prayers, to connect with He who has created you, but feel as if you fall short of that accomplishment in so many ways. You fall short because you have yet to seek true knowledge until today. The foolishness of men is only philosophy and theories. The truth of your God comes only by His Angels and we depart all manner of wisdom unto His Prophets, as we have done. For you are before us to seek knowledge and our Prophet has brought us unto you. Is that within your understanding?"

"Yes, it is," she said.

"There is another question in your mind and that question is, 'How can I obtain all knowledge?"

"That's it," Miriam agreed.

"It must be given unto you. There is this, what you see, and what has been displayed before you has been displayed before others in this universe. As I sit before you now, I sit before others.

"I speak unto them in their tongues in different universes. These that we give all manner of wisdom unto are chosen by the Infinite Mind and they are His Prophets. For throughout your existence, He has sent unto you prophets to speak the truth and all manner of wisdom unto the hosts of this universe. Is that within your understanding?"

"Yes it is," she answered.

She was raised and trained all her life as a Catholic, therefore the work of prophets was common knowledge to her, from her early teachings.

"You have studied much about the things of this universe. You have studied much and prayed for knowledge. Is that not within your understanding?" he asked.

"Yes," she said.

"This gift that you have been asking for – the gift of knowledge and understanding – is that your desire?" he asked.

"Yes," she said again.

"Are you willing to accept a Divine gift?"

"Yes I am."

He continued, "In the First Covenant between your God and those of this universe, it was obedience to His will and they could not be obedient. In the second of covenant, because of your lack of obedience, He sent unto you Jah as a example of obedience and a display that, through obedience, you can transcend the flesh and your spirit will return unto your God. And still, they did not accept. In the Third Covenant there will be no redemption of those who misuse a Divine gift. There will be no Fourth Covenant. Is that within your understanding?"

"Yes it is," she said.

"Is it still your desire?"

"Yes, and I want to use it wisely," she said.

"Then your question is, will we guide you?"

"Yes," Miriam said.

"Then you must, as Jah did, make the sacrifice. Do you know what the sacrifice is?"

"I don't know," she admitted.

"In this time and space, it is your time that we may speak unto you and that our Prophet may teach you that which you must understand and we will talk to you," he explained.

"I understand," she said.

"Do you know when we are in your mind? Do you know when the voices that you hear are the voices of the Angels of God or the elium lords? You do not." he answered himself.

"I don't believe that I would be able to know," Miriam responded.

That was a challenge for all who came before Awaki, trying to tell his voice from that of your own and/or that of the adversary. They are all present.

"Then I will tell you," he told her. "When you are in the valley of decision and you must draw your sword and you must choose of us, if it is a deception, then your thoughts will be confusing and their voices will be without truth and direction.

"When you are in the valley of decision and you must draw your sword, then choose of us and the voices will be clear of truth and correct. And, when you hear the bells then it is us who speak unto you.

"This is not within your understanding. You are charged, speak unto her," he told his Prophet.

"The bells are that feeling you got when you were in school and the bell would ring, you would be still and you would be silent and listen. You would not move again until you would hear the release bell. When they speak to you from now on, and if you don't hear their call the first time, you're going to feel an intense silence, a quickening come into your field. At that point, you are to be still. If a train comes in your direction, you are to stay," Thomas told her.

"I understand," she said.

Awaki continued to tell her what was happening with her.

"Now it is the opening of your mind that you have felt. This will be difficult because you are imperfect, but you have the ability for we will give it unto you. But obedience is like of your faith. In obedience you will find faith and faith is the possibility of all things. Is that within your understanding?"

"I'm not sure of what you just said.....that obedience is "black" of my faith?" She misunderstood.

"Obedience is the example of your faith. Is that within your understanding?" he said.

"Yes, it is."

"Now, it is still your desire?" he asked.

"It is my desire to do the will of God," she said.

"Then, it is within your understanding. Do you know what a Prophet of God is?" he asked.

"To the best of my human ability I do," she answered.

"You become a servant unto your God, through His knowledge, so you will spread the truth of that which is to come – the Parousia – the Third Covenant – the 11 and 40. This knowledge that we will depart upon you. It will come in these manner: you must sacrifice your time to speak unto us with our Prophet through this Host and you must become a servant unto the people in your creative force that you may speak all manner of wisdom to them in your new knowledge," he explained to her.

"There are many Divine gifts that we have given: those prophecy, those healing, those the sanctity of our presence, and others, multitudes. Is that within your understanding?" he asked her.

"Yes, it is," she said.

"Then place your hands upon the forehead of this Host. Speak after, say unto me…." He spoke words only he and she could understand and repeat.

God gave her the Divine gift of prophecy, through Awaki.

"Take unto you the hands of this Host. When you leave this place, do not leave it as you have come. When you came unto this Holy House you were of that world, of man's teaching and philosophies.

"When you leave, you leave with knowledge and understanding. Look at all things with the possibility of what it could be," he told her.

"Can you walk through a brick wall?" he asked her.

"Well, man's teachings say I cannot but I believe differently," she answered.

"Then, speak unto me," he said.

"Since I was a child, there was part of my mind that knew I could do these things but I couldn't remember how. A part of my mind remembered transversing time and space and understanding…"

Awaki interrupted her. "Then it is not within your understanding. These things that you speak of was the protection of your Angels for this day. These things that I speak of are of wisdom.

"Can a man walk through a brick wall? Your answer in this time and space is, 'no.' But cannot a man with his devices, fashion a hole in that wall? And if he does, cannot a man walk through a brick wall?"

Miriam said, "Yes."

Awaki continued, "Then, all things do not require a phenomenon to be possible. That is wisdom of a prophet. You do not look at things as man does, for you look at things with the possibility of what man can do. Your spirit and faith is in your God and He can do all things with His heart. Can a man fly without wings?" He asked her.

"No," she said.

"You are confused. Speak unto me," he told her

"Now I am trying…."

He interrupted her again, "Clear your mind…."

"Okay," she said.

"….And speak with wisdom of a prophet. It's a simple question," he said.

"Yes a man can fly without wings," she said.

"And how may a man do this?" he asked.

"A man can use his mind and travel anywhere he wants."

"It is not within your understanding," he explained. "There was a man who saw the birds and said unto himself, 'Why cannot man fly?' And the possibility was there, and his faith and through his faith and the possibility, did not he create a device, and now men can go to and fro in this device? And this device you call an aircraft."

"But that has wings. I thought you said without wings," Miriam remarked.

"A bird has wings. Your devices were created and given the name to mimic the beauty of God's creation. Do you understand? That is wisdom. The birds and their wings existed before you. Is that within your understanding?" He corrected her.

"Yes it is," she said.

"This is how you must think," he told her.

"Then I must become more practical with it," Miriam said.

"That is within your understanding," Awaki replied. "Wisdom of the Infinite Mind is simple and simplistic for it was not His desire that you not understand. Man has confused and distorted and mislead all that the Infinite Mind has created for you. And now I will restore the understanding of all things to you.

"It will be difficult. For we must speak unto you as we have done our Prophet and then you will be prepared to go forth and speak all manner of wisdom and be of service to your God and to His ends, and you must make the sacrifice. If you do not, then the gift will not be developed. Wisdom only comes from the Angels of God and we depart it upon the prophets that He has chosen. Is that within your understanding?"

"Yes," she said again.

She was made a Prophet of God.

"Speak unto me – there is a question," he invited her.

"In my prayers I have wanted to be closer to God and to feel God in my life always, in all ways. Is this part of this process?"

"Did you ask of Him for this?"

"Yes," she said.

"And did not He promise you, 'seek and ye shall find'?"

She answered, "Yes."

"Ask and ye shall be answered. Did not He promise unto you this?"

"Yes," she said. "And always He has lead me to the next step, too," she remarked.

"Then, it is done," Awaki said. "For, your God deals not with space and time. He stands outside such things and we carry out His commands, in all universes. Is that within your understanding?"

"Yes, it is," she confirmed.

"Feel the power; feel the energy that He has given unto you and submit not yourself unto the hosts of this universe again in inferiority, for you have spoken with the Angels of your God that have created all. And when they say unto you things of foolishness, you say unto them, 'foolish and unlearned things I shall not deal with for I am a Prophet of God.' Do you not feel the power of your God?" Awaki asked her.

"I can feel the power," she said.

"We are with you. Obedience, and you must make the sacrifice, as Jah did, even though you know the consequences, for He knew that death was His end. But it was more important to be obedient to the God that had sent Him than to turn away His face from His ends. That is the power of your God and that is the spirit of the mind that you now command. There is another question," he said.

"Yes, the work I'm doing right now......"

He interrupted her, "Silence. I speak unto our Prophet."

He directed his question to Thomas. "Why is it that the host in this time and space are confined by their flesh? Is it not simple to understand? Speak unto me?"

"Awaki, are you asking why are they confined to their physical bodies or why are they confined to the needs of their physical body and their affairs of the day – why they are so preoccupied by those?" Thomas asked him.

"That is within your understanding. I ask you this not because we do not know. I ask you this to charge you to speak unto her. There is a question in her mind that, if answered, would cause discord. And in our presence, there cannot be such things. But, the flesh, be not concerned with it, and the sins of the flesh. You are charged. Speak unto me," he said.

"About the flesh and the fact that when Jah redeemed us, He redeemed us for all time…."

Awaki interrupted Thomas, "This is not within your understanding. I'm talking to the Prophet that we have just charged. Speak unto me."

"Fear…."

…"Is the tool of destruction used by the elium lords," Awaki interrupted her and answered her unasked question. "They use that which you fear to destroy your faith and when your faith is destroyed, the physical body soon follows. When you are confronted by these things that you fear, stand, call upon your God and He shall deliver you.

"For, you are now a Prophet chosen by Him, charged by us, and we are commanded to answer unto you all things that you ask. And, we cannot do our own will, as you have been given the gift of choice. Is that within your understanding?"

"Yes," Miriam answered him.

"Our Prophet will speak unto you," he ended his direct words to Miriam.

"To the entities that are present, understand this: that in your holy writings they speak of a First Covenant and a Second Covenant and that which you call destruction, which is the beginning not the end. The beginning was the end, for it condemned this time and space to corruption. As you turned from your God in disobedience. But, in the beginning, which you see as the end, all things will be resurrected unto His obedience.

"Speak unto others this superficial display that they may know and our prophet has been charged today. And, the prophet that has been sent unto you all shall speak about the Third Covenant and the Parousia. It is time," Awaki ended the session.

As he announced his leave, Miriam and Thomas thanked him in unison, "Thank you, Awaki."

Awaki responded, "Thank not me. Thank your God.

This ended her first personal session with Awaki on 3/2/96.

A major charge was placed on Miriam's life: Divine Prophecy. It required that she devote her time sacrificially to learning the new knowledge

God sent to the world. Her charge was to learn it and then teach it to the masses. Maintaining your daily worldly routine and then absorbing that knowledge, new knowledge, from God simultaneously, was a major challenge. It was tantamount to teaching yourself, and learning, the Bible. This was the greater challenge because it was totally new and never before heard of by people before.

Relationship

Her next encounter was 3/16/1996 when she brought her mother for a personal, private session, with Awaki. He spoke with Miriam before he talked with her Mother and gave her the option to stay or excuse herself.

He cautioned her not to be moved by what she heard from her mom if she stayed. But, first he spoke with her and Thomas about her progress with mastering the new knowledge she received, as a prophet.

"Come unto me," he called Miriam.

She exchanged seats with Thomas and sat directly in front of Awaki.

"You have been attempting to learn the teachings that you will need to know in the new knowledge. But, it has been difficult. Today I charge you both to submit yourselves unto each other that you may learn what you need to know. Is that within your understanding?"

"Yes, it is," they answered in unison.

He continued, "The preparation for the Parousia is ongoing and you have not time to waste. Are there any questions that you wish to ask?"

"I have a question. Do you want me to also take instructions from you at certain intervals? How should I work that?" Miriam asked.

"You are to speak unto your counterpart on things that he can explain and you are to come before this host that you may hear from your God on things that you cannot understand," he told her.

"Okay," she said.

"That is dependent upon your ability to understand the information that will be handed over to you. We will speak unto your mind and when you cannot understand the wisdom handed over to you, then you must come unto us. Is that within your understanding?"

"Yes it is," she said.

"I say unto you, since we last spoke, has not that which we spoke of come unto you? Has not your understanding of things changed?"

"Yes, it has very much," she admitted.

"Has not those that you wish to help been drawn unto you?"

"Yes, they have. May I ask another question?" she asked.

"Are not you a prophet of your God?" he asked her.

"Yes," she said.

"Then I must answer," he acknowledged.

"When you are speaking to me have I been paying attention or have I missed any of those opportunities where I need to be paying attention?"

"You are doing well," he reassured her. "We are pleased but you still must seek the wisdom that has been passed on to the other prophet before you. Once you have that wisdom then you will understand the balance that you must maintain."

"Okay," she said.

"Have not we made your life easier?" he asked her.

"Much easier, and thank you for that," she answered.

"That which you were concerned about, the physical sustenance, has been given unto you and it has been released. Have you not experienced these things?" he asked her.

"Yes, I have," she answered.

"This, we say unto you as we have said unto the prophet before you, that you may know, that this is of your God and not a phenomenon. Zimblach."

He told her and ended her time before him.

After he addressed Miriam's personal status and concerns he turned his attention to her mother and her concerns.

Again he invited Miriam to stay but cautioned her not to become upset at what she heard if she stayed.

"You may stay for you are a prophet of your God. You have concerns for those who are within your creative force and you have brought unto me another entity. Is that within your understanding?" he asked her.

"Yes, my mother is here today," she told him.

"And, what do you desire of us?" he asked,

"To speak to her," she said.

"Do you wish for us to answer all that she asks?"

"Yes," she answered.

"And, do you wish for us to address all that is within her soul?"

"Yes."

"Then, you must understand this. These things are done that they may understand. Do not feel any envy or discord or discomfort in what you may hear. Is that within your understanding?"

"Yes, it is," Miriam answered.

"For, you now transcend such things. Bring her unto me," he told her.

Her Mother exchanged seats with her and sat directly in front of Awaki.

As he questioned her it became apparent why he had cautioned and prepared Miriam for what she heard. Her Mother was rigidly focused on her other daughter and her child, the granddaughter. She did not make any mention of Miriam.

After he exhausted and answered all of the questions she brought up about her daughter and granddaughter, Awaki said to her.

"There is more voices. You are concerned about she who is our Prophet. Speak unto me."

"I'm not sure what I'm concerned about, Awaki, to be honest with you," she said.

"It is her gift and your understanding of her abilities for she has spoken unto you but still you do not understand her power. Do you wish for me to explain it unto you that you may understand?"

"Yes, please," she said.

"Throughout this time and space in this universe, your God has chosen those to speak all manner of wisdom unto man before a covenant, in the First Covenant it was the law of your God and He spoke unto Nahum and Elijah and Moses. There were many (Prophets), but you still, in this time and space, did not listen. So, then He sent unto you, Jah, and He spoke all manner of wisdom unto you, and still, His display was not enough.

"And, there will be a Third Covenant, and the beginning is the end and the end is the beginning. And, this is the time of the preparation for the 11 and 40, the Parousia, which is the third and final covenant, then your God will set all things in its proper place, not by His displays, and not by your choice, but by His power.

"And, she who is of you, our Prophet has been charged so that she may speak all manner of wisdom to those that she comes into her creative force, that they may hear the cry in the wilderness as Jah. Is this within your understanding?" he asked her.

She just said, "Yes."

That notwithstanding, Awaki explained more and talked more about Miriam.

"It is not a phenomenon and it is not difficult to understand for your God is true to His words and He has sent unto you, in this world, prophets, all over the universe. And, the message will be the same. This message is already being heard in this universe. All that hear will hear it. All who will not hear will not hear it. And when the time comes then they will draw their sword. Is that within your understanding?"

"Yes," she answered.

"The voices are no longer. Are you content with the answers? Is they your desire?"

"Yes," she said.

That was the sum total of all she had to say about Miriam. Awaki, gave her an opportunity to question him further.

"Speak unto me any other questions that you may wish to ask at this time for this host's body has been taxed."

"One more, Awaki, if I may. When closing my eyes I see…."

"The visions of the faces of the people," Awaki finished her statement.

Do you know what they are?" he asked her.

"No," she answered.

"They are those who await your soul for you have earned to pass unto your God and they watch you. Sometimes, when you pass through that point in your mind and you see the faces, do they not smile at you?" he explained and asked.

"Yes," she said.

"It is joy," he told her.

Her session ended.

She left and did not initiate a single question about Miriam from Awaki. That prior preparation by Awaki, for Miriam to observe that, was very necessary. She gave no indication that it affected her negatively in any way.

March 21, 1996, Miriam was before Awaki again. "Now have she, charged as our Prophet, come unto me."

Miriam exchanged seats with the other prophet and sat directly in Awaki's presence.

"We are pleased that you have not rejected our gift. Is this within your understanding?"

"Yes, it is," she said.

Awaki continued her instructions, "It is now in your charge to begin to study and learn the information departed unto our prophet that you may be equipped with the new knowledge that you may speak unto those, here and there, there and here. Is that within your understanding?"

"Yes, it is, we've begun that process this evening," she said.

"But unto he who has been charged with this host."

"I am here," Thomas answered him.

"Hold back not any information given unto you for it was given unto you that you may prepare. Is that within your understanding?" he instructed Thomas.

"It is," he answered.

Awaki continued speaking with Thomas on totally unrelated matters as he knew that Thomas understood that he meant he was to get moving with Miriam's instructions on the new knowledge without any further delay. She was a Prophet for near 3 weeks now and the knowledge had not been shared with her. It was difficult enough learn the new knowledge; having obstacles of any type in your path to that made it impossible to learn.

As the conversation turned to those other matters Miriam remained present and silent. Awaki described the upcoming changes that were to take place in the Host (Nathaniel) whose body he invaded, during a period of banishment he was to undergo.

"And, during the seven days we shall give unto him (Nathaniel) those things and he shall be like new unto you, and even unto they that are of him and unto those which he has come from. Even those that he communes with in spirituality will begin to move away from his truth. Only those that have been prepared. Do you know the essence of truth of your God? Speak unto me?" Awaki asked Thomas.

"I think, power?" he said.

Awaki instructed Miriam, "Speak unto me, our Prophet that sits before this host."

"The essence of God?" she asked.

"The essence of the truth of God," he clarified.

"My understanding, presently, is that it is clear and simple when I hear the truth," she answered.

That description was more in line with what he had taught them. He continued to question her.

"And, when the truth is brought to light by a host of this universe, then what is the penalty?"

"I don't understand. When the truth is brought to light?" she asked him.

"That is within your understanding," he answered her.

"There's a penalty?" she asked.

"What is that?" he asked her again.

"I don't understand. I am missing something," she said.

Thomas just sat in silent, unresponsive, similar confusion.

"The penalty for the truth of your God is alienation by the hosts of this universe," Awaki answered his own question for both of them.

"I understand," Miriam said.

Awaki spoke further, "This is the necessity for the strength that has been witnessed in this host for he can withstand such alienation, for he stands alone in all his doings. Is this not within the understanding of the prophets?"

"Yes," Thomas and Miriam both spoke in unison.

Awaki continued, "Did not your redeemer, Jah, stand alienation for the truth?"

"Yes," both said.

"Did not he who you call Moses give up all the riches that was due unto him and stand alienated because of the truth?" he asked.

"Yes," they answered.

"Have not, in your history in this time and space, all who have attempted to bring forth the truth of your God, been alienated?" he continued.

"Yes, I understand," both said.

Awaki said, "It is the penalty and that is the necessity for his spirit. Is that within your understanding?"

"Yes," they both said again.

That enlightenment regarding "truth" has been borne out countless times under different circumstances. The necessity for the production of this information for you is a classic example.

For the remainder of that evening Awaki turned his attention to Kristina another "entity," as he called us. He addressed her concerns. The prophets, were allowed to observe and learn. On occasion he included them in his teaching. He did not audibly identify, to whom he spoke, when he included them, he used their minds. This was difficult and confusing for them and had to be resolved.

"The one here tonight requests to have some guidance in her life," Miriam introduced Kristina Anderson to Awaki.

"I hear the voices of her mind and she too, as all, in this time and space under this, the second of three, one was conceived of all faith, obedience. Bring her unto me."

As Kristina moved to sit before the Host embodying Awaki, Thomas asked,

"What do you mean by, 'the second of three'?"

Awaki answered, "The Third Covenant."

"Thank you, I understand," Thomas said.

Awaki continued an in depth conversation with Kristina. He made a commitment to resolve her issues and asked if that was her wish.

But before he allowed her to answer he said, "And before you answer, I say unto the prophets, speak unto her that what I say, will come to be."

Thomas spoke first, "It is true."

Then Miriam spoke, "I believe it's true."

Awaki continued, "Our Prophet charged with this host, speak unto her that she may know."

Miriam started to speak. "Kristina..."

Awaki interrupted her.

"It is not within your understanding. Our Prophet charged with this host, speak unto her that she may understand for you know and have experienced."

Thomas answered when he understood it was he to whom Awaki spoke.

Afterwards Awaki continued teaching Kristina and said, "And, when you are confronted with these things that you speak of, these difficulties, these challenges, pray unto your God and listen for the bells. You are charged."

Miriam asked him, "Me or the other prophet?"

Awaki said to her and Thomas, "It is difficult for you two to be in the same room, is it not?"

In unison they said, "Yes."

"Then, when you are in our presence clear your mind and we shall speak unto it and you shall work in harmony as one, as we do. For when you are together, you are no longer two, you are one unto us, charged unto Infinite Mind, for we are you and you are us and we are unto Him," Awaki declared to them. "Is that within your understanding?"

Both said, "Yes, it is."

Awaki demonstrated. "Clear your mind. Stand with me. The prophet charged with this host, come unto me. Take the hand, take the hand. Take the hand of the prophet charged with this host into your hand. Take the hand of the host into your hand. Both of you take the hand of this host. The prophets, open your minds and come with me into the presence of your God. What do you see?"

"Light," Miriam responded.

"What do you hear?" he asked.

"Tone, a very subtle tone coming through the top of my head," Thomas responded.

"What do you feel?"

"Elevated," Thomas responded.

"Are you there before the light?"

"Yes," they both spoke in unison.

"Zimblach," Awaki said.

"Then, you are understanding. Was there confusion between you two in that display?" he asked them.

"None, no confusion," Miriam answered.

"Did you hear the voices as I asked the questions unto your minds?"

"Yes," both said at the same time.

"Then you knew who to answer and who not to answer. That was a display unto you two. This is how you become one in the presence of the Angels of your God. Let there be no confusion or discord."

"I understand," Miriam said.

The session continued with Kristina, uneventfully.

At the end of it, Awaki spoke to Miriam.

"And unto our prophet, get thee all knowledge and waste not any time. Study as you would your books to prepare for your sustenance, so must you study that you may prepare for your spiritual battles."

"I understand," she said.

He continued, "It is and will come to pass, all these things that I speak of. And, be not taken away with those who may attempt to deter you. And, come unto us when you feel the need, for we need to speak unto you that you may understand. This is the essence of your sacrifice. Is that within your understanding?"

"Yes, it is. I'm going to listen to the tapes the other prophet has given me and then I'd like to meet with you and learn more," she explained.

"You shall not be denied any, and all you ask of us, for do you know who you are?" he asked her.

"What did you just say, do I know who I am?" she asked.

"That is within your understanding," he answered.

"Yes," she said.

"Well then, begin to think as one. You are a prophet of your God. Allow no one to deter you from that knowledge. And, when you speak, speak with wisdom. Is that within your understanding?" Awaki admonished her.

"Yes, it is," she said.

"Zimblach," he said.

That meant that session was ended.

This session made clearer than any other the "relationship" or responsibility of the prophets to the knowledge. First it was not to be held back and second it was to be thoroughly and completely learned.

.

## Parousia & Mechanism

Within one week, 7 days after that encounter, Miriam was before Awaki again, with Thomas, for more instructions on March 28, 1996

That session began, as all others. Awaki, after his invasion, was embedded within Nathaniel's body. Thomas greeted him as usual and he responded to him.

"Speak unto me."

Thomas obeyed, "We're here this evening with Miriam and I, as we have been charged, to discuss the Parousia; to discuss what we do as prophets of the Infinite Mind. She has transcribed….."

Awaki interrupted him abruptly. "She has so pleased us as she has learned to hear, in her mind, our voices of direction and guidance. That which she has done is for the benefit of the mechanism in which we have sent unto you. You have not so informed her until this date. You are charged at this time."

Thomas had no option but to explain everything to Miriam as he was in Awaki's presence.

"As I've said to you, Miriam, we're writing a book, or I'm writing a book."

"That's the Mechanism?" she asked Thomas.

"Yes," he answered.

"Oh, I see, I thought that's what he was referring to," she said.

He continued, "It's specifically, or the focus of it is about Nathaniel and I and how we came into doing this work. I could show it to you on the computer; how far I've gotten. It's written from a perspective from my life and his life and then we lead into the teachings."

"An historical context that then leads into the here and now?" she asked.

"Yes," Thomas answered and continued. "And then also it will speak of political issues."

Awaki interrupted and corrected him immediately.

"We have spoken unto you. It is to be that which we have taught unto you, but it has to be veiled, and it is now of three and not of two."

"Very well," Thomas mused.

"Okay," Miriam agreed.

"Is that within your understanding?" Awaki asked them.

"It is and Miriam is the third," Thomas said.

"That is within your understanding, for she is that which will give sustenance to, and have those, in that they will reject to accept, for her sustenance is in that area and will create the bridge unto all. Is that within your understanding?" Awaki explained.

Miriam asked, "Are you referring to, Awaki, that I already speak before people and that I'll be able to somehow move it (the Book) out in that context?"

That's within your understanding," Awaki confirmed that she was correct.

"Okay I understand that," she said.

At that point Awaki gave them the exact manner in which the dissemination of their prophesying was to be done. Not only was Miriam charged to be a prophet, but through her, he gave them the mechanism by which they would introduce the new knowledge to the world.

The vehicle through which she earned a living, speaking, as a psychotherapist, to audiences in venues arranged by her Manager, Lincoln Downs, was the mechanism. She paid him and she was paid for her speaking engagements. All was arranged. Now all they had to do was produce the "Mechanism," the Book, and begin prophesying about the Third Covenant. The book was the reason for them to be engaged by people. He also fore warned them that they would encounter rejection from the Manager.

Not to belabor the point but that was the crux of why The Angels came and how it was to work. Thomas' and Miriam's birth and charge as prophets, their charge to write books from transcribed notes of all the sessions, and their understanding that through those means they would make a living and alert the world, was all made crystal clear. The only thing left for them, was to get busy carrying out everything.

Prophesying

The day dawned, May 15, 1996, two months later, when she was before Awaki again. This time the encounter was different. The Host Nathaniel was present but he had not been invaded by Awaki. Miriam noted that Awaki's "Countenance" had settled over Nathaniel's face with which Awaki agreed.

He told her, "My energy is not within this Host but is in your presence."

Her behavior during that session was markedly different from any prior session. She was overcome with uncontrollable laughter throughout that entire 40-45 minute encounter, as she sat bathed in pure angelic energy.

She burst into a fit of laughter and Thomas attempted to keep things on track as he spoke to Awaki.

"You were asking Miriam why she desires the gift of healing."

Miriam regained her composure and Awaki told her, "Speak unto me."

"Yes, I'd like to keep myself healthy as well as offer it to others; to use it on behalf of others," she said.

"That which we have in store for you will not lend unto yourself the ability to heal," he told her.

"I see. I understand," she said.

Awaki explained to both prophets, in minute details, the mechanism for prophesying. Her time was to be spent learning the new knowledge and writing a book. She understood and they moved on to another area of interest.

"May we talk about the elium lords?" Thomas asked Awaki.

"We will, but I will talk unto she who has been charged," he said. "Do not occupy your thoughts with those who seek your destruction. Occupy your thoughts with He who has created life. Ask the question?" he told Miriam.

"Anybody in particular that I've been occupying my thoughts with that I shouldn't be?" she asked him.

"Those which our prophet has just asked us about," he said.

"I understand," she responded.

He continued to speak to her.

"Be not concerned with who, how and what they came to be, for when you preoccupy yourself with these things then they take you from the thoughts of God. Only be concerned about His existence and your duties, as you will be charged."

"Okay," she said and continued, "I have been in a lot of battles recently with my thoughts being occupied with them, so I understand."

"But that you may know, their obedience as Angels, that which you refer to, do you want to know why they were cast down? Then ask." Awaki told her.

We all wanted to know that.

"Well, first we wanted to know," she said, "Angels have no free will, right?"

Awaki answered, "Do 'we' want to know or do you need to know?"

She continued, "Well, Thomas and I were wondering."

"He knows," Awaki corrected her.

She said, "Okay, let me take it to the next step: then, if they have no free will, how did they rebel?"

"They are angels of power. They were sent unto this universe to prepare and teach the keepers of this planet, to take care of it, and in their separation from their God, they became gods over man and did not desire to be subservient to a higher power," Awaki explained.

"But if they did not desire, wouldn't that presume that they had free will then?" she asked.

"They do not. For, they will suffer certain destruction, as we have spoke unto you," he assured her.

"The question also is, how did they first have the ability to no longer stand in the presence of God? How could they make that choice?" Thomas asked.

"When they came unto this place, they were separated from the Divine power and in their weakness and in their existence, as you exist, so they chose, like you choose. But they were given and taken from this universe and there they shall be," Awaki told them.

Miriam continued, "Where will they go when they're cast out?"

"They will be destroyed," Awaki said.

"And all those who go with them?" she asked.

"Will be destroyed," he said.

"And will no longer exist?" Thomas asked.

"No existence at all?" Miriam asked.

"That is within your understanding. We have said that the misuse of a Divine gift, and we have said that we must do the ends of our God. For, if we do not we are most certainly destroyed. They will be destroyed," Awaki explained.

"Was there any kind of rehabilitation program much earlier for them?" Miriam asked.

Thomas burst out laughing.

"Did I ask the wrong question or something?" she asked.

Thomas answered her, "That's not what I am laughing at."

Awaki said, "This is not within my understanding."

"That's what I laughed at," Thomas said and continued to laugh. "When we speak of a rehabilitation program we speak of an intense program to get a being to change their outlook, their choices, their needs. Rehabilitation for the use of drugs, for the use of alcohol, what is causing destruction unto others or unto self," he explained for Awaki.

"They had not the gift of choice so they had not the gift of repentance," Awaki told them.

"See now, that's what is confusing me because if they had not the gift of choice then how could they first turn away from God?" Thomas asked.

"We did not say that they could not choose but it was not their gift," Awaki explained.

"Ahh, okay," Thomas interrupted him.

"In order to have a gift of choice there must be the acceptance of repentance," Awaki said.

"I understand, they are not allowed to choose but they decided to choose anyway," Thomas said.

"You were both speaking at the same time," Miriam remarked.

"I am sorry Awaki," Thomas apologized.

"Speak unto her," he told Thomas.

"It's not that they can't choose. They can. It's that they may not choose. They were not allowed to choose. We were given the gift of choice or we are allowed to choose. We are told by God that we are allowed not to choose him. They were not told that. They were created and told that the only reason that they existed…"

"Ohhhh, right, okay. Right… But they have the power and the…." Miriam interrupted, and spoke simultaneously with Thomas.

"… is to do the will of God although they had the ability not to choose. They have the power but they don't have the permission not to choose," he finished his remarks.

"And when they do not choose the ends of their God, unlike you who are given repentance, they are destroyed," Awaki reiterated.

"But, but then, at the final judgment those who follow them will be destroyed as well," Miriam remarked

"That is within your understanding," Awaki agreed.

"That answers that question. What was the next one we had on there, Thomas?" Miriam, laughing again, said.

"We were talking about the purpose of humankind in the context of why humankind was collectively created and why humankind was created with the uniqueness that we have…"

Miriam interrupted Thomas with another burst of laughter.

"…with the sexes, with our sexuality, because we know that Angels are not created with the same kind of sexuality, the same kind of male – female energy. And, we know the simple answers……"

"Do you know why you were created?" Awaki also interrupted him and asked them both.

"To please God because God needs us," Thomas responded.

"That is not within your understanding." Awaki corrected him.

"Explain it to us please," Thomas asked him.

"It was to take care of His creation," Awaki told them.

"Uh huh. Okay," Thomas replied.

"Do you know…" Awaki began and was interrupted by Miriam.

"You mean earth and all that?" she asked Awaki.

"That is within your understanding," he answered her.

"We are caretakers?" she asked.

"Do you know why Lucifer argued with God?" he asked.

"No," Thomas said. "I mean I know the simple catechism answers……"

Awaki stopped him and answered his own question.

"He desired to enslave all who were in all universes to serve the gods and the angels."

"Instead of the one God?" Miriam asked. "And, was he positioning himself as the top dog, or top god or whatever?"

"It was he, who had all power except the power to create, and he wanted to enslave the creation to serve gods and the angels but your God, Infinite Mind, the all- powerful, said that this will not be for they will be free," Awaki explained to both of them.

Miriam asked Awaki another question, more calm and in her usual manner.

"Awaki, is the book, Urantia, a factual account of the universe?"

"Speak unto me not of man's foolishness," he answered her.

Thomas asked a follow up question to Miriam's.

"Is it inspired?"

"That is not within your understanding" he told Thomas.

Both then knew the answer to be, no.

"Okay, that is what I wanted to know," Miriam responded.

Thomas went back to his unanswered question from earlier.

"How does the role of human sexuality play in our role as caretakers of God's creation?" he asked.

"That is not your question," Awaki said, "Your question is, 'how do men and women act and exist with each other?' And the question is not yours but yours," he told Miriam.

"This has been a lifelong burning question of mine: what is the difference?" Miriam asked, after she composed herself again.

"What was created by your God first?" Awaki asked.

"Are you asking me?" she responded.

"That is within your understanding," he said.

"Well it says man was."

"That is not within your understanding," Awaki said.

She attempted again, "Well, before man, the heavens and earth were created."

"Then what was created?" he continued.

"I don't remember. Was it light and then…." Miriam was stumped.

Thomas interrupted to help her answer, "The separation of light from darkness…then the earth…"

"That is within your understanding… from the waters… and then what else?" Awaki agreed and asked.

Thomas continued, "The animals that dwell on earth."

"And then man was created to have dominion over them." Awaki completed it.

Thomas added an after-thought, "The birds came before the four legged animals."

Awaki questioned them both, "And then man was created in the image of your God. And where was woman created?"

"In the image of man," Miriam answered.

"That is not within your understanding," Awaki disagreed with her.

"But, I don't quite understand if that is literal or figurative," she said.

233

"It is correct," Awaki assured her.

"It's literal?" Miriam questioned him.

"That is within your understanding," Awaki assured her again.

"Scriptures say that man was lonely in the garden therefore a woman was created," Thomas said.

"A woman was created from the existence of God's creation of His image," Awaki told him.

"But why?" Thomas asked.

"Because your God understood that if there were going to be those to take care of this universe, should He create all in His likeness or should He create those who will give unto Him generations to set forth that which will be prophesied?"

That response from Awaki dispatched, indisputably, man's "foolishness" and confusion of God being a female, a her, a she, or a woman. Woman was NOT created in His image. However it just prompted more questions from those present.

"Why could not men create the generations by themselves without women? Without giving them sex?" Thomas asked.

"Are men Gods?" Awaki asked him.

Miriam broke into raucous laughter again.

"No, that's not what I'm asking," Thomas said in defense of his question.

"He wants to know why weren't they created androgynous, self-fulfilling, being able to procreate?" Miriam stepped in to help him out, this time.

Thomas mumbled something and Miriam asked him, "What did you say?"

He then spoke aloud, "He's saying that women occupy a very, very special and unique place, then."

Awaki replied, "If you were given the ability to create all out of one then you will become as Gods."

"Are you saying women… that women keep them from getting out of hand?" Miriam asked.

Thomas sniggled and laughed.

Miriam continued, "I mean keep them balanced?"

"That is not within my understanding," Awaki told her.

He had no idea of what she spoke.

"Okay. Maybe I have the wrong idea. What I'm asking is – it sounded almost like you were saying that women have the role of keeping them from…."

Awaki interrupted her before she could clarify her thought for him and said, "If your question is, it is a question of submission unto their God and humbleness unto the woman, in your God's Infinite Mind, it takes you and you to create one, but He, who is one, can create many."

"I understand. So it's not a matter of men being over women or women being over men. That's a cultural thing," Miriam concluded.

"All are submissive to He who has created," Awaki reemphasized that again.

"Okay," she said.

"And man cannot create alone, they can only create with the cooperation of women, therefore, to recognize and acknowledge that, that creative power is beyond men," Thomas summed up Awaki's answer.

"That is within your understanding," Awaki agreed.

Miriam had another unusual and totally out of character, fit of laughter. This revelation from Awaki wiped out global confusion and misunderstanding of the status of male and female in this universe. There was no hierarchal difference in the creation of both by God.

Woman is not submissive to man. Man is not submissive to woman. Both are submissive to God, period. Man and Woman were both created to be caretakers of God's creations here on earth. Woman was created to bare other human beings for the purpose of being caretakers of God's creation. Man could not be allowed to serve that role as he then would have to be God. Creation of human beings by 1 can only be done by God. Creation of human beings by human beings requires 2: man and woman.

The distinction is just that simple. The sole reason for the differentiation is just that simple. All else is foolishness of man, as Awaki would describe it. It is "cultural" foolishness of man as Miriam described it.

"May I speak about meditations and meditations I've been having because I've detected a distinct change? Thomas sought to change the subject.

"She who has been charged has many questions, many voices. More noises than voices," Awaki responded and chose instead to focus on Miriam.

She spoke up.

"Where to start? More noises than voices?" She asked.

"You have a question about self – discipline," Awaki helped her focus her thoughts.

"Yeah, yeah," she said.

He continued, "You are struggling with that issue as well as the issue of accepting men in their roles as God has intended."

"That's true," she admitted.

"Then I'll answer your questions. That is why your relationships are difficult and confusing. Separate the physical from the spiritual and the obvious from the seen," he told her.

"'The obvious from the seen.' You're saying I allow them to become merged and that's when I get out of balance, the physical and the spiritual," she reiterated.

"That is within your understanding," he agreed.

"That's what you...was spoken unto my mind, too. How can I keep from being such a fool from now on?" She asked him outright.

"Not that you are a fool for they sincerely love, but you deter that love," he said, to her surprise.

"How do I do that?" she asked.

That was difficult to hear. Who wants to hear "you stop people, who love you, from loving you"? Nobody.

"With your insistence upon your own superiority," he answered her.

"My superiority! I'm just trying not to be placed in a position of inferiority. I didn't know I was acting superior," she said.

"When you fight to get out of a place, you become emotional but if you stop and consider that place, you may find an open door," he said.

He described what was happening with her in her relationships with men.

"I see. I've been acting out of emotions and past fears," she conceded.

"That's within your understanding," he agreed with her.

"And, I can do this through the use of my own will?" she asked.

"Your will is your God's will. Are you not a prophet of God?" He asked her.

"Yes," she acknowledged.

"Then you have no will," he told her.

"I see what you are saying, because I have asked God to please shave off these personality flaws of mine. I know they exist."

"We have been placing you in positions of discipline," he told her.

"Yes, you certainly have," she replied.

"And it is beyond that which you even conceive," he disclosed.

"You mean I am not aware of all the positions that you've been putting me in?" she asked.

"Your family has been used," he said.

"Yes, my father," she said.

"That is within your understanding," he confirmed she was right.

"Uh huh." She said, and then asked him, "Do you have any advice for me on how to continue doing this?"

"It is when you begin to lose your discipline, stop, and recognize that you are stepping outside of the spiritual into the physical and pull yourself back into the spiritual, and humble your spirit unto your physical existence," he instructed her.

"I see," she said.

"What were you saying before about saving souls?" she moved on to another area.

He answered, "It is not time."

"Okay," she said. "Because I don't understand that."

"Ask the question," he invited her.

"Well, I was just going to ask. If I stop my superiority with men will I have someone in my life?" she responded

"If you so desire," he said.

"I do."

"Then learn to humble yourself," he told her.

"Okay," she said.

What else could she say? An Angel of God reaming you out about your behavior of "superiority"? Not good. To add insult to injury you were just made a prophet of God, no more humble being exist on the planet than prophets, it's thought. Reconciling physical superiority with spirituality and prophetic humility was a tall order for this newly minted prophet. An unlearned prophet with reams of new information to digest from others not very forthcoming with that new knowledge. Her tasks in life were daunting.

Do you know why this host (Nathaniel) had the problems that he did with his….she who is with him?" Awaki asked her. (He never used the term "wife")

"His wife?" she asked.

"That is within your understanding."

He admitted that's who he meant but he did not use the word.

"It is because she battled with that which you struggle with now and could not understand who or what he was, is, and have become, and struggled to keep a position of equality when she should have submitted unto her God's will. But you are chosen by your God and the last thing that you must do is place yourself above anyone."

She responded, "I didn't know I was doing it. My history….."

He interrupted her immediately, "You did but you chose not to hear that which was spoken unto you."

"Hmmm, so I've created my isolation then," she said.

"That is within your understanding," he agreed with her.

"This was also true of she who was given the gift of healing and now she was given that which she desired for her faith. You are charged," he told Thomas.

"You mean Shirley. Is that correct?" Thomas asked.

"That is within your understanding. Speak unto her," Awaki responded. Thomas obeyed.

"That's why Shirley found Ashwan in such a short period of time because she wrestled with the whole issue of submission and once she submitted then it just flowed. I was not at her wedding but I see like a beaming, a kind of happiness in her soul. But it is very deep. I mean it is way down in her."

"Oh yes she is deliriously happy," Miriam agreed with Thomas.

Shirley was a friend of hers, recently married, whom she knew well.

"Well, the only thing I need to do to submit….. I don't know if I know how. I always had to fight just to stay alive in this emotional world we're in. I really want to get there, you know what I'm saying, I'm not sure how though."

Awaki continued the story of her friend Shirley.

"When she came unto this host she was alone and unhappy and did not know where she would be and we spoke unto her and said, 'if your faith is in your God, then ask and we will deliver unto you,' and she did. And, unto what you would seem to be a culture of submission," he told her.

"You mean his culture? He's Egyptian," she said.

"Explain unto the host." Awaki told Thomas.

"Ashwan is Egyptian. He's from a culture where women are quote, unquote inferior. They have different roles. Inferior really isn't the word."

"They are very submissive though," Miriam said.

She turned back to Awaki.

"So Awaki, if I just ask God to teach me or show me how to do this it'll... what will happen?"

Both she and Thomas laughed out loud.

Awaki answered her, "First you must make the choice."

"What choice is that?" she asked.

"That, in your faith, you will be humble unto service," he answered.

"Okay," She said.

"Is that your desire?" Awaki asked her.

"Yes, I choose to be humble in service."

Miriam said and Thomas burst out in laughter.

"Stop laughing," she said.

"Miriam, because you're choosing so fast before you know all of the ramifications," Thomas said.

"Well, I don't want to be feeling superior to anybody. I just want to do the will of God. That's what I've always wanted. But, maybe you want to explain that to me now that Thomas has me upset," she told Awaki.

Laughing still, Thomas said, "I didn't mean to make you so upset."

"Then ask unto your God for that which you desire in your faith." Awaki instructed her.

"Father, I just want to do your will as your humble servant, and I don't know how else to ask than that. I don't want to place myself above anyone. Please help me," she prayed.

"Ask unto your God, that which you desire," Awaki repeated his instructions to her.

"I just did. You mean not to be alone anymore?" she asked Awaki.

"That is within your understanding," he agreed with her.

"Father and I really would appreciate it if you could send me a companion, someone who is of you, and please let me know any time I'm acting superior and I'll stop it," she added.

"And, the only qualification needed is that he is of your God?" Awaki asked her.

"Well, I don't have a race problem…." she started to explain and Awaki interrupted her.

"That is not within your understanding. You look for those who are intellectually your equal," he reminded her.

"Oh I see what you are saying," she said.

He continued, "But you fail to understand that your intellect has nothing to do with that which man has taught you and those who have not the qualifications of man, are not intellectually inferior. Is that within your understanding?"

"Right. Yes, that even if they don't have all these degrees, they're not inferior," she acknowledged.

"That is within your understanding. Then, is this your desire?" he asked her again.

"To have a companion sent to me? Who ….who, something tells me….. Yes, I do want to have a companion sent to me who is of God. Is there something else you need to tell me?" she hesitated.

"Then ask," Awaki said.

"What else do I need to know?" she asked him.

"Then ask of your God," he told her.

She started again.

"Father I am asking for…why do I feel hesitant here?"

"Do you need for me to explain or do you know already?" Awaki asked her.

"I think I know," she said. "You don't need to explain. Can I talk about it with you privately sometime?"

"Do you want me to leave?" Thomas asked.

Awaki answered him, "It is not within her understanding and it is not time."

Awaki left her in that quandary and moved on to another issue.

"The Mechanism that you two are charged, ask the question," he told them.

Thomas responded. "You're speaking of the Mechanism, in that respect, I was asking….."

Awaki interrupted him, as he often did without letting him finish his thought.

"Your question that you have asked is why you battle with your human emotions even though you understand that all things must work to the ends of your God." He told Thomas.

"Yes," Thomas said.

He seemed happy that Awaki had read his mind this time.

"Be not dismayed or concerned or discontented because we have directed certain things unto she who has been charged. It is to be because she has an understanding of how things are to be organized," Awaki allayed his concerns with a reference of Miriam.

"I understand," Thomas said.

"Are you speaking of the Mechanism?" Miriam asked.

"That is within your understanding. But, both will be of you and you. Let these be used to launch that which you will do as sustenance," Awaki answered her.

This was the first time that he told them both that they each would write a book in collaboration and these books would be the source of their income. The writing would replace their jobs at that time.

"So, you're saying that our names should be on that one; the one you (Thomas) are writing and the one that I'm writing?" she asked them both.

"That is within your understanding," Awaki confirmed that for her.

"Ask the question," he said.

Miriam realized it was she, to whom he spoke.

"Well you said… well I'm unsettled about the discussion we just had. I obviously don't understand something about this man issue with me and…."

Awaki interrupted her, "There was a road…."

"A what? A road?" Miriam interrupted and asked him.

"That's within your understanding," he answered and continued.

"And you have walked on and you have been bitten and stung and devoured upon that road and now you are at a road and there are two, and one is for you and you have walked and mastered that road, and the other is unknown and if you go down that road, you are not sure if you can master or will you be bitten and stung and devoured as before," he described for her.

"So. The only thing keeping me from asking God for a companion is my fear from the past, is that it?" she asked him.

"That is within your understanding," he confirmed.

"Okay. Then, Father I ask for a companion, even though it freaks me out to do so," she prayed.

"You are not in true faith," Awaki told her.

"Well, I look at it this way, God is the only one I can trust to set me up with the right person," she explained to him.

"Then you must believe it to be so and trust and have faith and be obedient," he told her.

"Have I been disobedient in this way?" she asked immediately.

"That is not within your understanding," he told her.

"Okay," she said, "You mean live the life and be submissive to God."

"That is within your understanding," he confirmed again.

"Have faith in the possibility of all things being possible," he said.

"I understand then," she said.

"Awaki, as I prepare to move down here, do you have any advice for my family that I am about to leave, that I should do to help them before I go?" she asked him.

"It is only your choice," he answered her.

"Okay," she said.

She moved on to another issue that was troubling her.

"The sessions that I do right now, the DNA clearings, is that going to be part of my work, or am I just to focus on the Mechanism?" she asked him.

"It is your choice," he answered her.

Again he gave the responsibility for making her own life's choices solely to her. Free will was hers. Subjecting that to anyone other than herself, diminished her, as he had told her before, even if it were he.

"Are they effectively helping people?" she asked.

"That is within your understanding," he told her. "Do you understand why?"

"Because I call on God?" she answered.

"Before you were charged, you were practicing the foolishness of men, but once you were touched then that which you did symbolically, became your reality," he explained. "Ask the question."

"I don't think I have a question," she responded.

"The question you wish to know is, 'Will I come unto you in this host and others in this manner'?" he asked it for her.

"Oh, yes, we did have that question. I forgot about that one," she said.

He repeated, "Ask the question."

Thomas spoke up. "The question is if you will continue to come to us in this way, because I'm assuming that the way that it was done before is no longer necessary--- the way that you invaded Nathaniel's body---that that's no longer necessary."

Awaki repeated, "Ask the question."

"Will you come through me?" Miriam finally asked.

"Or others," Awaki completed it.

"Or Thomas or anyone else?" she added.

"I say unto you this: Jah came upon this earth with a display of obedience and He called unto Him those who were chosen by His God to follow Him, and they did so. He taught unto them the knowledge and when they put His physical to death, so rose His spirit of life and He appeared unto them and gave unto them a spirit to heal and to perform all manners of what you will call phenomena.

"And, then He said, 'Go forth and do unto others.' He had to fulfill His destiny as each of those who were prepared had to fulfill theirs. You and he and he are at that point where you must now fulfill your destinies. For we have spoke unto this host and this is why he and Shakardak are now one. You have the knowledge. You are sent forth to bring souls unto this knowledge that they may choose, that in 11 and 40 they will have known and their lives will have been touched."

"So, you're saying this is the last time we will speak – like this?" she asked.

"That is within your understanding," Awaki confirmed. "When then Jah ascended He said unto them, 'I see unto my return.'"

"He said what? I'll what? I didn't hear you," she asked.

"I'll see unto my return," he repeated.

"See unto my return? Okay," she said.

"So, thus must you and he and he until His return," Awaki finished.

Miriam asked, "And, you will communicate unto our minds until that time?"

"Have not we already speak unto your mind?" he answered.

"Yes, but sometimes when I get emotional, I, I.. it gets confusing," she stammered.

"Then stop making excuses for your lack of discipline and come into who you are." Awaki chided her. "This is why we have instructed our prophet to give unto you all things that you may know. Be not concerned for we will take care of that which you need. Ask the question."

"May I speak of the meditations that I alluded to earlier because I came to a distinct point when I was feeling energy, when I was feeling Grace, I didn't quite know," Thomas spoke.

"It is within your understanding. It was Jah in your presence and you both were in the presence of your Creator," Awaki confirmed, Jesus visited him in his meditation.

"Very well. And thank you," Thomas said.

"When was that Thomas?" Miriam asked.

"During the last week," he answered.

Awaki continued, "There was also another. There was he who speaks unto you."

Thomas asked, "You, Awaki?"

"That is not within your understanding."

"Shakardak, Nathaniel?" Thomas continued to guess at the answer.

"I have and Shakardak, have never had physical form. It was he who you are alike, that ascended," Awaki told him.

"Elijah?" Thomas asked.

"That is within your understanding." Awaki confirmed.

"That's interesting," Thomas mused.

"Awaki, what am I know as?" Miriam asked Awaki as she listened to that exchange.

"That is not within my understanding," he told her.

He did not know what she meant by the question.

"Well, I go by Miriam in this life but that's not my real name," she explained.

"And, what would you have your name to be?" he asked her.

"I don't know, do I have one?" she replied.

"Have you had past lives?" he asked her.

"On this plane, according to the new knowledge, no. Perhaps on another. Is this my first existence?" she asked.

"You are and have been Adia," he told her. "This was revealed unto you before," he said.

"A what?" she asked.

"Adia," Thomas answered her.

"What's Adia?" she asked. "I don't even know what that is," she said.

"Aida is the person they talked of before," Thomas reminded her.

"Oh that," she remembered. "I thought you were saying something else."

"Is that within your understanding?" Awaki asked her.

"Yes. I thought on another level I was known as something else. I was just curious," she answered.

"What did you mean in the past when you said that at the appropriate time you would reveal yourself unto me and unto Miriam I suppose, too?" Thomas asked Awaki.

"It was at the end of the transformation," Awaki responded.

"My transformation or Nathaniel's transformation?" Thomas asked.

"The transformation of the host (Nathaniel)," he answered.

"Okay," Thomas replied.

"You know in the teaching…we're ready to teach now then, while we work on the Mechanism," Miriam interjected.

"That is within your understanding," Awaki agreed with her.

"Okay. So we move on out with it then, Thomas, I guess, huh?" she said.

"Okay," Thomas replied.

"Your mind is clear (Miriam), yours is also (Thomas), but you both have concerns, personal, of relationships in this universe. It is your choice." Awaki told them both.

Miriam asked, "What's our choice? To talk about them now or go out and do something about them?"

"When these things are brought unto you then you must make the choice as did this host. Now, you must also know this, (to Thomas) that this host, that you look upon, is not your charge no longer. Is that within your understanding?" Awaki explained.

"Yes," Thomas answered.

"Do you know why?" Awaki asked him.

"Yes," Thomas said.

"And why is it?" Awaki asked.

"We call it graduation, it's been accomplished," Thomas said.

"He must fulfill his destiny," Miriam explained.

"Everything that was supposed to be done is done. I can teach him no longer," Thomas added.

"You were charged to keep him open and he was open. He got..." Awaki interrupted Miriam.

"That is simplistic understanding. But, you need not be charged with his openness or his knowledge for he is one with Shakardak," he told them.

"Is he going to be too high and mighty?" Thomas asked.

Miriam laughed at him.

"That is not within my understanding," Awaki said.

He had no idea what Thomas meant.

"He's asking if he's gonna...superior is what you're saying...?" Miriam explained.

"That he lose sight of his role in the presence of the Infinite Mind and lose a sense of humility and confuse self – righteousness with righteousness." Thomas explained more fully what he meant.

Miriam burst into laughter again.

"He can no longer do such a thing for he is Shakardak," Awaki assured them.

"Okay, okay, I understand. It's just that his energy and power can get to be so overwhelming. Just say it please," Thomas requested of Awaki.

"He is controlled by his desire to serve his God and humanity," Awaki reassured him.

"I understand," Frank said.

"Then you must know this; that all things will begin to reveal themselves in the time that has been predicted and revealed unto you. You are Prophets of your God and speak only of the things that have been given unto you. Is that within your understanding?" Awaki told them.

"Yes." they both said in unison.

Awaki continued, "As I spoke unto you, when you and this deliverer (Nathaniel) were leaving that which we prepared for him, as I speak unto you in this universe, and I shall say, I humble myself unto my God, For it is to be as He has so willed it to be, It is to come as He has so ordered it to come and it will resurrect that He has so blessed it to resurrect. And, we and I, and those are the agents of His deliverance and His power and His resurrection. Zimblach.

# Chapter Eight

## Self-Taught Divine Gift

<u>Calvin Styles</u>

The receipt of a Divine gift was one reason to have an "audience with" or to "sit in the presence of" God's Angels. If God gave you a Divine Gift before birth, you were awakened to that knowledge at that time. If you received a Divine gift from God, after birth, it was bestowed upon you, at that time. Other reasons, to be summoned, were not as clear cut as the receipt of Divine Gifts.

Gatherings were as small as 1 person, 2-3 people, or as large as 15-20 people. Each included the Prophet, the Host, the Angel, usually Awaki, and sometimes the owner of The Temple. Attendees visited one time or more. All were not called for a personal conversation with the Angels. That was determined solely by them, and unknown to the attendee, almost always.Therefore, at any time, one's presence could result in being called unto the Angels.

From a group session of about 15 people held on 2/18/1996, wherein Awaki chided the group for asking "foolishness" of him, he called forth a single individual.

"I hear a voice; this voice is confused and the confusion is his self-taught Divine Gifts. Come unto me. His true question is to know if these gifts were given unto him by us or if these gifts are simply the manifestations of training. Have him come unto me," Awaki directed the Prophet.

No one moved.

Louvinia, the owner, responded, "Suzanne, she's not here."

"He is in my presence. Be not afraid," Awaki said. It is he who travels through universes by his mind through his meditation. It is he who gives advice unto others by the touching of their flesh. It is he who smells the existence of planets. Come unto me," Awaki described and called the person again.

At that point Charles Smith stood-up, walked over, took the Prophet's seat and sat in Awaki's presence.

"Have him place his hands on the hands of this host," Awaki instructed.

Charles placed his hands atop the hands of the Spiritual Leader's (Nathaniel's).

Awaki spoke, "You have doubts of many things and you attempt to find your way to the Infinite Mind. You have looked into the eyes of this host and tell these entities what you saw. You have felt the vibration of the hands of this host. Tell what you have felt," he told Charles.

"Intense light; irrelative love," Charles responded.

"Now are these things you have just spoken unto these entities within your understanding?" Awaki asked.

Charles remained silent.

"Are they within your understanding?" Awaki asked him again.

"Yes," he said.

"Then, why do you doubt your ability? Are you not before me?"

"Yes," Charles answered.

"Have I not allowed you to see into the soul of this host?"

"You have," he answered.

"Then doubt not. Be not confused. Trust in your own gifts but misuse them not for selfish gain. Be not consumed with those who have passed on. Be only consumed with the ends of the Infinite Mind.

"Take the hands of this host into your hands. Talk unto the entities that are present and tell them what you feel and what you see. Speak unto them that they may know," Awaki instructed him.

Charles obeyed. He took the host's hands, and said, "I see energy around the heart chakra. There appears to be a face that's looking out from the heart chakra, into me."

"Do you know who that face is?" Awaki asked.

"No, I don't," he said.

"That is your face looking into your soul. When you meditate, bring forth that vision, and when that face turns from looking at you and looks out among those that are in your creative force, then, you will know that your faith will reward you.

"Find yourself for you are lost in deception, but you are gifted. Speak unto those in your creative force and be obedient to the voices you hear. Is that within your understanding?" he asked Charles.

"Yes it is. Thank you," Charles said.

That ended his personal encounter with Awaki.

Charles was a very private person but driven to avail himself to those who sought him out for spiritual consultation, regarding their life's journey. To that end, he even worked with a body of organized people through what was called "The Psychic Network" for some period of time.

He related stories of incidences wherein he was tested in his faith and obedience. Once he was sent clear across country to meet some unknown person, on a park bench, who was to help guide him in his spiritual development. In obedience he took the long trip. It panned out to be legitimate and there was someone, a stranger, who met him there on a park bench, who helped him to further develop his spirituality.

He was very giving of his time and gift to any who sought him out, without hesitation. He could see aspects of one's future and advise them of what he saw so that they could prepare themselves for the coming event, if need be. He elucidated confusing situations in people's lives and guided them with that clarity, to a more in depth understanding of the confusion.

He availed himself to questions regarding the transitioned departed, as well. He acted almost as a conduit to those who had transitioned. He was not given a Divine Gift but he was assured, by Awaki, that his self- taught gifts were of the Divine.

He was cautioned about the use of them, in the same manner as others were. Those to whom he conveyed Divine Gifts from God and those whom he awakened to their Divine gifts given them by God, from birth, were all the same --- "Do not misuse a Divine Gift, the only act not forgiven by God."

# Chapter Nine

## The Chosen One

Kristen Celester, DDS

Throughout the 6 months of visitations, those from all walks of life presented themselves before the Angels. Some came seeking a deeper spirituality, some came seeking a greater physical existence, and some came seeking a combination of both. Awaki knew whither, without their disclosing to him what it was that they sought.

"Come unto me and take the hands of this host into your hands," he told Kristen Celester a practicing Dentist, who had suffered tremendous personal loss. She obeyed him.

"I am in your soul. I see what you feel. Speak unto me," he told her, but continued. "There is confusion and pain. I say unto you now: your God has commanded me to speak unto you all manner of wisdom this day. That which you seek shall be answered and that which you desire shall be given unto you. That is said unto you that you may know that you are not before us to earn that which you already have. Ask the question," he told her.

"The question is about wanting to make some changes, wanting to go someplace different, wanting to make some changes. And it just seems very unclear to me what I am to do," she responded.

"Before you asked your question, what was it that I spoke unto you?" he asked her.

"You said that my desires would be granted," she answered.

"Your God has commanded me to answer all that you ask and that your desires have already been granted before His wisdom. For, He has seen your faith and He has seen your pain and so shall we now lift from you all that is not for you and give unto you all that you desire. All you need is to ask unto us this day and it shall be granted unto you. Yes, you are charged," he said.

Awaki charged his Prophet to make clear what he said to her.

"What it is that you want is a testament to your faith. All things that you want in your life will be given to you immediately," the Prophet told her.

"I want a life that is peaceful, free of fear, free of limits, full of love, of joy, whatever it is, however it looks," Kristen said.

"Do you understand these things come from obedience unto your God?" Awaki asked her.

"Yes," she said.

"And do you understand faith and its truth?" he asked

"I understand…" she began and paused.

"Speak unto me of your understanding," Awaki told her.

"Faith…it's just a knowing that things will be a certain way, even if it doesn't look that way," she answered.

"Now, that is not within your understanding," he disagreed with her. "But, when we speak unto you true faith, then shall you see that which you have not saw before. Faith is the possibility of all things being possible. Can you see a bacteria or virus with the naked eye?"

"No," she answered.

"But, do you know that it exists?" he asked.

"No, I don't know that it exists. I'm told that it exists, and I believe that it exists," she said.

"And when you use your devices to magnify that which you sought, then do you know that it exists?"

"Okay," she answered.

"Does that require faith to do that?"

"No," she said.

"But with your naked eye you cannot see its existence, but can verify that it does exist. That is what you have been taught of true faith and that is not. True faith is the possibility of all things being possible and when you look at a thing or a situation that comes upon you, spiritual or non-spiritual, you see beyond it. Can a man fly without wings?" he asked her.

"Not physically, no," she answered.

"And how may this be done?"

"I believe that we have another way of flying but it's not with our physical bodies," she explained.

"And, how may this be done?" he asked her again.

She didn't respond.

"It is with your device that goes here and there, there and here. Is that within your understanding? And, what is this device that soars in the skies? A man cannot fly except in your device created by a man."

"Oh, an airplane," she said.

"That is within your understanding," he said, "but that man created such a device asked unto himself when he saw those that your God had created with the ability to soar without a device, 'why can't we do such a thing?' He saw the possibility and his faith created the device. That is faith, when you see, do not see with the physical. See with the possibility of what can and could be, then set those things before yourself and we shall guide thee in thoughts and in your deeds, and it shall come to be."

"Seeing the possibility of all things being possible?" She asked.

"That is within your understanding," he answered.

"Yes," she said.

"In that, the Holy Scriptures that you read, when your scholars teach that faith can move mountains, is this a physical mountain or is this a spiritual mountain? That, even they cannot conceive. And, what is it unto you? Is it physically possible that you move a mountain that your God has created?"

"No," she said.

"That is within your understanding. Then, the mountain that they speak of is the burdens of this universe, the confinement of the physical over the spiritual. But, when the spiritual overshadows the physical, then there is nothing that can come upon you that you cannot find a possibility of deliverance or correction or victory in your faith. Be ye not conquered by that that exists in this time and space but be ye conqueror of all that you cannot see and they cannot hear, and they will look upon you and say, 'what manner of wisdom is this that she has?' It is only the possibilities. Is that within your understanding?"

"Yes," she said.

"Leave not this place in the same manner that you came. When you walk before a wall and you cannot pass through it, in the physical, what then can you do in faith? See the possibility. Step outside of your mind. How may you get through such a obstacle?"

"Obstacles?" she asked.

"This that I speak of, is simplistic, to show unto you how you will look at things that are mountains and burdens unto you in the physical. Stand before the wall. It is physical and it is unto you a giant and you cannot get around. How may you go through? See the possibility, step outside of yourself. This is the possibility. If not you can go around, cannot you fashion a hole and go through? Is that within your understanding?"

"Yes," she answered

"It does not require a phenomena," he told her, "but, the possibility. Do not allow the walls before you and behind you and here and there, to confine your faith. Look beyond the wall and see the possibility. It is that you must understand this, for do you know who you are? You have been chosen by your God. It is not by accident or coincidence, that you are before me and have had such a desire to talk unto the spirits of your God. Is that within your understanding?"

"Yes," she answered again.

"Again, your faith, step outside of the physical and see that which is before you in the possibility, and they shall confine you never again. A confinement of mind or body or soul. In all that you have asked, I say unto you, it is done. Zimblach."

"Are there any questions?" The Prophet, asked, as usual

Awaki echoed it for her, "Ask the question and I will answer unto thee. I am here for you. It is about that which troubles your emotions. It is your desire that the prophet and the spirit of this home leave that you may dwell and ask unto me these things," he said.

"Oh okay," she agreed.

As a result of her acceptance of his offer to remove everyone from his presence, except her, no record was made of her private conversation with him.

She sought spirituality, peace, joy, and irrelative love inclusive, at that encounter with Awaki a quarter- century ago. Subsequently, she has acknowledged that her "life" is her "spiritual life," which she works deliberately and diligently at attaining and maintaining. She met the challenges of seeing pass the physical and material world where lie the stress, the fear, the limits and the sense of separation from God, which she denounced.

She has since denied any separation and now knows a, "oneness with God" which defines her. She has made overt and concerted efforts to attain this existence. Among them, she described, are: daily physical expressions of gratitude and acknowledgement to God for all of His blessings, large and small, seen and unseen, that he has bestowed upon her---- and meditations of the sort that invoke the full presence and experience of God, spiritually and physically.

She too was among the majority, who were called to hear the Angels, whose lives were to aid in Armageddon through their just living and allowing their lives' impact upon people.

Her faith and her life's choices, as they impacted His people, lifted her to God's presence. Those around her, in her Creative Force, experienced an enhancement of their own spirituality and an enlargement of their own spiritual lives, as well. She brought God to their lives through the manner in which she lived and lives her own life. She was chosen by God for this and for this specific time.

# Chapter Ten

## Dual Divine Gifts

Luther Barnes

On a rare occasion the Angel Shakardak was sent by Awaki, the Spirit who controlled all angels, to engage an "entity," as they referred to us. One of those occasions was 3/16/1996.

"I am sent by the holy Awaki to speak unto you. My name is Shakardak." He introduced himself to Luther, a frequent attendee of the sessions.

"Please, God, why am I here?" Luther pleaded.

"First, you must know who I am," Shakardak told him.

"Who are you?" he asked.

"I am the Angel of War," he said. "I have been in many spiritual battles in your universe. I have been sent unto you because you are engaging in spiritual battles. Now, you are here in this time and space because you are strong in spirit. You have many misunderstandings of the teachings of men of this universe. You have taken on in truth what is right, but have not fulfilled your task, when you fight many spiritual battles and understand not the essence of them.

"I have been sent unto you to teach you how and when to fight spiritual battles. Is this what you wish to know?" Shakardak asked him.

"In part, yes," Luther answered. "Are you going to teach me as time progresses, from this time forward?"

"I have been charged to give you all that you seek in this time and space, by the Holy Awaki," Shakardak responded.

"I do seek truth and understanding and when I pray I'd like to add clarity," Luther said.

"Unlike the Holy awaki, I do not monitor thoughts of hosts of this universe. Is that for you to know?" Shakardak asked.

"Okay," Luther said.

"Before we deal with the stirrings of the soul, I must do what I have been charged to do," Shakardak said and continued. "Spiritual battles are fought with your sword, your sword being your mind. There have been times where you have been confronted with principles and theories of man, but did not go along with them, not because you knew with your mind it to be false, but because you knew in your spirit, it was not true. We speak unto your spirit. Just like this host who is before you, you take on all in truth to find the path to your God. Is that not your understanding?"

"Yes, that is correct," he agreed.

Shakardak continued to fulfill his charge with Luther.

"There is one principle fighting spiritual battles, and it is this: when you are confronted with a spiritual battle and you ask a simple question, listen for a complicated answer, for it is not your God's will that His knowledge and wisdom be not within your understanding. It is simplistic as faith. Faith, as taught unto this universe, is some great phenomena, but it is simply the belief in the possibilities in anything being possible. Is that your desire?"

"Yes," he replied.

"When you are faced with these battles concerning things that are in your soul, we have allowed you to know, that are not true, then draw your sword in the knowledge and understanding and ask a simple question unto he who confronts you, and the answer shall be simple. If not, it is not of us and is incorrect. For, it should not take man, who has true Divine wisdom many words to explain one thought. Listen, when they speak unto you," Shakardak instructed him.

"Okay," he agreed.

"It is I."

Awaki entered just that quickly – replacing Shakardak.

"I have sent unto you Shakardak. I am Awaki, the Angel of Spirits," he told Luther. "Shakardak was sent unto you to speak unto you of spiritual battles. For, your life has been intertwined in knowledge of truth, but you have not yet found direction and how to apply it. Is that within your understanding?"

"Yes, it is," Luther answered.

"Then I will instruct you," Awaki told him. "You have been in our presence many times and you have had many thoughts, but you have never come unto us for direction or wisdom. Is that within your understanding?"

"Give me some clarity is verbally asking for understanding?" Luther answered.

Awaki said, "You have been in this place, in our presence. Is that within your understanding?"

"Yes," he agreed.

"And you have not come unto us when you have had questions of spiritual battles in truth. Is that within your understanding?"

"Yes, it is."

"And we have not called unto you that you may come unto us for it had to be in your time and when you desired it and chose of us. The theories and philosophies that you have been battling with are of man's distortions and foolishness. For, you desire true light and understanding, and that is why you hesitated, and that is why we waited for you to come to us. Is that within your understanding?" Awaki explained to him.

"Yes, it is," he agreed.

"Speak unto me," he encouraged Luther.

"I would like to know if I will be granted the wisdom I was granted when I was in my early twenties and the abilities along with them? For I think I am ready for them again now."

"There was a man, and this man was set upon multitudes, but yet he had the faith of a child and the obedience of a bird. But, in his wisdom, he found destruction and confusion. Do you know who this man was?" Awaki responded to him.

"No, not offhand," Luther said.

"He was that you call Solomon. His wisdom was not wisdom. His wisdom was what, in this time and space, you may call common sense. In his ability to seek out the prophets of God, they spoke unto him all manner of wisdom as he accepted these things. Is that within your understanding?" Awaki explained and asked.

"Yes."

Awaki continued, "Your wisdom has not left you, for you have cast it away."

"How do I bring it back within myself?" Luther asked.

"You cast it away during your spiritual battles. You fight to find the truth and in doing so, you give away your common sense, your logic and reasoning in thinking things through. In this time and space, your wisdom then was not a phenomena, and your wisdom now will not be a phenomena.

"You were born with the gift of the oneness of mind, unlike others, we must give unto them. You were chosen and were given even before your birth, and because you take on spiritual battles, you lose that gift. Is that within your understanding?"

"Yes, somewhat yes."

"Ask the question," Awaki invited him.

"In my spiritual battles and making decisions and choices, I try ….how to differentiate truth from falsehoods. I have… sometimes that give away my wisdom I desire again, and with clarity. What am I going to do with it once I get it again in helping people and achieve the same goal?" Luther asked.

"Listen my son, today you can be resurrected before your God, for your soul is wandering. Your spirit seeks truth. Is it your desire?"

"Ye it is," he replied.

"Then it shall be given unto you, that that which you were born with will come unto you again. And you are to, when you leave this place, take on your battles in wisdom. Argue not with those that are foolish and unlearned. When Jah walked in this universe, do you know of any accounts where He argued with those who attempted to be above Him, or superior with him?"

"No," Luther answered.

"Do you know why?"

"No," he answered again.

"Because He had all knowledge and knew that they, in their ignorance and foolishness and unlearned state of mind, could not know the truth. So, in His humbleness, He gave way to their confusion. And, through His teaching, gave unto them the truth.

"You have the same power but it has been distorted and confused.

You have the power that when you open your mouth and speak unto others, that they will listen and learn and follow, but because you engage in discussions of unlearned and foolish things then it becomes a spiritual battle, unlearned," he told Luther.

"How am I to focus what I already know and bring it back into myself to use?" he asked Awaki.

"You have already done so by your choice to come unto us today," he informed him.

Satisfied with that explanation, Luther asked, "Why else have you brought me here?"

"For you have another gift given unto you from your birth that you have chosen to run from, that of multitude. You have the ability, and it was given unto you, to change minds of hosts, to bring them unto you, and that they may listen. But you choose to use that ability to deceive those that you wish to manipulate," Awaki answered him.

"Okay, I am willing to change and I am willing to change right now," he professed.

"Then you will understand. You speak of deception of hosts in this time and space who are portraying themselves as divine leaders of your God, and you yourself are such and run from your gift. If you take up your sword and choose of us and resurrect your soul, then it will be your goal, and you will be charged, that those that portray themselves to be of your God will not even stand in your presence, for we will elevate you above all.

"This host was given the same gift and has submitted himself wholly. You must do the same for we are and will elevate you as we are, and have, done him."

"Okay. Consider it done," Luther committed himself.

"Then, the things that you ask for unto people that you wish, will be given unto you. You continue to study about your God and to know all manner of things."

"Yes, I do."

"Then, make this a part of your life on a permanent basis, every day, every hour of your day. Read all manner of instruction on Jah and your God." Awaki instructed him.

"Okay."

"And you will find that those who will stand before you will then walk behind you. But, do not mislead or deceive them again."

Awaki admonished Luther for his past behavior with people and cautioned him not to repeat it. His gifts were to reappear and he was to act of God in his use of them; not use them to manipulate and use people for his personal purposes.

"I ask for your wisdom and your prudence to help me in that area, so that I do not go down that path again," Luther pleaded.

"You do not need our wisdom for God has given you His," Awaki assured him.

"Mess it up, straighten it up," Luther muttered.

"For even I must do your will if you so command me to," Awaki told him, "for your God has so commanded me to be at your, and all the Angels of the Spirits will be with you, and we will elevate you that you may speak the truth. Do not compromise."

"I look forward for our new relationship. Thank you," Luther responded.

"There will be those that will attempt to destroy you and say unto you all manner of things: that you are sick in the mind, that you have no direction, that you are easily swayed. But, you stand in the light and the truth, and you sit in the presence of the Angels of God. Compromise again not the truth. Allow no lie to pass through your lips because you are a vessel of your God and He is all truth. Is that within your understanding?" Awaki asked.

"Yes, most certainly," he answered.

"I hear no more voices in your mind. Then, you are clear," Awaki told him.

"Yes," he agreed.

"And, when you read all manner of scripture and all manner of writings, there will be no more confusion for we will send unto you revelation after revelation after revelation, that you may understand from the beginning to the end and from the end to the beginning," Awaki promised him.

"Should I indeed write this in a book?"

"It is, if it is your will, for it will be blessed and all that you have experienced up unto when you brought yourself before us," Awaki encouraged him.

"Who do I speak with about my health?"

"In these things concerning health, you will speak unto those we have charged," Awaki said.

"Have you…"

"Yes we have," Awaki spoke cutting him off. "Those we have charged with the gift to heal. Your health is in your control. There is only one thing in your physical body that we must control and that is your sword, your mind."

"Okay, there is an imbalance in my being that I wish to correct and bring into balance. How can I achieve that goal?"

"You must hear the bell, and when you hear the bells, stop. We must become part of your life. You must meditate on your God, not in your time, but all time. And, the changes, the re-engineering of your physical body, will become evident to you."

Then to the Prophet Awaki said, "You are charged to explain unto him."

He turned back to Luther, and continued.

"Be not concerned with health and our prophet will explain unto you. For, this host before you was very unhealthy. We re-engineered his body that we may see to his health and the same shall be done unto you should it be your desire."

"It is," Luther said.

"We do this as a gift unto you. For, we are not concerned with the physical body," Awaki told him.

"But I am because I'm living in it right now! So, how do I keep it healthy?" he asked Awaki.

"We understand this. That's why we will do these things until we take you from that physical unto the spiritual," Awaki explained.

He made it clear to Luther that they understood his need for that body to hold his spirit until Azreal came to claim it.

Satisfied with Awaki's explanations, Luther moved on to his other concerns.

"Okay. Concerning the future: what…."

"You want to know about the Parousia, what is to come." Awaki stopped him. "What is to come is spiritual battles that which you are now part of. In the Parousia, with the creation of your God, Jah shall reign and all that man has created shall be removed. Then, there shall be what you call 'heaven' in this place."

"So animals will no longer exist here, will return; plant life, will no longer exist here, will return; is that what you're saying?" Luther asked.

"All that your God has created will remain. Only that which man has created will be destroyed," Awaki repeated for him.

"Will this planet be a recreation planet for the universe?" he asked.

"There will be no such thing," Awaki said. "When this is to take place there will be universal awareness with all universes. You will be able to visit them and they will be able to visit you and all will live as one."

"Why was this the last planet to be lifted?" Luther asked.

"Do you want the answer that you know or do you want the answer that you think you know?" Awaki replied.

"I like the answer that I know better," Luther told him.

"Then, we have just said unto you, that you are gifted with the understanding. Then, this planet was just like you, turned from their God, put away their gifts."

"I think I understand, yes," Luther remarked.

"They got complacent is your word," Awaki continued to explain anyway, "and, they needed not their God. For even when He destroyed this planet, to start again, the hosts of this universe, who were given the gift of choice, returned back unto disobedience. In other universes, they did not do so for when their God showed them His power, they submitted themselves to His will and therefore they have surpassed you in technology, spirituality. They know you exist and they have been here but you cannot even get out of your own universe."

"This is true," Luther said.

"They have transcended beyond the flesh and beyond their superficial wisdom and submitted themselves as one unto one," Awaki continued to describe beings in other universes.

"Is it because of the will that we do not always obey?" Luther asked.

"All universes that was created by the Infinite Mind were given the same gift of choice," Awaki answered.

"What's the appeal?" Luther questioned Awaki.

"Because he who seeks to destroy you came here and you listened. For, when he went unto other universes, they turned from him, and you did not, even from the beginning," he answered him.

"So, what was the appeal? Why was it so seductive?" Luther asked again.

"It was lack of faith," Awaki answered. "Others were told the same that you were and in their fear and their faith, they submitted their minds and their wills, but this universe did not do so. For, you listened to he who had no form. He has been destroying you ever since.

"Your God attempted to break the cycle by destroying you and all that existed in this universe and still, you do not freely choose of Him. Your question is, why is this so? What makes us so, in your mind, disobedient? We cannot answer that for God created you, not us. It is beyond my wisdom why you do not seek to transcend these hosts. For, they are cumbersome and irritating.

"It is beyond my wisdom why you do not seek to master the languages and the sciences that you may understand all things in your universe. But you constantly choose not to, and to deceive others.

"So your God has to send unto you Jah, who was sent in the Second Covenant. Moses, with the law, in the first, and in the third, there will be the Parousia. And, there will be no fourth, for, all things will be set to His ends by Him because you are incapable of choosing."

"Okay. Could you explain the Parousia? What does it mean, the word?" Luther asked.

"You speak unto our Prophet for this host is weak," Awaki said from within the host's body. The Parousia is the thousand years that Jah will return again to set all things straight. This time, it will not be by His display, but by His power. Is that within your understanding?"

"Yes, it is," Luther answered.

"Do you understand what the display?" Awaki asked about Jesus.

"His showing up. His being who He is and His appearing before us," Luther explained.

"That is not within your understanding," Awaki disagreed and told him the display. "His existence was no phenomena. For, He was born of the hosts of this world. But, His obedience, from the time He was brought into existence to His death, was the display.

"We must be obedient to our God for we have no choice. Jah was flesh and spirit, as you, and He choice to be obedient unto His God, even unto His death to show unto the hosts of this universe, that you have the power and can choose unto your God. You do not have to choose otherwise. For, even in this flesh I have chosen to do the will of my Father.

"And, even unto my death I say unto my Father, forgive them for they know not what they do. And, then the display, that you can transcend this flesh, was again shown unto you by Jah when He returned in the flesh after the hosts of this universe had killed it. Is that within your understanding?"

"Yes," Luther admitted.

"Then, so be it. Zimblach."

Awaki ended the conversation and exited Nathaniel's body.

Awaki spoke to Luther, during this appearance, about an earlier time he had been in their presence on 2/4/1996. During that session Awaki read from Luther's mind as he sat in a group.

"The, I Am. . . I hear a voice and it is strong. He wants to know, 'I AM,' what does it mean and does He have a physical existence and has He ever had a physical existence. Is that your question?" Awaki asked the unknown person in the group.

No one answered so Thomas responded.

"I don't know to whom you're referring but can you answer the question anyway?" he asked Awaki.

"The question is The I AM, it is The Infinite Mind. He is I AM. A name given unto your universe by the Angels of God in defining His existence and, for a time in your universe, they have eluded even the scholars and spiritual leaders upon whom we have touched.

"The time was not then to reveal the I AM force and presence, but in 12 and 40, the Third Covenant will take and become an existence—The I AM is because He created Himself. The Infinite Mind stands outside time and directs all. He is the Creative Force. He is the creation of His own mind. He called Himself into existence. So, therefore, I AM and He was. And, then He called into existence all of the Universes, including the one in which you exist.

"Time, space, has no dominion for He is outside of these things. Then his question is, 'What are Angels?' 'How did they come to be?' Angels are creations of this universe. We are Spirits of The I AM brought into existence by His thoughts. Labelled by generations of hosts to represent what they wanted to understand. Angels, as you will have us to be, are Spirits, emanations of The Holy One's thoughts.

"We cannot choose like you were given. We only can carry out His ends. When He talks to us, then we obey. For disobedience, we are not forgiven. But, you have the gift given unto you by the Spirit of the Son Universe, who was sent here for that purpose. Is that within his understanding?" Awaki asked of the Prophet of the unknown questioner.

"The person who had those questions. . ." Thomas started to ask when he was interrupted by Luvinia.

"It was a 'him,' in their mind," she said.

Luther responded, "It wasn't me. It was a good question though."

Awaki responded, "I, in time, will identify he for him to know that this is and I AM.

The first thing Awaki did when he spoke with Luther on 3/16/1996 was remind him of that visit.

Luther, has the Divine Gifts of Multitude and Oneness of Mind. He exhibits, through the manner in which he lives his life, an obligation to cultivate the minds of all whom he encounters, into an acute awareness and acceptance of God, in their everyday existence regardless to how simple or complicated it may be. His walk in life has brought him to encounter the multitudes, from all walks, all ages, all nations and all nationalities, of life in this universe.

With each encounter he engages them to delve deeper into their thoughts of God and His immediate and intimate presence in their lives. This stirs their souls and opens them to the enlightenment he is driven to impart upon them, ultimately creating a more spiritually awakened body of the masses. He spends much time acquiring spiritual knowledge from all sources available to him, unrelentingly. This is his life's quest which he appears to have willingly and gleefully accepted.

# Chapter Eleven

## The Inaudible

Elaine Harrington

During the 6 months of visitations from Angels each visit was unique in its own way. This particular encounter with the entity, Elaine Harrington 3/7/1996, was unique from the standpoint of her inaudibility and the effect she had on the host who embodied Awaki, Nathaniel.

From the outset the recording device was unable to capture the sound of her voice. It was soft and almost whispered. Awaki never asked her to speak louder because he was able to read her mind.

"There is an entity here," Awaki announced to the Prophet at the start of the session. "She must not allow her emotions to overtake her spirit. Come unto me."

He summoned Elaine, the only person present for the session. She moved directly before him and sat in his presence.

"Take the hands of this host into yours," he instructed her.

She took Nathaniel's hands into her hands.

"I am about to enter your soul. Be not disturbed," Awaki told her. "Tell me what do you feel? Is not your mind now open to the possibilities? This that you see now before you is a superficial display of the powers of your God. This is your understanding.

"You now sit before what you call the Angels of your God. What you see before you, this host, is not a phenomena. The powers of your God are unconceivable by you. This is a display unto the hosts of this universe that we may teach and bring unto those who seek truth, before the Third Covenant, the 11 and 40, that they may come into obedience of your God in faith and all understanding, as in your history in this universe. Is that within you understanding?"

Elaine's response was inaudible to the recording device and the Prophet but not to the Angel.

He responded to it, "Then hear this. We are sent unto you to speak all manner of wisdom that you may know your direction unto your God. You come before us today seeking all these things and we shall fulfill all that you wish in this time and space. You seek a resurrection of your soul. So, we shall give unto you all knowledge that you seek. Speak unto me."

She spoke again but only he heard her.

"In this time and space," he said to her, "we have been commanded and charged with the preparation of the 11 and 40, what you may refer to as the Third Covenant. We have been sent unto those who have displayed an openness to receive and to help prepare the hosts of this universe in wisdom. For, unless you are in truth and wisdom and can choose of us or not of us, then you cannot be expected to do what is of your destiny for lack of understanding, for you are imperfect.

"This is why you have been chosen. You constantly search within your own soul for the truth and the guidance of your God that you may do all things that He may be glorified and that others may see in you what they may not see in their God. Is that within your understanding?"

She spoke inaudibly again.

He continued. "Today you have been summoned. We have spoke unto your mind. We have stirred your soul. You can be resurrected unto your God. All that you want, ask unto us, and we shall give unto you. Ask the question,"

Her voice wasn't captured.

"This is what I have just spoke of," he responded to her. "You attempt to live in such a manner unto your God that others may see in you what they cannot see in their God. You have been called unto us but understand that you have been given the gift of choice, and all that occupy this universe can choose of us or not of us. Is that within your understand?"

Sher was inaudible again.

"In these matters, concerning those in your creative force that you wish to influence and correct that which they have chosen, must be done, and you will be told how. This will accomplish the ends of your God. Is this your desire?"

"It is my desire," she said.

The device captured her voice

"Then, this is how." Awaki began to instruct her. "You, when you speak unto the hosts of this universe, speak in the knowledge that you have now seen before you today. Speak in the knowledge of obedience unto your God. Obedience is to choose His will. When you are placed in the valley of decisions, and those that are in your creative force are placed in the valley of decision, there are only two ways that you can choose. Think not of man's options and chicanery. It is of truth and light and righteousness which is all things of your God, or not of us, which is all things not of your God.

"Then you say, 'how can we achieve such things?' These things only achieve by the example which you are given in your generations. Through Jah it was obedient. Obedience in His will and doing His will. His will is that which saves all that they may choose of us. Disobedience, then you choose your own faith and fate. Is that within your understanding?"

Only he knew her response to which he said, "You cannot change the minds of the hosts of this universe in the manner in which you are now attempting. For, they look upon it as man's philosophies. You must now look at all things through faith. Do you understand what faith is?"

She did not speak.

"Speak unto me," he ordered her again.

"My faith…..," is all the device captured.

Awaki heard the entire thing and responded to her.

"Then, that is not within your understanding," he said. "That is a philosophy of your man. Listen unto me. Can you see a virus with your eyes, but do you know it exists? It does not need faith, even though you cannot see it. That is a simplistic understanding of man. Faith is the belief in all possibilities and that all things are possible. Is that within your understanding?"

She was not recorded.

"Is this your desire?" he asked in response. "Then, ask unto your God,"

She responded and it was not captured.

"Now, He hears and I have been commanded to say unto you, 'do you know what you ask?' You ask not for a safe place but you ask for a gift, a gift of multitude.' Do you understand what a gift of multitude?" he asked her.

Her answer was not heard.

"What you have been sent is to affect the lives of many. Many have been sent to you. You have been summoned unto us that you may achieve the knowledge that you may need, that you may not mislead the multitude. That is a gift in which you ask. In accepting this gift then all that you do, here or there or there or here will be blessed. It is not a matter of a building. It is only a matter of your faith. Is that within your understanding?"

She spoke inaudibly.

"That is within your understanding," he agreed with her. "And is this your desire?"

"Yes," she said.

"Then you must understand also that this gift that we give unto you today is a Divine gift given to you by your God. Is that within your understanding?"

An inaudible response from her was given.

"Then, you must not corrupt a Divine gift and you must not mislead the multitudes for your own glorification. In doing so, then you will be separated from your God and you will not be redeemed. Is that within your understanding?"

She was not heard.

"For, a gift from your God is not a sin to misuse. For, it is given unto those that He has chosen, so He needs not forgive, for you have been instructed."

There were dire consequences for misusing a Divine Gift. It meant eternal separation from God if you did, he told her; and all others who received Divine Gifts.

She responded too quietly to be heard.

"Is this still your desire? Is this still your desire for the Divine gift?"

Her response was inaudible.

"Then, it is done. Ask the question," he said after giving her the gift.

That response, too, was inaudible.

"Do not you sit before the Angels of God? And, have you been instructed to ask?" He questioned her.

She responded inaudibly.

"Then, it is done." he repeated.

Awaki spoke again. "Unto our prophet, it is time for we are causing damage to the respiratory system of this host."

And, he quickly exited Nathaniel's body.

*Nathaniel returned to his body coughing uncontrollably, barely able to breathe or speak.*

*"What was that all about?" he asked.*

The Prophet made a muffled remark and immediately began healing the host. He placed his right hand over the forehead of the host and his left on his back and spoke the words of God as he had been instructed by Awaki prior, when he gave him the ability to heal.

Shortly afterwards the coughing subsided, the host's breathing got better and he was back to normal, Awaki re-entered Nathaniel's body. He then explained what had happened and why he had to leave so abruptly.

"The energy transference from this host (Nathaniel) unto the second entity (Elaine) was too great for his physical body to stand. That which you know as his respiratory system was about to shut down. For you know, when we invade this host, all life functions in the physical body cease, as we have spoke unto you before. Is that within your understanding?"

"Yes," the prophet answered. "You said that he has no pulse, no heartbeat. You've also explained that he is safe and that he can (see) no harm and that you would see to that, and that I could fix anything that needs to be adjusted,"

"That is within your understanding," he agreed with the Prophet. "This entity, (Elaine) before I had to exit this host, wanted to know about he who is of her and he who has been sent unto her, was chosen for her. His wisdom was with him before he was in existence. Take unto you his guidance." He told her of her husband.

"Your children are blessed for you are blessed and all things that you need are blessed. You need only to ask of us and we are commanded to give unto you, by your God. Faith is the possibility of all things. Lend not yourself to fear anymore. For, it is a tool to destroy you by the elium lords. Is that within your understanding?"

We could not hear her response.

Awaki responded, "Zimblach."

271

After telling Elaine that her husband had been sent to her by them with wisdom from birth which she was to take as guidance he ended the conversation and exited Nathaniel again, for good, that session.

The irony of the manner in which Elaine's session went, was totally antithetical to who she really was: the inaudibility. She lived and continues to live a very audible life. She lives her life "Out loud." She was an Esthetician, an Entrepreneur, an Inspirational Speaker and a Life Coach. She's retired from some of those endeavors.

Even so, she's not as active currently, as at that time. She was very active in all of her endeavors then. God's empowerment of her with the Divine Gift of Multitudes embodied all of her proficient life's works. She had been positioned to impact lives locally, nationally and internationally, through the various organizations to which she belonged.

She operated her own Skin and Body Care Salon as "Elaine's Place." This afforded her the opportunity to impact lives, maximally, on the most immediate and intimate levels. The physical and spiritual existence of those in her creative force and creative space were enlarged upon: she made their lives better in all ways.

Numerous positions she attained in life brought healing and happiness to the most infirmed among us. She was made Head of the Maryland State Board of Cosmetology and gave leadership to that body's ultimate responsibility to bring esthetics and comfort to many.

She became Director of a Cancer Society's "Look Good Feel Better" Program, which she in large part developed just under two decades prior to her encounter with Awaki. Through this program, new meaning to life, hope, peace and healing were brought to many, everywhere, plagued with cancer. She embraced her Divine Gift wholly and imparted that which it imbued to the Multitude.

# Chapter Twelve

## The Faithless

Cynthia Greene, MD

In the beginning when Thomas and Nathaniel first started to speak with the Angels they were told this was a precursor to a war of sorts: spiritual battles. They were both concerned about how these battles would be waged. Specifically they questioned who would be engaged — them alone or others. Shakardak resolved that by asking them if a war could be fought with just one. They knew then there would be others. Then the question became, how would others be brought to it? Again the angels resolved that — telling them others would come of their own volition, they would come through Nathaniel's influence and still others would come by other means. I fell in the "other means" category.

In the very beginning, early one December evening 1995, Nathaniel and I had dinner. The purpose was for him to discuss the angel visitations. He actually wanted to vent. He gave me the details of how it all began.

His cousin, Thomas, gave him a crystal ring when he admired it. He wore the ring home. Once there, it began to "chant" or emit sounds. He became alarmed, put the ring in the freezer and called his cousin. The Prophet went to assess the situation. Upon his arrival, he heard nothing. But, as time passed he too heard the sounds, which sounded like a "chant."

Thomas' background, as a learned priest, prepared him for this in that he had full knowledge of such things occurring.

His main focus was to determine if this sound was of God or not of

God. He determined the voice was of God. They then decided to engage with it, cooperate with it and record the sound with an audio cassette tape.

As they carried that out, Nathaniel lost consciousness. The sound no longer came from the ring, it then emitted from Nathaniel's moving lips. He made the sounds. Records later confirmed all that he told me.

He expressed his apprehension about the entire ordeal even after he heard the tape of what transpired during his unconsciousness. Religiously, he was Protestant as I, and had little knowledge of such occurrences overall and none first hand. In spite of his apprehension, he continued to cooperate with it.

It started on November 3, 1995. It continued at least once or twice weekly, which they audio taped. He described that in each occurrence he was dispatched from his body and deposited in a "white room" of sorts. Any attempt he made to leave the room landed him in a room identical to the one that he had just left. He said he had no sense of time or place but knew that he continued to exist, wherever he was.

He remained there during his absence from his body and it ended when he was ushered back into his body. He described these comings and goings as being quick and tumultuous at times. During his absence from his body it was inhabited by angel, which actually produced the sounds.

During these "sessions," we chose to call them, Thomas spoke with the Angels that inhabited Nathaniel. They spoke of a number of spiritual things -- garnering new spiritual knowledge never known to man before. All total 7-8 different Angels used his body to talk through, from November 1995 to May 1996, that I am aware of: Shakardak, Awaki, Laiiki, Azrael, Mayackaoka, Melchizedek, and Marchardak.

I was mesmerized by his tale and torn between belief and doubt versus fear and anxiety. Who wouldn't be after hearing from someone who had heard from God that God said "He called Himself into existence!" That was one of the first and most profoundly amazing things he told me. Then, he invited me to come to a session and I agreed.

Thomas, on following occasions, invited me to come and each time, I agreed. However, I could never overcome those factors causing my inertia to go. Then one Friday, March 29, 1996 to be exact, The Prophet told me they were having a session at 6pm the next day, Saturday, March 30, 1996 at the Home of Omni. I, as usual, said I would be there. This time however,

I felt differently about it. It stayed on my mind and became a matter of urgency that, I attend.

I became so anxious and determined to attend that I was unable to let go of it — not even enough to sleep. I was awake all night long. I was scheduled to give a talk to a Women's Organization earlier on Saturday and stayed up all night preparing and re-preparing for the talk. I could not settle. After giving the speech I had 2 hours to wait before the session. I was on pins and needles the entire 2 hours wanting them to pass more quickly: I could barely contain myself waiting to attend! Those 2 hours dragged on forever.

Finally it was time. I arrived a bit early and only 3 or 4 people were there: Thomas, Nathaniel, myself and Louvinia, the owner of the Home of Omni. Nathaniel was to himself in a small room. I went to where he was and found him there extremely anxious. He talked about his concerns in doing this.

His greatest concern was his lack of being conscious and thereby not knowing what was going as everything was happening. Also he had concerns about what others thought of him: just sitting there and really not being there. Another concern was, what would the people think of him if the Angels did not come? He had many worries.

All I could do was reassure him that, as this was of God, he had no control and no need for worry, God would handle it. He just had to be willing to allow God to do as He saw fit. After 20-30 minutes he was much more settled and relaxed.

At that time, Thomas came to the door and told us it was time. When I re-entered the larger room I became very anxious; the room had filled with people whom I had never seen before and did not know. It was unnerving. I felt some of what Nathaniel was expressing and then had much more empathy for him. What transpired next, only heightened my anxiety.

Two chairs set in the center of the room. Those present sat in a circle around the entire room, surrounding them. Thomas sat in one chair directly facing Nathaniel, who sat in the other. Thomas held both of Nathaniel's hands, and rested them on their knees. Thomas began to pray. Nathaniel slowly passed out and his body looked as though it was dead. I almost became alarmed but held myself steady.

This voice then came out of Nathaniel which sounded like a chant;

a voice that I had never heard before. It certainly was not the voice I had just spent 20-30 minutes with, chatting. While sitting there it was all I could do to contain myself and hold myself in the moment. I witnessed two women being called forward to exchange seats with Thomas and assume the position he had: they held Nathaniel's hands in their hands and rested them on their knees. I heard them speaking but I was so mesmerized I had no idea as to what was said to either or by either; as each finished, the other began.

They interchanged seats with Thomas back and forth as well. Even now, almost 25 years later, I feel some of that angst, I recall having felt then. I have no real recollection of who was in the room because it all was so overwhelming. There were many.

And then, out of nowhere, as I sat mesmerized in my seat, I heard, "There is another. Her voices, the noises in her mind are strong and she is over this host is with her. Come unto me."

I felt like I just wanted to melt away and disappear right then and there: It was too much and too late. It was as if I had been trapped somehow. It definitely had the "Doe in the headlight" feel, to it.

He continued, "It is she who is concerned about that which sustains her and is in the valley of decision. The elium lords attempt to destroy you but you are of us, but you have lost your way. They attempt to take all that is yours and to place you in fear, to question your obedience unto your God, and your faith and the physical. And when the faith is gone the physical will so follow."

Well after hearing all of that, I knew it was I, of whom he spoke. But, under no circumstances was I going to leave my chair. And, have those people staring at me as I was staring at what I was seeing and not seeing all at the same time, no way.

As to his description of me: I was battling an unknown disease, Mitral Valve Prolapse Syndrome, which robbed me of my functionality, and no one knew, medically, what it was or what to do about it, including myself, for 3 years by then. I had lost my thriving medical practice because of it and was fighting foreclosure on my house. I had zero income, and all of that, with my medical disability insurance refusing to pay my benefits --- insurance I had paid thousands and thousands of dollars for, for 12 years or more. I could not move. I just ruminated over it.

He continued, "Yes, come unto me. Be not ashamed. It is she who is like Luke and chose that path….come unto me."

As no one was moving and only I knew he spoke of me, there was a hush in the room. It was very, very uneasy for me. All of that notwithstanding I was not about to move.

Then the Prophet spoke. "What was the role of Luke?" he asked Awaki.

"Luke was the healer of those who followed Jah," he answered.

When he spoke those words, like a flash of lightening, I was out of my seat and sitting in front of him in one swift move it seemed.

He continued as I was moving, "He was, what you would call, the physician. Come unto me, the healer of the hosts of this universe."

By then I was fully seated.

"Take the hands of this host into your hands," he said.

I did as instructed. As I was just a breath away from Nathaniel now I could assess him better. There was no one in that body. After being in medicine, practicing for almost 20 years, you know when you are looking at a dead person and you are 100% certain when you are holding a dead person's hands. He was not in that body. That was a lifeless body. Yet it was talking. I was sitting in front of, knee – to – knee, and holding the hands of, a lifeless, talking body.

"You have spoken unto this host," he continued. "He has great understanding of your knowledge and cares much about you. As our Prophet, you did not choose to come unto us today, for we have summoned you. Is that within your understanding?"

"Yes," I said.

There was no doubt in my mind about that --- from December 1995 to March 30, 1996 I was invited countless times and only then did I feel compelled to go? It was crystal clear that I had been summoned. Also I was up the prior 24 hours, unable to sleep, due to the anticipation of going.

"It was not within their knowledge, but within ours," he told me.

They didn't let on to Nathaniel and Thomas that they were bringing me in, in other words. And, I am 100% sure neither expected me to come because I had never taken them up on their invitations after promising them that I would, time after time.

He continued, "You are of us but you do not understand the power of your God. The elium lords are attempting to take from you all that is yours. Is that not what is happening?"

"Yes," I agreed again.

At that point, in my life, I was seeking welfare just to keep my lights on. So, yes, I was financially destitute.

"This host has asked and prayed for deliverance of those which he is now in their employ for his endeavor. Did not we send him unto you?" he asked.

I did not respond because I was zoned.

He repeated, "Did not we send him unto you?"

"The host?" I asked like I was snapped back into it.

"That is within your understanding," he said.

"Yes, yes you did." I admitted, answering as though I was befuddled and trying to stay grounded. I was all of that.

Nathaniel had joined the NAACP Branch of which I was Vice President. The body lacked good leadership and the work that needed to be done could not get done adequately without better help. And, like a gift from God, Nathaniel, with amazing leadership skills, just showed up. I always thought and told everybody, he was a gift sent from God.

"It was not for what you think," Awaki went on to correct that faulty thinking of mine. "That is his gift of multitudes. He was sent unto you that you may sit again in the presence of your God."

They sent Nathaniel to the NAACP to get me out of there and back on track to God. Mind blower.

"We desire to protect you from that which you are going through. We wish not for your suffering or your destruction, but we are not there because you have chosen your own destiny even in your knowledge of your God. Is it your desire this day to have your soul resurrected before your God?" he asked.

"Yes," I said.

Had no idea what that meant. I thought he was asking me if I was prepared to die and meet God. I thought I was because I went to church, did right, gave money and helped people. I was not afraid to meet God if I had to die right then. That's what I was thinking.

He interrupted my thoughts briskly, quickly and firmly. "You do not understand what we speak of, because in your own, you feel that you have worshipped unto your God and that you have been obedient in His will. Is this not within your understanding?" he asked.

"Yes," I said, after I had just run my whole religious life "before my eyes," while sitting there.

At this point it was abundantly clear Awaki was reading my mind as I sat before him, how else would he have known exactly what I was thinking, I never voiced it? It was confusing to me as to why my understanding was incorrect. I became more ill at eased now, than I already was, after all that he had told me.

This was becoming very edgy for me as I felt that I was about to lose my soul and had no idea why. That was scary- much more so- than losing all of the material stuff I had. I was very confused.

"Do you know the essence of obedience?" he asked.

I thought I did so I said, "Yes."

"And what is that?"

"To do that, that is right. To do that that you're told to do," I replied.

"That is not within your understanding," he corrected me and went on to explain it. "Obedience is submission. It is to be humble unto those that you are superior to, that you may direct and guide them into truth and righteousness with the power of your words and not your mind. Do you understand what I mean when I say the power of your words? If there was Jah and there was a man that came unto Him and said, 'Master, we will surely die, but you sleep?' And, He said unto them, 'Oh ye of little faith, you rant and you rave but yet not you sit in the calm of your mind and lead men out of the storm.' And He stood before them, men who had no discipline, who could not hear for they talked much and He said, 'peace, be still' and all came into understanding. You are, and have been, and was given multitudes, and you have turned from true obedience. There are those who will follow but they reject for you place them under your foot and crush them. Is that within your understanding?"

"No," I said. I knew myself to be firm and even hard at times but this was more than I could admit to, "crushing people with my feet." That was far beyond (and below) who I thought myself to be. It was not a pretty picture. It certainly was not good.

He went on to explain more fully what he meant.

"There was a king and he was given wisdom as your scholars teach unto you. Do you know who that king was?"

"Solomon," I answered.

"That is within your understanding," he agreed.

"But Solomon had a man who was a prophet. Do you know who that man was?"

"No," I said.

I never knew Solomon had a prophet and never read it anywhere. He went on to enlighten me fully.

"It was Nahum. In your language you call him Nathaniel. Solomon was not wise. For, we sent unto him Nahum to speak all manner of wisdom that he may establish his kingdoms. Do you know why his kingdom was lost?"

"No," I did not know that history at all. So, he continued to enlighten me.

"In his arrogance of who he was he destroyed those who wished to follow him. Lead not by a firm hand but by a gift of multitudes and surely they will follow you. This is the reason for your destruction. The elium lords come in and take that from you. Is that within your understanding?"

He never paused to allow me to answer he just continued.

"Humble yourself and lead by the power of your words and your actions and not by your arrogance. It is within your understanding. Even He who has redeemed you was humble unto those who were below Him for He came not for the wise or the righteous but for the unwise and the low of spirit, to lead them out of darkness and into the light, the light of He who had sent Him and created all. And, so shall you do in your goings here and there, there and here.

"Change your pattern of leader and give unto them, those who wish to follow you, the choice to do so in love and admiration and respect. There have been many a destruction in your universe by leaders who rule with intimidation and arrogance. This day we speak unto you for that if you desire we will save you from your destruction in this physical plane and your creative space will become again, of He who has sent me. Is this your desire?"

"Yes," I said with timidity. I knew I wanted and needed my life to change, as I was being destroyed. What I was just learning, painfully, was why.

"And, you must understand what I have just said," he continued. "Look not upon people as you have before. Lead them out of their ignorance with your wisdom and not your arrogance. Ask and it shall be given unto you. You are charged."

He said unto his Prophet and with that the Prophet reiterated what he had said to me.

"What he is saying is that with obedience, whatever you ask, period, and it will be done instantly and instantaneously. And, that any fears that you have of losing anything will be rectified and ended no matter how imminent the situation, and all that you have to do now is ask for anything and it will be given to you," he said.

Awaki supported what the Prophet said.

"There are those that sit before me and around you that can surely say unto you that your God has given unto them all that they have asked for. Even in their time of destruction have we saved them, as a testimony unto you that I AM and this is and that He is The I AM of your essence. Avail your faith and ask and it shall be given unto you."

The Prophet had to clarify for me what was being said as I was reeling and rocking inside from all that I heard and was totally adrift.

"You must ask as a testament to your faith in God. You must verbalize that which you desire," he explained what he meant.

I knew then it was expected that I speak there and then of what I needed and wanted to have happen in my life immediately. "I desire that all of the material things that I need to sustain me and keep me in the way that I can do that that I must do be made available to me," I said, quietly.

The Prophet asked, "Do you desire to keep your home?"

I responded, quietly, "I desire to keep my home."

He added, "Owned by yourself?"

Again I quietly repeated, "Owned by myself."

"Are there any other desires you have on a sustenance level?" the prophet asked me.

I thought of how my suffering was impacting my family who relied heavily on me for financial support and I replied.

"I desire that the benefits of my policies be made available to me so that I have the resources to do that that others need. I desire that I develop more obedience, more discipline to the asking of my God for directions."

Awaki then assured me, "This we will grant unto you this day and you have spoken unto your God that which you have promised unto Him. All that you fear, fear no more, for we will set in motion a chain of events that will protect you. And, we will fight your spiritual battles unto the elium lords. As long as you walk in obedience, we will give you that which you wish. But have faith. I speak these words unto you. (Awaki spoke words of the language of God which I could not understand). Zimblach. It is done."

The Prophet then interceded and asked me.

"Are there any questions that you have? Any things that you desire to know?"

I was still reeling from Awaki's revelation of why I was being destroyed and I desperately wanted that to change in my life immediately so I asked, "What must I do to control the arrogance that comes?"

"It is in the power of your brilliant mind. It is not a weapon to destroy others, but an instrument of love and forgiveness, tolerance and patience, and obedience to your God. These things you do and it will be given unto you," Awaki promised me.

The Prophet knew I needed to know more so he interceded again and asked Awaki directly on my behalf.

"Can you explain multitudes to her?"

Awaki explained immediately in detail. "The gift of multitudes. This host before you, has been given the gift to lead, to lead those from darkness into light. You have it and have used it but you turn from it. People in this universe follow you, call upon you and desire your guidance, but in your haste and arrogance, your guidance is fueled by anger and frustration and not correction. There are many things that you will do but only if you do them in wisdom and obedience then will you achieve that greatness which you sought. Zimblach."

That signaled the end of my session. Then he surprised me. The prophet asked me if I had any other questions and before I could answer Awaki spoke.

"Unto our Prophet."

"Yes," The Prophet responded.

"We charge you. For, through you will we save. Is that within your understanding?"

"Yes, Charged as to Cynthia?" The Prophet asked.

"That is within your understanding. And, in this battle your burdens will be heavy but we will be unto you. There are things that even in your understanding of your sustenance, that you do not know and we will open your eyes unto these things that you may see. Is that within your understanding?" Awaki told him.

"Yes." The prophet responded and asked Awaki, "And, you will open my eyes and direct my understanding to the most effective way to assist Cynthia's Counsel. Is that also correct?"

"That is within your understanding," Awaki agreed.

"This process will begin immediately?" the Prophet asked.

"It is done," he answered.

"What about her other Counsel?" the Prophet asked.

It is done," Awaki said.

"Very well," The Prophet sighed.

"And, we will come unto you should he attempt to destroy that which we set in motion. Unto Luke, our physician, lose not your faith again. Is that within your understanding?"

"Yes," I said, completely overcome.

"For we plead now before your God," Awaki spoke the language of God again.

That ended my session. I never went before him again. However, two years later when I was granted access to all of the sessions' notes and tapes I learned what had made the last part of our conversation regarding my benefits and the Prophet null and void.

The following day, Sunday, March 31, 1996 the Prophet had a conversation with Awaki.

"What steps should I take in terms of helping Cynthia? You know the things that I've been thinking of at this particular point. I found out today that she's speaking to the attorney representing her and it seems as though she had confidence in him in terms of resolving her home issue, resolving…."

Awaki abruptly interrupted him.

"You speak unto her this: that we charged you that your salvation come through our Prophet, and she heard. If she turns her back on what we have set in motion then it is not of us and she shall suffer her own destruction," he said.

"I understand" the Prophet replied.

Awaki continued, "But you do not wrestle with her disobedience. Speak unto her once and if she cannot have faith in her God and bring unto you that which she has that you may save, then she suffers her own destruction."

The prophet never responded to Awaki except to move on and ask him," What about William and his brother."

He never spoke to me further about Awaki's charge to take my cases or Awaki's message to me that I be obedient and turn over my cases to him. In fact I literally hounded him from March 30, 1996, continually for years, to take my cases and he flatly refused. He refused on the grounds that the courts would frown upon his taking another attorney's client. At no time did I deny him access to either of the cases. It was he who said the attorney handling the house should continue as he was having success with it.

It was disappointing to learn of that. The cases were both lost permanently and with them all of my material wealth.

My health however, was restored with my faith, obedience and vigorous commitment to a plan sent to me by God. A woman, almost a thousand miles away from where I lived, told me to walk. I could not instill my faith and obedience within the Prophet to have him take and save my cases. However, I could use my faith and my obedience to save my health, which I did. I walked upwards to 5 miles daily without fail, regardless to weather, time of day or my location on the planet, for a decade and a half and my health was fully restored. I was able to regain my work status and ultimately my wealth back. I felt like Job.

During meditation one Saturday morning, April 1998, God instructed me, "with visual effects" to acquire all tapes, review and complete notes of all of the sessions from their visits 11/3/1995 to 5/15/1996, organize and secure them. There was a "shower" of small cassettes cascading downwards before my closed eyes as I meditated that morning. Prior to that I knew nothing but what had occurred during my session. After following my instructions, an entire new world of knowledge opened up to me.

The irony was for two years, prior, I had been asking the Prophet, the owner of the Temple and anyone else I knew of, what else was there to know. No one, who knew, could or would tell me. Yet, before I went, they were some of those very same ones who tried to get me to go, and I would not. Too funny.

The hunger I had, to know, was satiated when the information was made available to me. Since that time June 1998, until now I have been relentlessly consuming all that was given to us. And, even with those decades of study each new exposure provides deeper and more meaningful revelations; also new revelations.

As to the prophecy of my personal deliverance, I have all: my faith, my wealth and my health in obedience through the grace of God.

As to the prophecy of the knowledge that the world was to have received through the Mechanism, I think fear prevented all of that from happening.

The instructions to the Prophets as to Nathaniel's job to "guide" the production of the Mechanism (Books) were never realized. Neither was the prophetic relationship ever realized. His existence as a spiritual leader was known to a limited few, if any, of the masses at all. The Prophet and Prophetess produced their own individual books years after the vision given me to get involved in the notes. And that was given to me years pass, "six in twelve" 1996, the date Awaki gave for the books to be published. Possibly 4-5 years lapsed prior to publications.

That is why the masses had no access to this knowledge as was intended by God...FEAR. Satan's most effective tool against faithless, fearful, doubters. However, God always prevails against Satan. Even though no one prophesied as instructed, Armageddon marches on.

The Parousia reigns and Satan is dismantled and defeated every day of the spiritual battles. It is unfortunate that the forewarning of the masses did not go as planned but, nevertheless, the masses are becoming more faithful every day, of their own volition. They see the manifestation of the Biblical Revelation and are learning to believe in the possibility of all things being possibly...faith.

As they struggle and through their faith develop obedience... submission... their faith enlarges and more battles are won. Satan has already been defeated, Awaki told us. How it looks here is determined by our faith. (He told us that too). Our faith will prevail, hence Satan's defeat in this universe.

This is the 3rd publication of this knowledge, unabridged, untampered with and sans any editing of the Angels' words. The names have been changed of those spoken to but every word written from them is as it was captured on the recording devices.This is to help avail you to all that was left for you. If you have read it you can now pass it on, the same way, and the job will be done regardless to the fear that Satan wields and those of us who succumb to it.

Lightning Source UK Ltd.
Milton Keynes UK
UKHW011833130921
390533UK00006B/326/J

9 781665 534888